AF889826

BODYS ISEK KINGELEZ

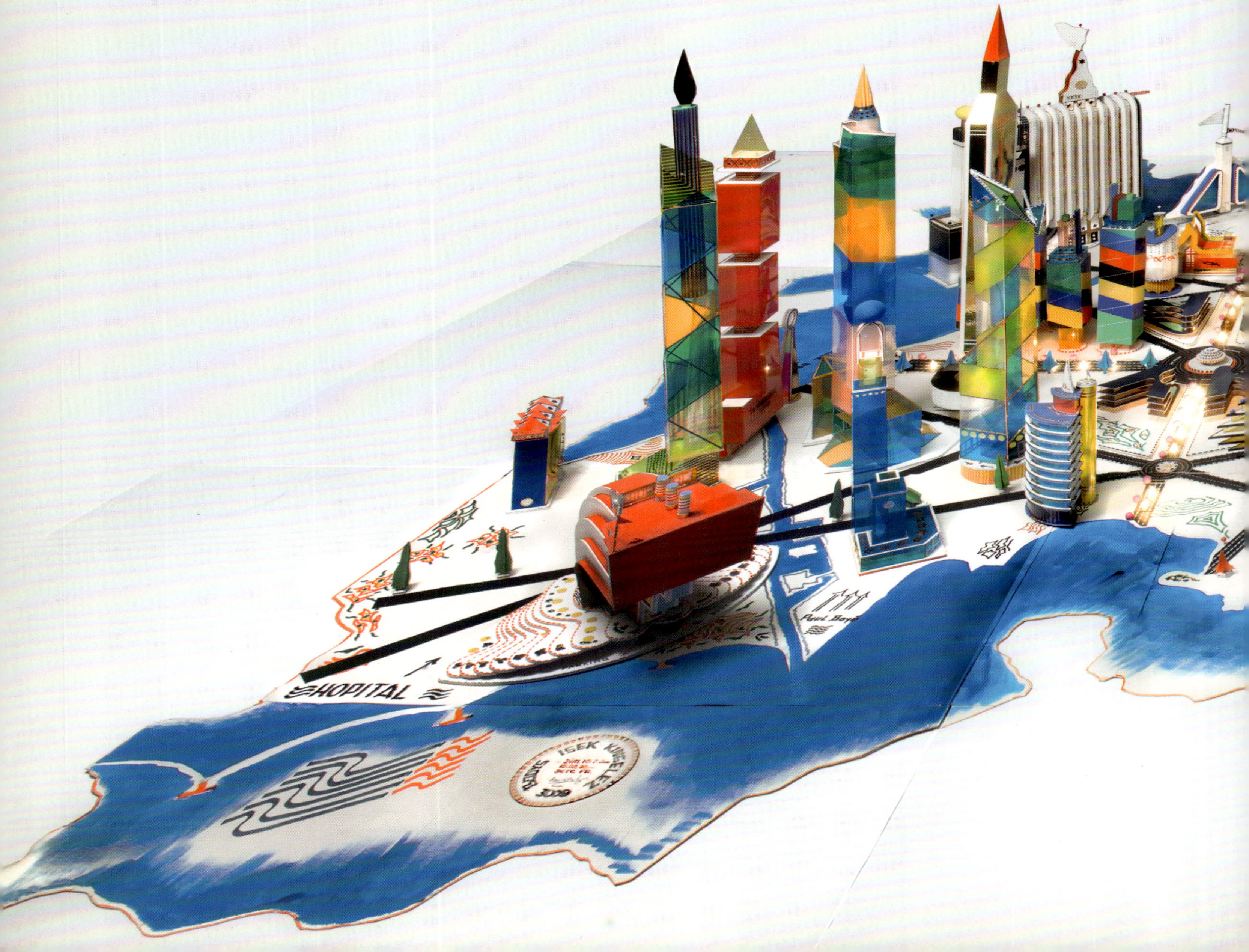
HOPITAL

BODYS ISEK KINGELEZ

SARAH SUZUKI

The Museum of Modern Art, New York

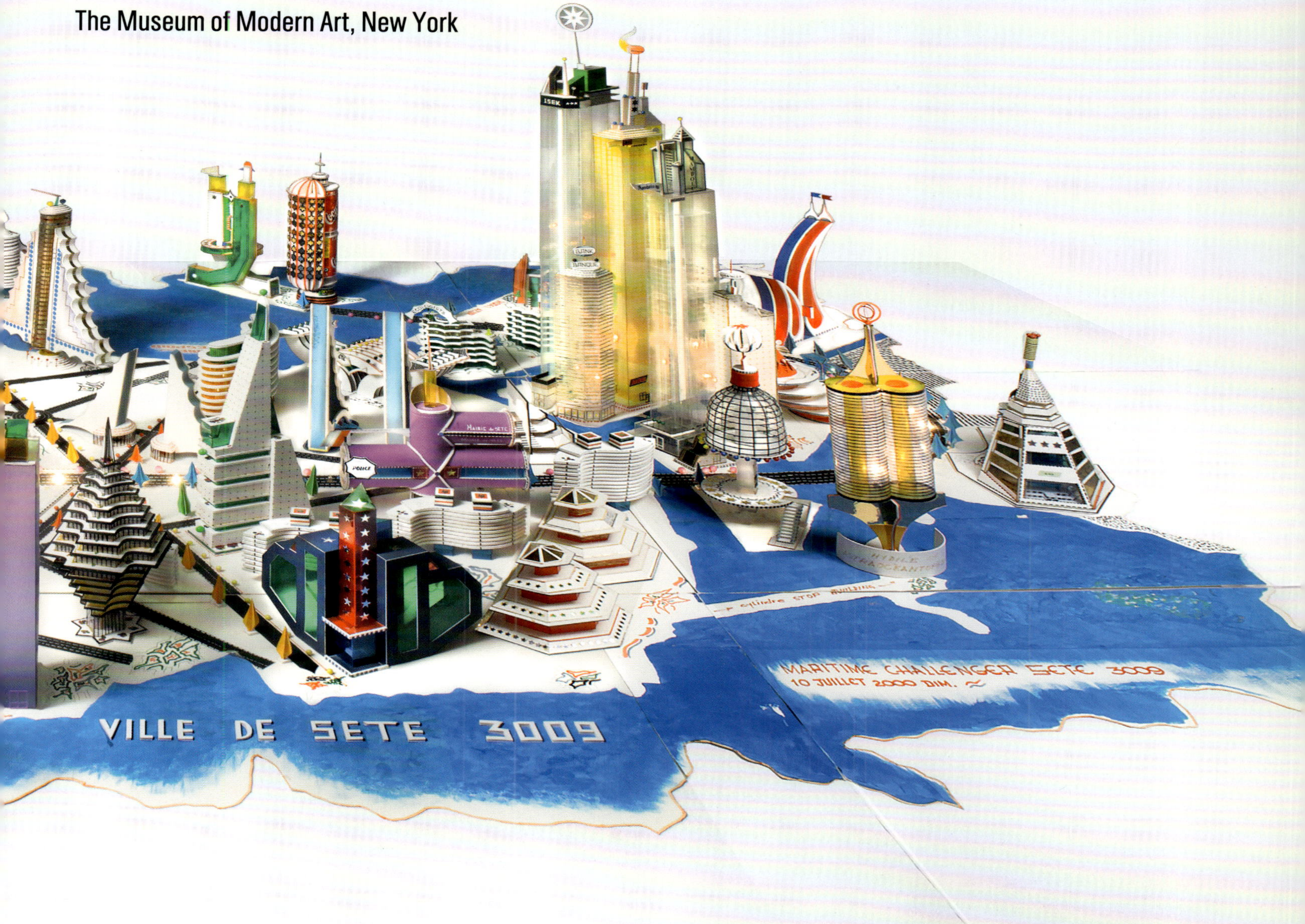

Published in conjunction with the exhibition *Bodys Isek Kingelez*, organized by Sarah Suzuki, Curator, with Hillary Reder, Curatorial Assistant, Department of Drawings and Prints, at The Museum of Modern Art, New York, May 26, 2018–January 1, 2019

Allianz

The exhibition is made possible by Allianz, a partner of contemporary art at MoMA.

Major support is provided by The International Council of The Museum of Modern Art.

Generous funding is provided by The Friends of Education of The Museum of Modern Art.

Additional support is provided by the Annual Exhibition Fund.

Major support for this publication is provided by The Dale S. and Norman Mills Leff Publication Fund.

Produced by the Department of Publications, The Museum of Modern Art, New York

Christopher Hudson, Publisher
Don McMahon, Editorial Director
Marc Sapir, Production Director

Edited by Rebecca Roberts
Designed by Naomi Mizusaki, Supermarket, New York
Production by Marc Sapir
Color separations by t'ink, Brussels
Printed and bound by Gorenjski tisk storitve, Kranj, Slovenia

This book is typeset in Akzidenz Buch. The paper is 150 gsm GardaMatt Smooth.

The essay by Sammy Baloji was translated from the French by Jeanine Herman.

The English translation "Maquettes of Post-Modes Art" was first published in *Gagarin* 7 (2003): 72, as "Scale Models of Post-Modes Art." www.gagarin.be. The English translation "The Essential Framework of the Structures Making Up the Town of Kimbembele-Ihunga (Kimbéville)" is © Bodys Isek Kingelez and Serpentine Galleries. It was first published in *Big City: Artists from Africa* (London: Serpentine Gallery, 1995), 50–51.

Published by The Museum of Modern Art
11 West 53 Street
New York, New York
10019-5497
www.moma.org

© 2018 The Museum of Modern Art, New York. Artworks and writings by Bodys Isek Kingelez are © 2018 Estate of Bodys Isek Kingelez, unless otherwise noted. Certain illustrations are covered by claims to copyright noted in the Photograph Credits. All rights reserved.

Library of Congress Control Number: 2018936170
ISBN: 978-1-63345-054-7

Distributed in the United States and Canada by
Artbook | D.A.P.
75 Broad Street, Suite 630
New York, New York 10004
www.artbook.com

Distributed outside the United States and Canada by
Thames & Hudson Ltd
181A High Holborn, London WC1V 7QX
www.thamesandhudson.com

Printed in Slovenia

Cover and page 38: *Ville Fantôme* (detail). 1996. See plate 28.
Title pages: *Ville de Sète 3009*. 2000. See plate 30.
Page 8: *Canada Dry* (detail). 1991. See plate 18.
Page 31: *Belle Hollandaise* (detail). 1991. See plate 16.
Page 32: *Place de la Ville* (detail). 1993. See plate 23.
Page 48: *Allemagne An 2000* (detail). 1988. See plate 6.

Contributors

Sir David Adjaye OBE is the founder and Principal of the global architecture firm Adjaye Associates.

Sammy Baloji is a photographer and installation artist based in Lubumbashi and Brussels.

André Magnin is the founder of the gallery Magnin-A, Paris, and former curator of CAAC—The Pigozzi Collection.

Chika Okeke-Agulu is Professor of African and African Diaspora Art in the Department of Art and Archaeology and the Department of African American Studies at Princeton University.

Hillary Reder is Curatorial Assistant in the Department of Drawings and Prints at The Museum of Modern Art, New York.

Sarah Suzuki is Curator in the Department of Drawings and Prints at The Museum of Modern Art, New York.

CONTENTS

Allianz

As a partner of contemporary art at The Museum of Modern Art, Allianz is proud to celebrate the first major retrospective of the work of the Congolese sculptor Bodys Isek Kingelez and the first substantial monographic presentation of his work in the United States.

Allianz believes that people want to live with courage rather than fear, remaining curious and exploring their world with an open mind and an abundance of imagination. Our engagement with the art of today reflects this belief, and we are honored to support exhibitions by contemporary artists who push the limits of their disciplines and challenge expectations and conventions.

Both as a company and as individuals, we are moved by the question of how people can live better lives in the future. With his infinite curiosity, imagination, and skill, Kingelez has shown himself to be an explorer of a new era. His spectacular, visionary sculptures shape a fantastical urban landscape that is prosperous and peaceful. They are powerful representations of the "city of tomorrow."

This unprecedented exhibition is accompanied by a virtual reality component that transports visitors into Kingelez's imagined tomorrow and enables them to see the future through his eyes. We hope that visitors will be inspired by this extraordinary artist and his vision of a better world.

#**ExploreWithUs**

Jean-Marc Pailhol
Head of Group Market Management & Distribution at Allianz SE

FOREWORD

An artist of tremendous and enduring vision, Bodys Isek Kingelez believed that art-making was "the grandest adventure of all"—a vocation with the power to serve his community, bridge civilizations, and contribute to the progress of science and the pursuit of a better life. Born in 1948 in what was then the Belgian Congo, Kingelez moved in 1970 from his home village to the city of Kinshasa, the capital of the newly independent Democratic Republic of the Congo (soon renamed Zaire). It was against the backdrop of this complex city, rapidly redefining itself in the years after Independence, that he would realize his artistic aspirations, creating fantastic paper sculptures that suggest utopian possibilities for global urban sites.

We are thrilled to present the first full retrospective of Kingelez's work, tracing the arc of his practice in its entirety. While he has long been included in important exhibitions of contemporary art, from *Magiciens de la terre*, at the Centre Pompidou in 1989, to the landmark documenta 11, in 2002, he has been the subject of very few solo presentations. *Bodys Isek Kingelez* unfolds as a chronological display of the artist's three-decade career, capturing the transformation of his work as it grows in scale and complexity from the early single-building architectural sculptures to the sprawling, futuristic cities of his later production. It is moving to see so many of Kingelez's *extrêmes maquettes*, as he called them, assembled in one place for the first time.

Although Kingelez was part of the group exhibition *Projects 59: Architecture as Metaphor* at The Museum of Modern Art in 1997, this retrospective may be for many of our visitors their first encounter with his work. His imagined metropolises offer a prescient articulation of the multivalent realities and potentials of the contemporary city, and his utopic, joyous vision for a global society—for a "better, more peaceful world"—seems pointedly relevant today. His distinctive voice adds immeasurably to the global story of modern and contemporary art we seek to tell at MoMA.

The success of our exhibitions relies on so many, beginning with my peerless colleagues at MoMA. Sarah Suzuki, Curator, and Hillary Reder, Curatorial Assistant, both in the Department of Drawings and Prints, have overseen every aspect of this project with enthusiasm and care. We owe particular thanks to Allianz for its significant contribution to realizing this exhibition. We are also grateful for the essential contributions of The International Council and The Friends of Education of The Museum of Modern Art. Additional support was provided by the Annual Exhibition Fund. Jean Pigozzi of CAAC—The Pigozzi Collection deserves my special thanks, not only for his loan of artworks but also for the ideas and enthusiasm he brought to our project. Lastly, on behalf of the Trustees and staff of The Museum of Modern Art, I extend my profound thanks to all the lenders who have entrusted us with their works by Kingelez, making this exhibition possible.

Glenn D. Lowry
Director, The Museum of Modern Art

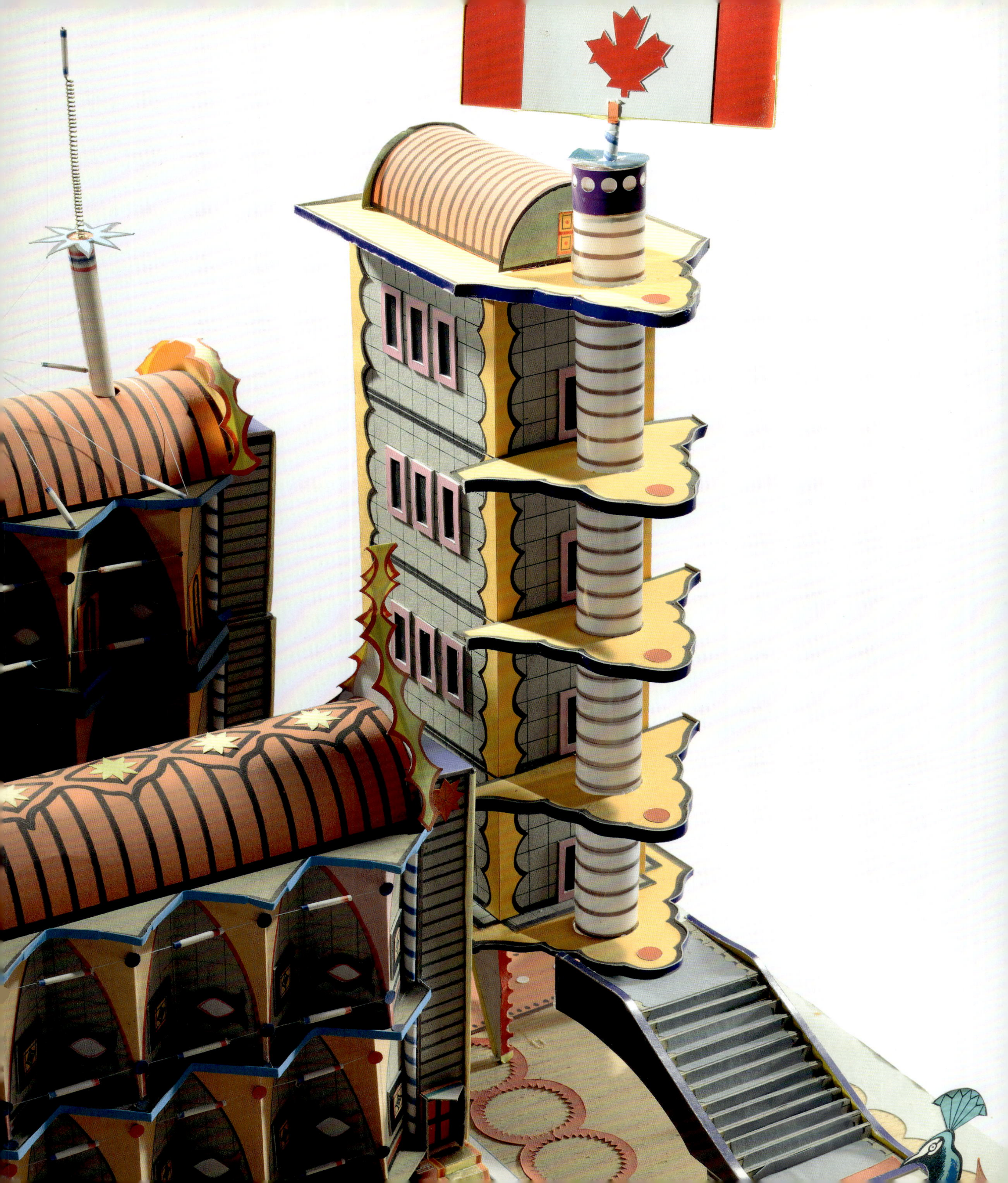

KINGELEZ VISIONNAIRE

Sarah Suzuki

The words and commentaries that I write express the vision that inhabited me even before I started the piece. First comes the name (the title) of the piece; secondly I wait for the vision to come; then I make it real. I never make preliminary drawings. The vision gives me all I need, even the shape and the colors. . . . I am a designer, an architect, a sculptor, engineer, artist.

—Bodys Isek Kingelez

Bodys Isek Kingelez is one of the unsung visionary creators of the twentieth century. A lifelong resident of what is now the Democratic Republic of the Congo, Kingelez developed a notably individualistic style that is beholden to no obvious artistic precedents. Beginning in 1978 with his very first artwork, the result of a feverish session with "some scissors, a Gillette razor, and some glue and paper,"[1] his oeuvre took a unique form, in sculptures of mixed paper and other ephemeral materials that suggest miniature architectural structures. Dazzling in color and decoration, the works grew in scale and complexity over time, from models of individual buildings to intricate cities complete with roadways, billboards, and public monuments.

Kingelez was a formidable figure. Remarkably self-assured, he believed of his work that "since time immemorial, no one has had a vision like this,"[2] and he aimed to be a force for good in the world, hoping, he said, that "architects and builders worldwide can try to learn from my perceptions so as to help the forthcoming generations. I'm dreaming cities of peace. I'd like to help the Earth above all."[3] He was a complicated person, at turns outgoing and reserved, and the making of his work was all-consuming; to some, he seemed most comfortable in the fantastical world of his own creation. Beauty was a paramount concern, not only in his art but also in his dress (see p. 37), and while he didn't go to the theatrical lengths of Kinshasa's famous dandies—the label-loving sapeurs—his personal style reflected the perfection he aimed for in his sculptures: "The shirt, jacket, and shoes need to be harmonious," he declared.[4] This holistic attitude and desire for harmony aligned with his aspiration to make the world a better and more beautiful place through his work.

Kingelez's practice, though unquestionably appealing to curators, critics, and art historians, has presented them a maddening challenge. In collapsing the boundaries between sculpture, architecture, and design, it eludes the categorization and classification on which institutional collections rely, and in its lack of known art historical precedents it evades the genealogy that we love to document and trace.[5] As a result, although Kingelez has been included in some of the most important visual art exhibitions of the last forty years—the groundbreaking *Magiciens de la terre* in Paris in 1989; *The Short Century: Independence and Liberation Movements in Africa, 1945–1994*, a paradigm-shifting show that opened in Munich in 2001; the acclaimed documenta 11 in 2002; and biennials in Johannesburg, Dakar, and São Paulo, among others—very little has been written about him and his work. This study is an initial step in correcting the dearth of literature on Kingelez, and it is my hope that it will lay the groundwork for future efforts.

As an American curator delving into the work of a contemporary African artist, I have referred to the scholarship of important cultural thinkers of the last decades. Okwui Enwezor and Chika Okeke-Agulu have set forth a number of considerations for the conceptual framing of the term "contemporary African art." They argue that the connective tissue of this "malleable" category is composed of the political and economic events that have shaped the continent, emphasizing the impossibility of considering aesthetic or conceptual strategies without taking into account postcolonial realities.[6] Enwezor has reiterated the importance of historical context in understanding the work of such artists: "In speaking of Africa today we need to ask how the struggles of independence, the problems of the national sovereign state, the expanding definition of national culture, citizenship, and cosmopolitanism (which are partially linked to economic malaise, social obsolescence, and political destabilization) define subjectivity."[7] In thinking through his approach to an art historical study of the black diaspora, Stuart Hall likewise has asserted the importance of working in a way that is "'historical'—that is, with proper attention to chains of causation and conditions of existence, to questions of periodization and conjecture—not just celebratory of a general and undifferentiated 'black presence.' I have been concerned to give it specificity; but also to read it *both* in its connection with, and difference from, other histories." He underscores the importance of attempting to "make connections between works of art and wider social histories without collapsing the former or displacing the latter."[8] In his review of the various strategies taken in analyses of African contemporary art, John Picton has suggested that the more successful approaches have focused on artists rather than attempting to identify or construct silos into which they might fit.[9] I take these to be calls for contextualization and specificity, so I will begin with the artist himself and explore his moment and milieu with an eye toward some of the histories, events, ideas, and experiences that likely shaped his practice. My aim is to inform the reader about who Kingelez was, how and in what context he made his work, what that work consists of, and how it has been received.

FROM KIMBEMBELE-IHUNGA TO KINSHASA

Kingelez was born on August 27, 1948, in the village of Kimbembele-Ihunga, approximately 370 miles southeast of the city of Léopoldville (now Kinshasa), the eldest of the nine children of agricultural laborers Maluba Abraham Kingelez (1908–1968) and Isek Mabo Bendele (born 1931).[10] He was baptized Jean-Baptiste, though as an artist he would primarily use "Bodys Isek Kingelez" when signing his works, styling the name in myriad ways, sometimes eliding letters, introducing hyphens, and playing with capitalization. This name honors the artist's ancestry: Bodys was his grandfather's name, and Isek descended from the matrilineal side.[11] His surname has deep and meaningful roots in the region. In the seventeenth, eighteenth, and nineteenth centuries, the small kingdom of Kakongo, on the Atlantic coast, was an important commercial center for the slave trade and for trade in resources such as ivory and copper, frequented by the Portuguese, English, French, and Dutch, among others. Kakongo's capital city was Kinguele, a homonym for Kingelez.[12]

Kimbembele-Ihunga was and would remain a potent influence on Kingelez, who later acknowledged the importance of his birthplace, saying, "Every artist on earth achieves self-expression through the most deep-rooted origins of their nature."[13] It was the subject of several sculptures—including the luminous *Kimbembele Ihunga* (pl. 26), his first work to accumulate a mass of buildings into a large, elaborate cityscape—and it remained a beacon of his past and an emblem of his hope for the future. "The town of Kimbéville flourishes," he wrote in a remarkable text that conflates the real village with his own fantastical simulations of its past, present, and future. "People flock here because the wind blows in off the sea and the mountains, refreshing its complex beauty in which all the heightened colors join forces constantly to create an environment where everyone can feel at home."[14]

Taught in his village by the Belgian Catholic missionaries who almost exclusively oversaw the local schools until 1960, Kingelez was a top student, and he later credited his early education with establishing a critical skill: "I learned calligraphy, which is so useful today in my work, from the Belgian fathers."[15] Many of his sculptures feature hand-lettering in a variety of styles, and his unique penmanship, both in all-caps printing and in tight, looping cursive, is a distinctive feature of his manuscript texts.[16] The priests who taught him hoped that he would follow in their footsteps and join the clergy, and though that didn't come to pass, religion played an important role in his life.[17]

Church architecture is a recurring motif in his practice, as evidenced, for example, in a small, early untitled work (pl. 5) that soars upward in three peaked tiers. Topped with a shining silver star, its facade is marked by multiple crosses in silver and gold, and its eaves are adorned with tiny foil bells. Kingelez often cited a divine inspiration for his practice—"No one could beat the strength of God that worked in me," he said[18]—and, with a typical lack of modesty, he classed his own occupation in relation to the glory of Creation: "God has shown us that He himself is an artist. He painted the mountains, he painted the plains. . . . It is our duty to follow in his example. He who follows His example, he who paints as He does, will be blessed. And that's why I am a small god."[19] In 1970, after receiving his high school diploma, Kingelez left his bustling village for the booming metropolis of Kinshasa. He was twenty-two years old.

AUTHENTICITÉ AND A CIVIC IMAGINATION

Already, at this young age, Kingelez had experienced an era of tremendous change. Enwezor has pointed to decolonization as one of the principal events of the twentieth century, and Kingelez found himself directly in the middle of this incredibly complex moment, straddling the colonial and postcolonial periods.[20] The territory that is now the Democratic Republic of the Congo had been settled for nearly ninety thousand years when the European explorer Henry Morton Stanley arrived in the 1870s, under the aegis of King Leopold II of Belgium. Leopold claimed the land as private property, ushering in a horrific period of violent domination of the land and its people—including forced labor, widespread disease, and punitive mutilation—that did not cease upon the territory's annexation as a Belgian colony in 1908. After decades of struggle, the independent Republic of the Congo was declared on June 30, 1960, by Patrice Lumumba, the country's first democratically elected prime minister (fig. 1). Fatefully for the young nation, Lumumba was arrested and then murdered just a few months later by a band of political rivals headed by Joseph-Désiré Mobutu, the chief of staff of the Armée Nationale Congolaise. With support from Western governments, including that of the United States, Mobutu seized power in 1965; he would remain the president and self-declared "Father of the Nation," eventually enjoying despotic, near-divine status, until his military dictatorship was overthrown in 1997.

In the late 1960s, Mobutu instituted a series of new policies designed to promote nationalism and cultural "authenticity" (a doctrine officially termed *authenticité* in 1971). He required that his fellow countrymen and -women adopt Bantu names, and he himself became Mobutu Sese Seko Kuku Ngbendu wa Za Banga, usually shortened to Mobutu Sese Seko, a moniker often translated as "the all-powerful warrior who, because of his endurance and inflexible will to win, will go from conquest to conquest leaving fire in his wake."[21] Léopoldville, Congo's capital city, was renamed Kinshasa in 1966, and in 1971 Mobutu renamed the country and its major river Zaire. Covering a range of traditional African leadership roles, he identified himself as both king and chief, statuses he underscored through his customary accessories: an elaborately carved walking stick and a leopard-skin cap (fig. 2). He developed a new style of national dress known as *abacos* (a shortening of *à bas le costume*—essentially, "down with Western dress")[22]—and promoted economic and political independence as symbols of national pride and identity. In the words of Zaire's former Commissioner of National Orientation, Sakombi Inongo, these doctrines should be understood not "as a reaction against the old colonizers and even less a vengeance, but as a positive affirmation of ourselves."[23] Mobutu also emphasized self-affirmation: "*Authenticité* has made us discover our personality by reaching into the depths of our past for the rich cultural heritage which was left to us by our ancestors. We have no intention of blindly returning to all ancestral customs; rather, we would like to choose those which adapt themselves well to modern life, those which encourage progress, and those which create a way of life and thought which are essentially ours."[24] It was in an atmosphere of pride in Zaire and hope for its future that Kingelez arrived in the newly renamed capital.

An extraordinary early sculpture, 1980's *Kinshasa: Cité du 24 Novembre de l'Authenticité Africaine*, exemplifies the way in which Kingelez's work was shaped by

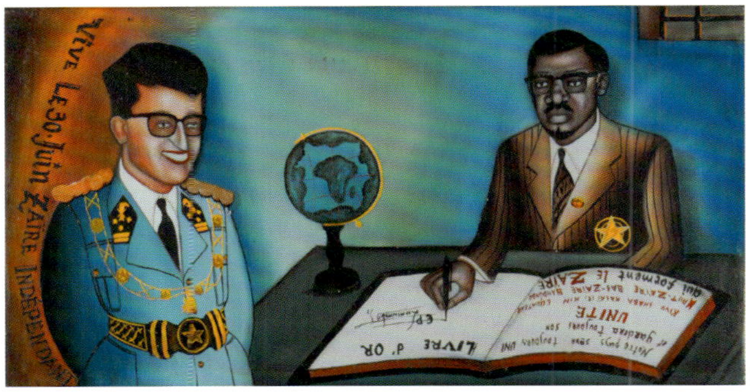

1. Tshibumba Kanda-Matulu (Congolese, 1947–1981). *Vive le 30 juin Zaïre indépendant* (Long live June 30, independent Zaire). 1973–74. Acrylic on canvas, 14 3/8 x 27 3/16" (36.5 x 69 cm). Nationaal Museum van Wereldculturen, Netherlands. The painting depicts King Baudouin of Belgium (left) and Patrice Lumumba, prime minister of the Republic of the Congo, formalizing the independence of the new nation on June 30, 1960.

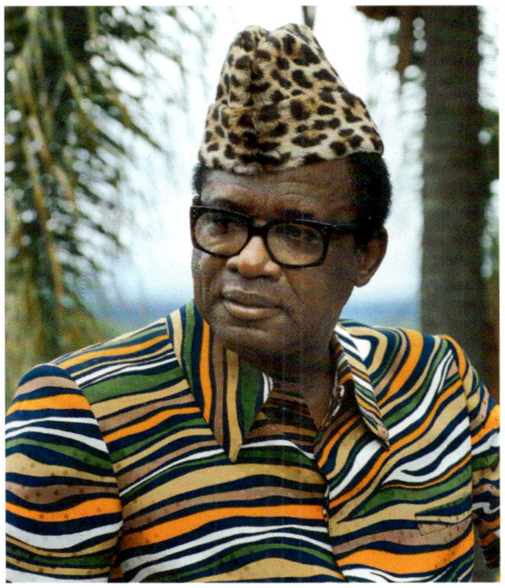

2. Mobutu Sese Seko, president of Zaire, c. 1985

post-Independence politics, suggesting the young artist's excitement about the nation's direction. A tableau of multiple structures, including a church and an elaborate, multistory building with several wings (see fig. 4), the sculpture is certainly the precursor to his later cities.[25] The date named in the title—the day on which Mobutu seized power in 1965, an occasion of celebration throughout his reign—is hand-lettered on a sign that soars above the rooftops. Closer to ground level, but still elevated, is a small, black-and-white photograph of Mobutu in military garb mounted on a wreathlike placard above a banner reading "*La République du Zaïre*." A medallion celebrates the iconic torch-bearing fist of the Zairean national flag (see p. 34), alongside a reference to Mobutu's political party, the Mouvement Populaire de la Révolution (MPR). Circling the medallion is the phrase "*Zaïre Alinga Mosala*," a traditional saying that, roughly translated, means "Zaire loves to work."[26] It was connected to *salongo*, a policy introduced by Mobutu that mandated civic participation and productivity in the name of "hard work and national self-reliance."[27] A group of four small hangars to the right of this signage, designated the "Artist's Village," points to another facet of *authenticité*, the desire for "the return of traditional art objects to Zaire so as to inspire contemporary artists."[28] All together, this complex small sculpture suggests an enthusiasm for Mobutu and his efforts in shaping Zaire. It was an endorsement of *authenticité* and *salongo* from an artist who believed strongly in civic responsibility—always orienting his own work to the collective rather than the individual (one never finds a private residence among his projects)—and who, in his own words, "devotes his daily life to excellence."[29] No other work would make such explicit reference to Mobutu's regime, though Kingelez's political engagement continued to manifest itself in sculptures that imagined a world untainted by corruption, greed, and economic disparity.

Kingelez would go on to make numerous works whose titles suggest the administrative, political, or governmental functions necessary for a successful democratic state. The handsome trapezoidal form of 1992's *Reveillon Fédéral* (pl. 20) evokes a kind of temple to democracy, with at least eight doorways marked in multiple languages, offering many ways to enter, and adornments referring to local fauna: a leaping zebra (reclaimed from a box of matches) and a horned impala. Kingelez wrote of this work in lofty terms, explaining his choice of palette: "The red and yellow symbolizes victory and absolutely reminds us of 'the Martyrs' blood' that ran through the meanders of this fight for pure freedom."[30]

The symbolic meaning of color was as carefully considered by Kingelez as it had been by Mobutu. The first iteration of the president's flag was blue with a yellow star and a red diagonal stripe, with red symbolizing the blood of the people's sacrifice; yellow, prosperity; blue, hope; and the star, unity. Following the adoption of *authenticité* in 1971, a new Constitution of Zaire was issued in 1974. Article 4 decreed: "The emblem of the Republic is a light green flag, ornamented in the centre with a yellow circle in which a right hand is holding a torch with a red flame." Hope was embodied by light green; unity by the circle, whose color represented Zaire's extensive natural resources; and the nation's revolutionary spirit by the torch-bearing arm, its red flames an honor to its martyrs. This approach to color and the use of the flag as a potent symbol of nationhood and pride were practices Kingelez would turn to throughout his career.

Air Force (pl. 12), made in 1991, recalls Zaire's military, the group from which Mobutu rose, and specifically the Force Aérienne Zaïroise, which had been active since about 1961. Though sober in coloration, seen from above the work is a riot of black, red, and white stripes; it is topped with a sign bearing an icon that recalls the Belgian flag. The structure's handsome facade is marked by a tidy grid of round windows and four-pointed stars set in relief. Of the star, one of the most prevalent motifs in his work, Kingelez wrote, "It's . . . the ultimate symbol of wisdom which has a double origin. The first, the spiritual origin, in the form of a star, represents humanity. The star is born as displayed in the sky. It's a magisterial symbol for which All Powerful God The Creator communicated to His people on earth. The second is the material origin of the star. It's the representation of equilibrium on earth."[31]

Medical infrastructure was also a key element of Kingelez's civic necessities. Suggesting the campus of a sophisticated medical center and marked with signs calling for silence, *The Scientific Center of Hospitalisation the SIDA* (pl. 17), also of 1991, was constructed in part of reused paper packaging from a malaria medication. Epidemiological history suggests that 1970s Kinshasa was the epicenter of the first epidemic of HIV/AIDS (*SIDA* in French); by the mid-1980s, when Mobutu banned the subject in the press, six to eight percent of the population was believed to be infected. Around the time Kingelez made the work, the World Bank committed resources to Zaire's newly established National AIDS Control Program, which brought condoms, screening kits, and a testing laboratory to Kinshasa, the only such facility successfully established by the program.[32]

KINGELEZ AND KINSHASA: 1970s AND '80s

Before conceiving of a career as an artist, Kingelez struggled to define his professional aspirations, considering various vocations inclined toward civic engagement. He had the idea of being a magistrate, but dismissed the notion because, he said, "I realized I was too strict and impartial to judge people suitably."[33] He also thought of becoming a member of the government, one of the "university-trained technocrats and senior civil servants" with whom Mobutu staffed his government, "to help build a better world."[34] In Kinshasa, he attended the University of Lovanium, where he focused on economics but took classes in a wide range of subjects, including, he later reported, "business, French correspondence, industrial and business accounting, [and] industrial design."[35] In time, he would put all of these skills to excellent use: his French in the drafting of the extraordinary, poetic texts that often accompany his works; the accounting skills in running a tremendously successful sole proprietorship; and his knowledge of design principles in the construction techniques that underlie his sculptures.

Kingelez has often been described as a self-taught artist or an autodidact, even though he was a university graduate with a background in industrial design, and spoke five languages.[36] It is true that he did not attend art school or a formal artist's training program; such opportunities were limited, even though, as the former Belgian colonial capital, Kinshasa had long been one of the country's centers of cultural production.[37] A rise in Christian missionary activity in the 1930s had resulted in increased Western-style educational opportunities for colonial subjects in Congo, including, in some cases, the creation of art schools or experimental art workshops.[38] The Académie d'Art Populaire Indigène, also known as "Le Hangar," was established in 1946 by Pierre Romain-Desfossés in Elisabethville (now Lubumbashi). As its name suggests, it sought not to inculcate Western aesthetic ideas but rather offered a free workspace and access to materials, with the only guiding principles that the artists follow their own creative impulses and not repeat themselves.[39] In a rather paternalistic process, Romain-Desfossés administered an entrance exam for potential new students, asking them to depict certain subjects. From the results, he determined the artist's area of speciality, either easel painting (which was considered prestigious) or decorative painting (a marketable skill, used in hotels or for public signage).[40] Alternately, the École Saint-Luc, established by Belgian missionary Marc Wallenda in Gombe-Matadi in 1943, offered a multiyear cycle of art instruction in sculpture, the most widely practiced art form in the region at that time, as well as drawing, casting, and other disciplines, with a focus on Western-style academic realism and naturalism. Wallenda's school relocated to Léopoldville in 1949, where it expanded, offering courses in painting, ceramics, and architectural drawing, and eventually, in 1957, metamorphosed into the city's Académie des Beaux-Arts.[41] These differing strategies eventually led to a seeming schism between the country's esteemed contemporary artists: those who produced "authentic" work like the patterned, flora- and fauna-filled drawings of Pilipili Mulongoy (1914–2007) versus those who worked in a figurative, more academic style based in part on Western models, like N'damvu Tsiku-Pezo (1939–1997), whose mural commissions adorned several presidential buildings.[42] In the 1970s, the situation was further enriched by the rise of the *peintres populaires*, or "popular painters," including Moké (1950–2001) and Chéri Samba (born 1956), many of whom had a background in commercial sign painting, and whose colorful, figurative work, inspired by daily life, created a new paradigm for contemporary Congolese art. Neither trained in nor belonging to any of these prevailing tendencies, Kingelez stood resolutely apart right from the beginning of his career.

In the mid-1970s, he took a position as a secondary-school instructor. By his own account, he was quite good: "They said I was an excellent teacher, as all my students passed the bac[calaureate exam]."[43] Meanwhile, the city continued to grow and shift around him. The population had swelled to approximately 1.3 million, a number that would grow to 3.4 million by 1990 and 5 million ten years later. As Mobutu's early championing of the new nation slid steadily into despotism and self-enrichment, the country entered a long period of political and economic instability, further undermined by the policies of the International Monetary Fund, which continued to provide loans to Zaire despite evidence of high-level corruption and insupportable debt, and by inflation and tax hikes that devalued wages. These failings were transforming Kinshasa into "a city where students do not study, workers do not work, ministers do not administrate," in the words of poet and journalist Lye Mudaba Yoka, a contemporary of Kingelez's. It was, however, a place of "great creativity and improvisation," he said. "To the outsider, the perception is chaos. For me it is not chaos at all. We've developed an informal system. And within this informal system, there's an organization."[44] Indeed, the music scene was thriving and gaining worldwide renown, the flamboyant self-expression of the city's sapeurs was attaining international acclaim, and the *peintres populaires* would soon be included in museum exhibitions around the world.

In the rapidly changing milieu of late-1970s Kinshasa, young Kingelez found himself feeling restless and unfulfilled: "I understood that I couldn't reach my goals as a teacher," he later said. "I needed to stake out more brilliant options."[45] In 1978 he terminated his teaching career without knowing what would come next. "I drew up a list of ideas in my little room. Then a muddled confusion set in me and lasted for more than a month. It was at this time that I became obsessed with the idea of getting my hands on some scissors, a Gillette razor, and some glue and paper. It felt like fate when I finally did procure this particular material, and things became clearer then. I put together a little house without quite understanding the meaning of it all. And this is what stopped the fatal hemorrhaging."[46] The drama of this event would be typical for Kingelez. He described the desire to make art as almost an illness, a pain that was alleviated by creation. He said of his process: "I can't stand any sound, not even a mosquito. I'm more aggressive with my kids. It's like I'm ill."[47] His family concurred. His second wife, Madeleine Mupanga, told him, "You're awful when you're creating a work of art. You're agitated, you're not happy with yourself. If your work isn't going as planned, you're touchy."[48]

Following the creation of this first sculpture, there was a quick succession of events: Kingelez made a second work, titled *Musée National*, which a neighbor helped him transport to City Hall, where—given its subject matter—the administrator suggested that he take it to the Institut des Musées Nationaux du Zaïre (IMNZ, now the Institut des Musées Nationaux du Congo). The institute had been established jointly as a cooperative enterprise (in name, if not in practice) by the Belgian and Zairean governments in 1969–70; it was launched with enthusiastic support from Mobutu, who viewed the traditional art of the region—the institute's focus—as powerful and persuasive cultural capital. The director general, Frère Joseph-Aurélien Cornet (1919–2004), a Belgian missionary and art historian who spent nearly thirty years in the country, was the person to whom Kingelez hoped to present the work, but before reaching Cornet, he was subjected to a gauntlet of interrogation.[49] One after another, a series of museum staffers suggested that the work, with its remarkable level of invention and accomplishment, could not be his, and that he had surely stolen it. In a misguided attempt to prove Kingelez a liar, they challenged him to make another work on-site, while they watched. Kingelez produced the sculpture *Commissariat Atomique* under these conditions, and the staff, so impressed by his artistic skills and the dexterity with which he manipulated his materials (and chagrined, perhaps, at their gross error), offered him a job as a "*technicien restaurateur*," repairing works in the museum's collection.[50]

By the time Kingelez started his new job, the collection of the IMNZ was estimated at between thirty thousand and thirty-eight thousand objects (fig. 3), built by modest transfers of works from the Royal Museum for Central Africa in Tervuren, Belgium, along with an extensive program of local expeditions and acquisitions.[51] Over the next six years, Kingelez worked on objects ranging from wooden sculptures to ceramic vessels. The job gave him access to supplies and materials, the opportunity to ponder what made certain artworks and artifacts worthy of collection and consideration, and, as he later noted, the chance to hone his technical ability: "These ruined statues led me to the pinnacle of my skills."[52] He took characteristic pride in the excellence of his work despite his lack of formal conservation or restoration training. "My perfection," he said, "was such that I was even mistaken for a forger. I never learned the metier but how little this mattered; I came from a traditional village where everyday I used to watch the men making masks or working at the forge. There was no need to learn, then, what I used to see all the time."[53]

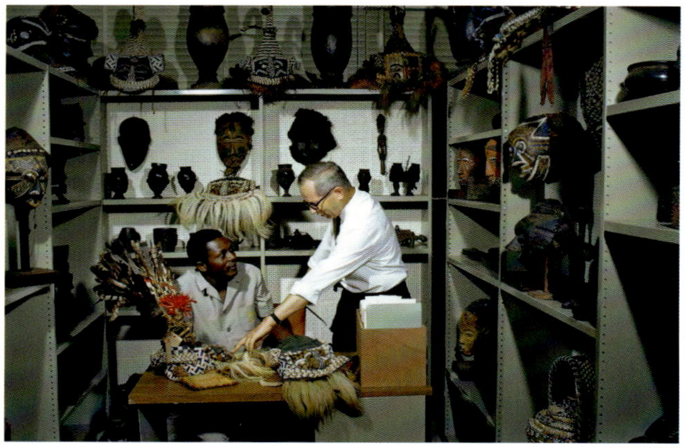

3. Frère Joseph-Aurélien Cornet, director of the Institut des Musées Nationaux du Zaïre (right), at the museum with an unidentified colleague, Kinshasa, 1972

It was during this period that Kingelez likely experienced the first significant interest in his work. While Kinshasa did not have a strong network of commercial galleries, exhibition spaces, artist residency programs, and museums, the city's French and Belgian cultural centers supported a number of artistic activities, and anecdotes and archival materials suggest that organizations like these were instrumental in helping Kingelez make his work more visible.[54] Around 1981 the architect Christian Girard traveled to Kinshasa in the employ of the French government for a series of urban-planning projects, and a colleague there suggested that he might be interested in meeting a man who was making what he called "strange models."[55] Girard visited Kingelez at the IMNZ, where he recalls seeing a shelf full of sculptures in the restoration office: miniature administrative buildings, churches, and amusement parks.

What is extant of that remarkably rare early work demonstrates that even at this nascent stage of his career, Kingelez had already developed many of the hallmarks of his mature style. The palette is predominately monochrome—a function of the paperboard and cardstock varieties that were most readily available—but it is accented with brilliant bursts of color from found paper and packaging materials. An untitled sculpture from 1980 (pl. 2) suggests that his ideas about how a work is conceived, composed, and constructed were then well established, as was his system of cataloguing the objects. The untitled sculpture immediately suggests an architectural form—a contemporary urban building. A symmetrical but dynamic rectangular prism, marked on the front face by ten rows of precisely hand-cut openings backed with white tissue, sits atop a series of flared fins cut from blazing orange cardstock. Triangular additions of gray translucent plastic protrude from its sides. The structure is topped with a skeletal sphere made of strips of black paper; its shape recalls the universal symbol for atomic energy, an icon Kingelez depicts in many works. In this, he was likely inspired by something close at hand: TRICO I, the African continent's first nuclear reactor, had been installed in 1959 at Kingelez's alma mater, the University of Lovanium. Established with Belgian funds in 1954 and initially overseen by Jesuit missionaries, the university aspired to be one of the continent's premier educational institutions, and it was the first in the country to provide a course of study for doctors, architects, and civil engineers.[56] In 1972 TRICO I was succeeded by TRICO II; the campus, now part of the University of Kinshasa, still hosts the research reactor and the Centre Régional d'Etudes Nucléaires de Kinshasa.[57] The country also contains the world's richest uranium mine, the source of the material used to produce the atomic bombs dropped by the United States on Hiroshima and Nagasaki in 1945.

This untitled sculpture includes an early example of the system Kingelez used to number his works throughout his career. In this instance, a round paper medallion, positioned prominently on the base of the object, bears the hand-lettered information "BODYS-KIS J. 58-27-11-80," signifying a work, number 58, made on November 27, 1980. Kingelez numbered every work he made, and he claimed that he made over three thousand.[58] Girard noted that when he visited the artist in 1982, the sequential numbering was already over two hundred; a 1980 work numbered 58 confirms the plausibility of the system, if not the later total.[59] Kingelez worked in a museum, so he knew that the cataloguing of artwork was critical. He had likely seen a lack of information confound and frustrate his colleagues as they struggled to date and attribute an object. He was also intimately familiar with the IMNZ's methodology for numbering the works in their collection: each object bore a unique identifier, composed of the last two numbers of the year it was acquired, plus the number of the lot or series and the position of the work within the lot.[60] Kingelez's use of this highly visible system of signing and numbering his sculptures ensured that the attribution of his work would never be at issue and positioned it, with both optimism and foresight, as if it were already part of an institutional collection.

Among the few published accounts of this early period of Kingelez's career is an article written by Girard and Jacques Soulillou, a critic, art historian, and cultural attaché who spent years running French cultural centers in Cameroon and Nigeria, among other assignments. In the October 1984 issue of the journal *autrement*, in a brief rundown of artistic activities in African capitals—from embroidery and photography to polychrome sculpture—they refer to three of Kingelez's early works by title (*Maryland University USA* [pl. 3], *Le Ministère Belge de la Guerre*, and *Le Palais Modeste d'Espagne de l'Antique Marine Commerciale*) and attest to the serious and substantial nature of his activities, which they describe as "architecture in paper."[61] A small black-and-white photograph of Kingelez's *Kinshasa: Cité du 24 Novembre de l'Authenticité Africaine* (fig. 4) bears a caption that erroneously identifies the work as made by "a Brazzavillois who works in an adminstrative office."[62] The authors testify to his unshakable belief in his talent and

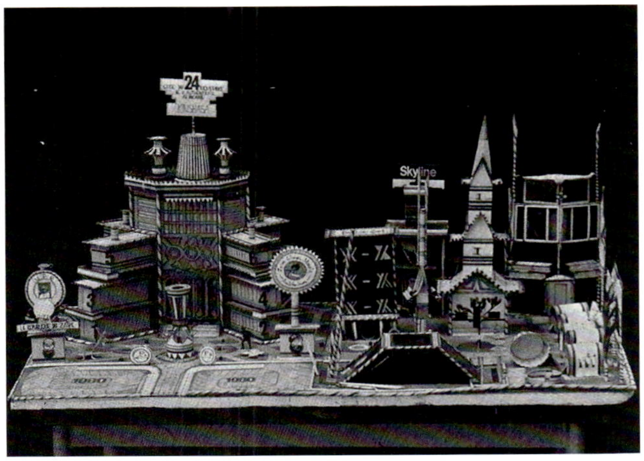

4. Photograph of Kingelez's *Kinshasa: Cité du 24 Novembre de l'Authenticité Africaine,* 1980, as reproduced in Jacques Soulillou and Christian Girard, "Une internationale de l'art urbain," *autrement,* "Les capitales de la couleur," ed. Bruno Tilliette, special issue no. 9 (October 1984): 278

his project, noting that he "claims the title of artist with vehemence, and waits for nothing more than universal recognition."[63]

DESIGNER, ARCHITECT, SCULPTOR, ENGINEER, ARTIST

In a later text, Girard recalled that on first seeing Kingelez's work, he was struck by its similarities to the architecture of Michael Graves, an American associated with postmodernism, perhaps because Kingelez's designs, like Graves's, embrace ornament and decidedly reject the modernist edict that form must follow function.[64] Girard assumed, likely correctly, that Kingelez had had no direct contact with work by Graves or with other buildings in the postmodern style, since he didn't travel outside Zaire until 1989. "I had never seen any other city," the artist later said, looking back at the moment he began his artistic practice. "For me, Kinshasa was The City; I had never seen any other, not even in photos. I had never traveled before. I neither read nor looked at magazines."[65] There were, however, many rich local architectural sources for him to draw on, from the Art Deco buildings of the colonial era that still lined the streets of Kinshasa, to the ambitious structures of the post-Independence period, and it is clear that the sculptures Kingelez began making feverishly in the early 1980s—which he soon dubbed "*extrêmes maquettes*"—had their precedent in the urban fabric around him.

Mobutu was personally invested in the power of architecture, which he harnessed to glorify his rule. In 1966 he opened the Presidential Domain of Nsele, an idealized shadow city in suburban Kinshasa built to host foreign dignitaries and international delegations interested in developing agricultural or trade programs with the country.[66] In 1975 the British writer V. S. Naipaul likened Nsele to a luxury resort, with amenities such as air conditioning and, according to one report, gold-plated bathroom fixtures.[67] Among the palaces Mobutu built there was a pagoda, designed and constructed by Chinese personnel already working at the site and intended to connect his reign to the splendor and power of the Chinese imperial dynasties. He also built a complex of pagoda-style buildings in his hometown, Gbadolite, deep in the country's northern rain forest (fig. 5). During his reign, he completely redeveloped Gbadolite, transforming it into an outpost of opulence and luxury that has been referred to as "Versailles in the jungle."[68] He built an airport (with an extended runway to accommodate intercontinental jets, including the *Concorde*), boulevards, banks, hospitals, and a Coca-Cola bottling plant, as well as multiple presidential homes, including an undulating multistory villa with an Olympic-sized swimming pool, known as the Palais des Bambous.[69]

One of the principal designers of the presidential complex at Gbadolite was the Tunisian-born French architect Olivier-Clément Cacoub (1920–2008). He was also responsible for high-profile projects in France and for the post-Independence leaders of North and sub-Saharan Africa, including palaces in Ivory Coast, Cameroon, and Tunisia. Known as the "*architecte du soleil*," for his penchant for warmer climes and his loose, playful style, Cacoub approached his projects with an organic freedom—"I make architecture like I make gestures," he said[70]—and a reformist spirit: "In effect, our era has definitively broken away from sad and somber offices with their narrow

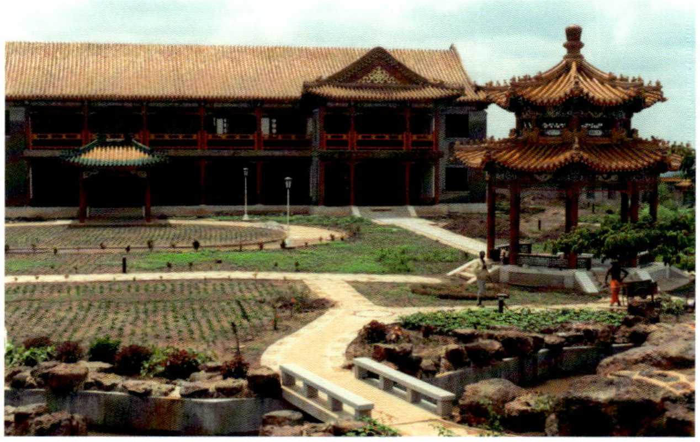

5. Private residence of Mobutu Sese Seko (construction began c. 1970), Gbadolite, n.d.

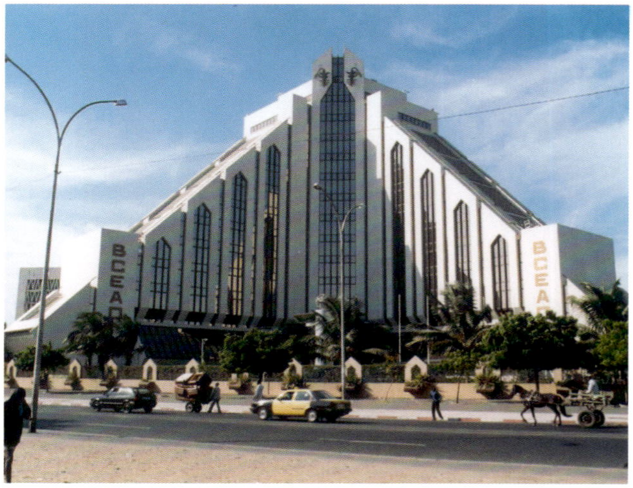

6. Banque Centrale des États de l'Afrique de l'Ouest (constructed 1975–90), Dakar, Senegal, 1985. Architect: Pierre Goudiaby Atepa

windows and their oppressive conference rooms. Light, sobriety, and functionality have made their way into our offices, our factories, our courtrooms, our laboratories."[71]

Cacoub's codesigner on the Gbadolite complex was Pierre Goudiaby Atepa (born 1947), a Senegalese architect known for projects throughout the African continent but most notably in Dakar. In 1973 Goudiaby presented a thesis on the ideal African city. Its first key feature, he said, is that it must be "profoundly African. The second, that it is turned toward an assured modernity. The third, that it is a solar city."[72] Known for buildings with improbable, sweeping contours, like his pyramidal headquarters for the Banque Centrale des États de l'Afrique de l'Ouest in Dakar (fig. 6), Goudiaby draws on myriad sources, from the handmade cloth his mother used to sell, to the baobab tree and the calabash, to Doric columns: "The Romans stole ideas from the Greeks, the Americans stole from the Europeans. Now it's our turn. I use whatever I want and make it African."[73] This attitude toward architecture, unanchored by Western conventions, is clearly reflected in Kingelez's constructions.

Although few locals outside the upper echelons of government had the opportunity to see Cacoub's work at Gbadolite, another of his projects was a prominent landmark in Kinshasa. The Tour de l'Échangeur (alternately known as the Monument to Patrice Lumumba, the Monument to National Heroes, and the Limete Tower) was planned to be among the tallest buildings in Africa; construction began in 1971, but it was never fully completed. Commissioned by Mobutu, the tower—four soaring columns topped by a structure designed to house observation platforms and a restaurant—was centrally located in the industrial neighborhood of Limete and visible from a great distance in all directions (fig. 7). Certainly Kingelez knew this futuristic monument, impractical in form but limitless in possibility, and it was evidently the model for his own skyward-thrusting work, *Approche de l'Échangeur de Limete Kin* of 1981 (pl. 4).[74]

In 1972 Cacoub was commissioned to design an international trade center for Kinshasa, the Centre Commercial International du Zaïre, an effort to position the city at the center of the African business world. It was envisioned as a complex of office towers, meeting halls, a six thousand–seat conference center, and a thousand-room hotel, but only the first twenty-story tower was completed before the project was abandoned.[75] Cacoub's model shows two trapezoidal buildings of different sizes, a skyscraper, a series of disc-shaped structures staggered at different heights, and an undulating, S-shaped tower set into a horizontal plane (fig. 8). Kingelez moved to the city shortly before the plans for the development project were announced to great fanfare; in its fantastical forms and iconoclastic layout, the model bears a striking similarity to the sculptures he would later build.

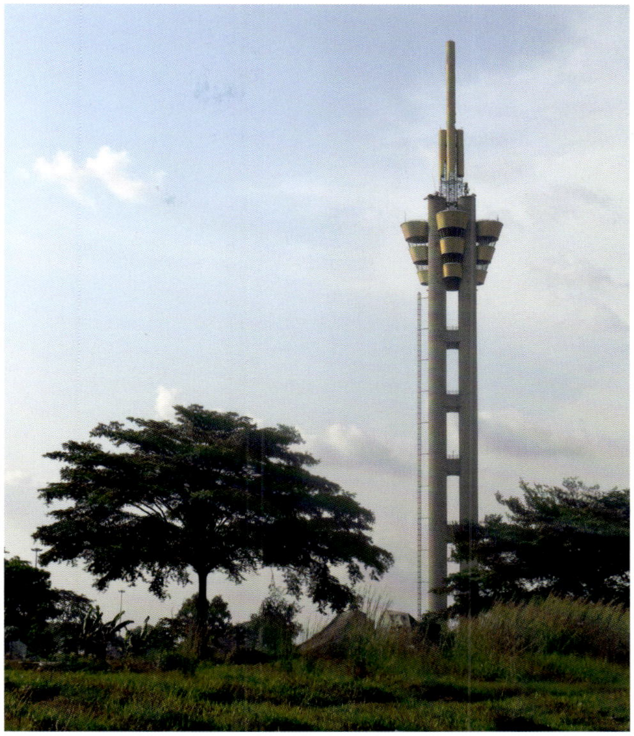

7. Tour de l'Échangeur (construction began 1971), Kinshasa, 2010. Architect: Olivier-Clément Cacoub

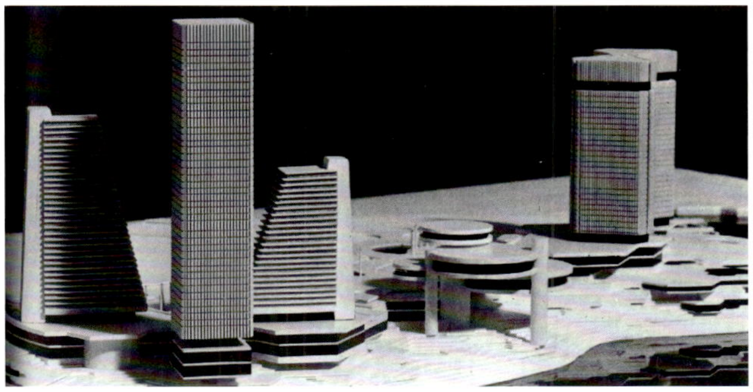

8. Model of the Centre Commercial International du Zaïre, Kinshasa, early 1970s. Architect: Olivier-Clément Cacoub

The connection between Kingelez's work and the practice of architecture has been discussed by several writers and curators. Ismail Serageldin has placed it in a category he identifies as "architectural sculpture," which is free, he writes, from architecture's responsibility to "retain a social and functional role, whether built with or without architects. . . . Architectural sculpture is liberated from such restrictions and can push form, texture, and color far into the realm of the imaginary, as it does in [Kingelez's] hands."[76] Writing about Kingelez's 2001 sculpture *Köln,* commissioned by Museum Ludwig, Cologne, Marjorie Jongbloed has likewise made the case for hybridity: "Kingelez's models are architecture, painting, and sculpture in one. They are hermetically sealed and impossible to enter; they have no inner life. In this regard, they only refer to architecture."[77] As to Kingelez's intentions, a friend of the artist commented, "Kingelez is not an architect and does not wish to be considered one. He is surprised when you ask him if he wants to see his works actually built."[78] Dan Cameron has intuited rightly that "the point is not so much that Kingelez plans someday to be able to build these structures, but rather that the act of imagining them and bringing them into existence, albeit through maquettes, represents an almost fervent idealism which over time will invariably have its impact on the types of visions that other, less poetic city planners may bring to bear on the future of other African cities."[79] That is to say, Kingelez is not an architect but rather the creator of a new and hybrid form. Drawn both from airy flights of imagination and the solidity of reality, his work proposes an idealized vision for the future, one that architects, city planners, and builders may one day be inspired by.

GLOBAL VISIONS

On June 30, 1969—Zaire's Independence Day—Mobutu, with King Baudouin of Belgium as his guest, inaugurated the first Foire Internationale de Kinshasa (FIKIN).[80] Held on what would become a permanent fairground in the neighborhood of Limete, not far from Cacoub's tower, the international trade and culture fair featured the participation of more than twenty countries and hosted nearly 600,000 people during its three-week run. The fairground's designer was the Congo-born, Belgian-trained architect Fernand Tala-Ngai (1938–2006), who would go on to design other municipal buildings in Kinshasa in the 1970s and '80s, including a residence for Mobutu (the Palais de Marbre, on Mount Ngaliema), the Supreme Court building, and the Hôtel de la Monnaie (fig. 9), with its scalloped base and brise soleil–gridded facade connected to an existing building by a bridge of four-pointed stars.[81] According to reports, the fairground was like an ideal mini-Kinshasa, featuring amenities such as new drainage systems, paved roads, public toilets, and copious parking, along with beer gardens and cafes, copper-roofed exhibition halls, national pavilions, and demonstrations of the latest in mining technology and energy development.[82] An amusement park was added the following year, including a carousel, a roller coaster, and a tunnel of love. A photograph from the period shows dozens of flags waving in the wind over landscaped grounds, with national pavilions (and Cacoub's tower, still under construction) visible in the distance (fig. 10). These pavilions, a staple of world's fairs, created something akin to a United Nations, with each sponsoring country showcasing the resources, technologies, cultural traditions, and specific histories it contributed to the global story. Newly arrived in Kinshasa, Kingelez was likely among the hundreds of thousands of residents who visited FIKIN in its early years, and it is enticing to think that his encounter there with an array of international cultures and styles, set within a cheerful, orderly microcosm of the larger, sprawling city, influenced his later work.[83]

Kingelez's sculptures are filled with evocations of nationally or geographically specific architectural tropes from outside Africa, like the tiered Asian-inspired forms in *Palais d'Hirochima* (pl. 15), of 1991, which the artist described as a homage to Japanese culture and a salve for the memory of the "intolerable tragedy imposed by the Americans in 40–45."[84] In addition to the fairground, the marvels of Nsele, and the architectural landmarks designed by Cacoub, Kinshasa featured a diverse range of building styles. A group of buildings nicknamed the *hollandaises*, or "Dutch houses," had been erected in the Gombe neighborhood around 1925 for the use of colonial functionaries temporarily based in Kinshasa (fig. 11);[85] they are evoked in Kingelez's 1991 sculpture *Belle Hollandaise* (pl. 16), with its swooping gables. Its central grid is backed with Christmas wrapping paper featuring a celestial Santa

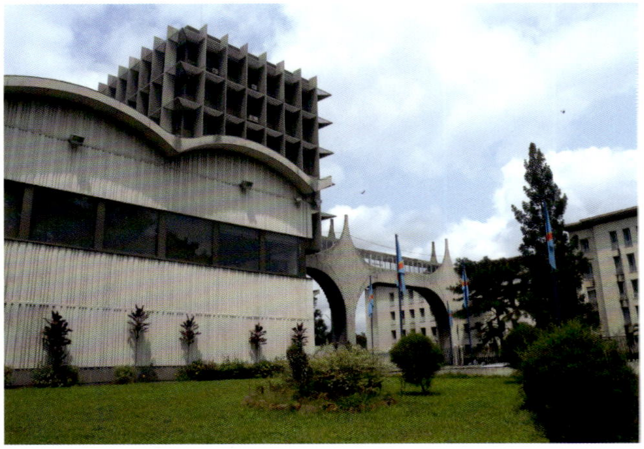

9. Hôtel de la Monnaie (constructed 1980), Kinshasa, 2010. Architect: Fernand Tala-Ngai

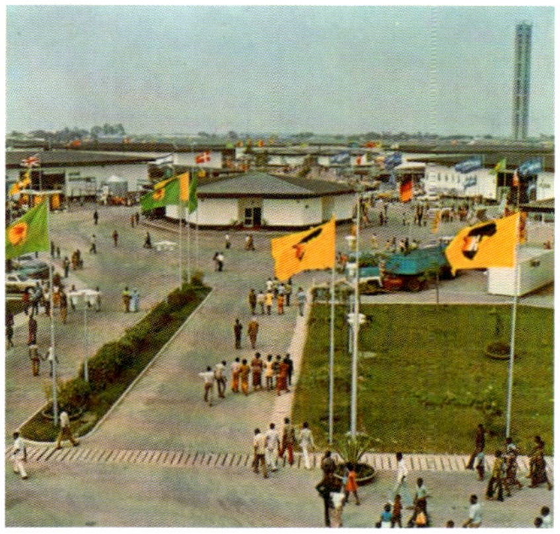

10. The entrance to the Foire Internationale de Kinshasa (FIKIN), 1971. Architect: Fernand Tala-Ngai

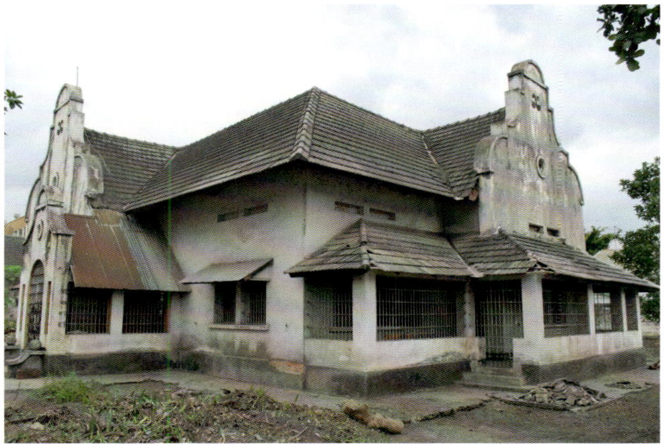

11. *Hollandaise* house (constructed c. 1925–26), Kinshasa, 2010

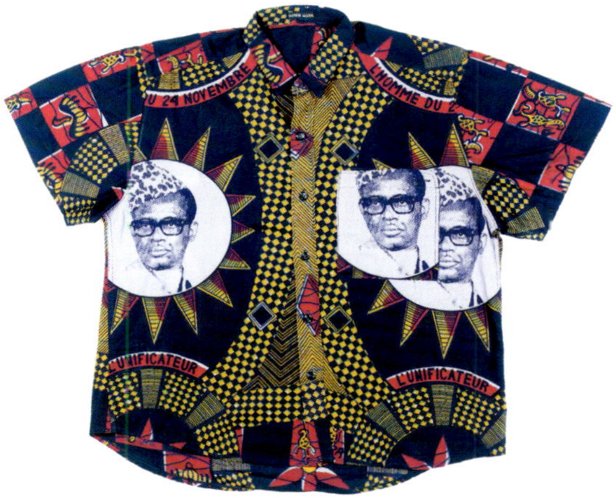

12. Wax hollandais shirt with a portrait of Mobutu Sese Seko, made after 1966. Nationaal Museum van Wereldculturen, Netherlands

driving a train full of toys across the night sky, surrounded by gift-giving cherubs and bare-bottomed putti, evocations of the North Pole that may have been prompted by Kingelez's experience in the chilly northern Netherlands the year it was made.[86] The title of the work might also refer to wax hollandais textiles, the colorful, patterned wax-printed fabrics that have been designed, manufactured, and exported by the Dutch for African consumption since the mid-nineteenth century.[87] Vlisco, the most prestigious producer of wax hollandais, has its flagship store in Kinshasa; it continually updates its roster of patterns, incorporating references to contemporary culture, from car brands to political figures (fig. 12).

With *U.N.* (pl. 27), Kingelez made a direct tribute to the United Nations, whose peacekeeping presence had returned to Congo in 1999 after a long hiatus, and whose blue-helmeted personnel were a common sight in Kinshasa. He created the work for *Dialogues de paix*, a 1995 exhibition in Geneva that celebrated the fiftieth anniversary of the founding of the United Nations and aimed to include artists from fifty countries on five continents.[88] Kingelez, who visited Geneva to deliver his work in person, recalled, "It was at the time of the war in Yugoslavia. We stood up for peace, artists from all over the world, but I was the most famous one."[89] His contribution was in some ways a striking departure from his earlier sculptures, and he referred to it as "an expansion" of his work.[90] *U.N.* has a decidedly asymmetrical overall form: a tall tower with a protruding arc and flared foot at left is paired with a fluted half-circle at right. And the tower's surface, unusually, has been impressionistically hand-colored and overlaid with a red grid. The interior of the half-circle is lined with narrow bands of black and silver and dotted with collaged stars, and the base is punctuated at irregular intervals with conical trees. A sweeping stair rises to an elevated platform ringed with flags. "The dominant color is clearly blue, the color universally associated with the United Nations," Kingelez wrote. "The stars are distributed around the form of the building. They represent the member countries, which I want to be equal. In this palace, peace is an indispensable tool for the democracy of nations."[91]

KINGELEZ IN PARIS: *MAGICIENS DE LA TERRE*

The 1989 exhibition *Magiciens de la terre*, mounted in Paris at the Centre Georges Pompidou and the Grande Halle de la Villette, was the first to bring Kingelez's work to an international audience. It would be difficult to overstate the reverberating impact of the show, which Cameron likened several years later to the act of "toss[ing] a bomb into the village square of the international art community."[92] Organized by curator Jean-Hubert Martin, with Mark Francis,

Aline Luque, and André Magnin, *Magiciens de la terre* was a pioneering and controversial attempt at creating a global contemporary art exhibition. It was planned with the express and primary goal of recalibrating the inclusion of artists from the "mainstream" and the "margins" of artistic production through the development of a checklist that would include Western and non-Western artists in equal proportion. This ambition was met in art history circles with deep suspicion. A preemptive take-down by Guy Brett called into question the project's potential for success, emphasizing the likelihood that it would end up flattening the artists' contributions into Western art world–approved sameness: "For have not the subversive and emancipatory projects of the 20th century avant-garde—from the surrealists at one pole, with their proposals to 'liberate desire,' to the constructivists at the other, with their plans to transform the environment—been reduced, first by the art market and then by the wider range of lifestyle, to the same bland range of designer-commodities?"[93] Martin has gone on to devote much of his career to attempts at dissolving the binaries of West/non-West, fine art/vernacular that plague many institutions, and in a lively, at times barbed and contentious conversation in advance of the exhibition, he seemed perfectly aware of the potential pitfalls of his project, refuting each of them in turn and asserting, "Our first concern is with exchange and dialogue, with understanding others in order to understand what we do ourselves."[94]

How was it that Kingelez, who at the time had no international profile to speak of, came to be included in the exhibition? The curators called on experts in France and abroad for suggestions and guidance as they began their exploratory research.[95] One source was Jean-François Bizot, the Paris-based editor-in-chief of the culture-oriented monthly *Actuel* and founder of the world-music broadcaster Radio Nova, whose work occasionally took him to Kinshasa. He was friendly with Samba, the *peintre populaire* whom he had commissioned to do a project for *Actuel* in 1982, and so was able to connect the exhibition organizers with him and make some suggestions about whom to see in Kinshasa. Martin himself happened upon the 1984 article by Girard and Soulillou in *autrement*, with its unattributed black-and-white photograph, and he put the artist on a list of figures to investigate.[96] He later called on Soulillou, then stationed in Douala, Cameroon, to help locate Kingelez, which he did in 1987.[97] Magnin made a trip to Kinshasa and met the artist; upon his debrief with the curatorial team back in Paris, there seemed to be little doubt that Kingelez would be included in the exhibition.[98]

A photograph taken in Kinshasa in 1988 (fig. 13) shows Kingelez sitting in a narrow, high-walled alley with three works intended for the exhibition. *Allemagne An 2000* (pl. 6) and *Paris Nouvel* (pl. 7) were included in the show; the third, *Brasilia*, was badly damaged in transport.[99] Kingelez had purchased some materials in Kinshasa with the money advanced by the exhibition organizers upon the commissioning of the sculptures, and while formally they are clearly connected to the earlier work of the 1980s, materially they are noticeably different. Gone are the collaged elements from reclaimed packaging and the palette dictated primarily by the discarded materials Kingelez was able to source. The new mediums include pencil, colored pencil, watercolor, colored paper and cardstock, silver reflective paper, and gold metallic paper (rolled to form tiny tubes), all of which the artist could have bought at a local stationery or hardware store. From this point forward, Kingelez used found materials less often, although he returned to them with gusto in the early 2000s. In an offhand remark, Jonathan Jones later wrote of the artist that "his delicate colourful follies are made from the unwanted detritus of city life. Kingelez incorporates any old rubbish into his architectural language—packaging of all kinds, bits of cardboard, shiny paper."[100] In fact, Kingelez always selected his materials with care, and even in the earliest works he did not use stained or discolored paper, despite the challenge that might have presented. Susan Vogel has noted that, "to us [in the West], objects of cardboard and paper seem so ordinary, transitory, flimsy . . . but in Kinshasa these materials mean the opposite. They are exotic, expensive, and imported. It's even hard to keep this stuff clean."[101] Later the artist proudly declared that he had thirty thousand dollars worth of imported art materials in the front room of his house.[102]

In both *Paris Nouvel* and *Allemagne An 2000*—one ebullient, the other restrained—there is a sense of equilibrium and order. The buildings are symmetrical, regular, predictable: an opening on the left is matched by an opening on the right, a structural riposte to the improvisation-dominated ethos of the city in which Kingelez lived and worked. *Paris Nouvel* is dominated by pristine colored cardstock and, for the first time, gold, which Kingelez would go on to use in many sculptures. The work itself is a veritable riot of color and form, with repeating horizontal bands of sky blue, dancing red diamonds, and bands of white—hewing to the French *tricolore*—plus snaking ladders of gold. *Allemagne An 2000* is almost austere in comparison, a rational, rectangular form of black, red, and white, suggesting the colors of both the East and West German flags. Each level is adorned with the same orderly forms: three circles and a series of vertical parallel lines, along with an odd protruding shape in light green—an abstracted letter "b" that serves as a kind of monogram for the artist and a reminder to viewers that "Bodys made it."[103] Elevated on a series of tiers,

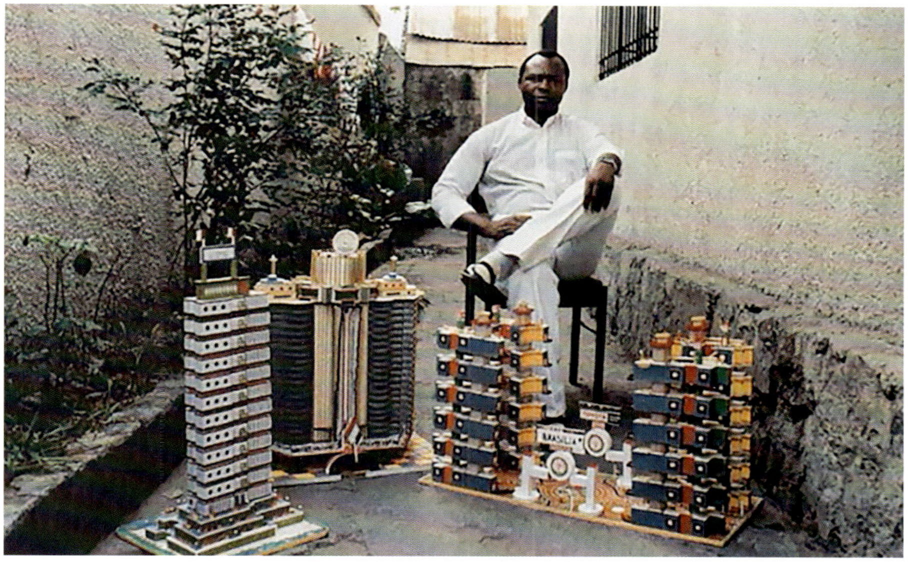

13. Kingelez in Kinshasa with *Allemagne An 2000* (1988, pl. 6), *Paris Nouvel* (1989, pl. 7), and *Brasilia* (1988), 1988

the building is surrounded by lanterns made of identical pins; lengths of yarn suggest trailing, verdant vines in round and rectangular planters. The painted base reflects Kingelez's inclination toward floral and star-shaped forms, which recur in almost every work. Both sculptures suggest a national character, early manifestations of this enduring concern.

The catalogue for *Magiciens de la terre* identifies each of the one hundred participating artists' country of origin and prints their responses to the question "*Qu'est-ce que l'art?*" (What is art?). Kingelez answered,

> Art, the rare product of great reflexive values, accompanied by serious movements of imagination, that the author of such invention turns toward the promises of dearer sacrifices of a better and hoped-for future.
>
> Art, with all its consequences of maturity, of creativity, is a hidden wealth whose cultivation requires patience, as well as respect of the talents which are specific to the latter in order to be commensurate with this knowledge.
>
> A vital necessity, art is a progress which marks the importance of a person, of a practice, or of a city that is developing harmoniously.
>
> Art is a higher knowledge of doing well in order to, in the end, live well, as it is one of modernism's types of individual and collective renewal.[104]

In this, his first published text, the artist's persona as a writer is fully developed. Lofty, high-minded, with big goals and ideals, he aspired to nothing less than a radical rethinking of the world around him. Just as he created his own visual language in his sculpture, he also began to invent new nouns and adjectives and new sentence structures to describe his philosophy and works. Kingelez had begun producing descriptive texts to accompany his sculptures in the early 1980s,[105] and by the late '80s and early '90s many of his new objects were paired with such a document. Virtually impossible to translate faithfully from the original French, the texts give another window into Kingelez's ethos and ideas. As Marie Lemeltier and Céline Soutif have written, these manuscripts have much in common with the sculptures they accompany: "In his texts as in his *extrêmes maquettes*, he presents himself as the creator of a new language. The artist imagines an unedited vocabulary and a rhetoric that form what he calls his '*langage bodysois*.' In effect, he uses fanciful words and syntax that reflect the demiurgic character of their creator. For the viewer-reader, the understanding of his texts requires abandoning all traditional or academic reference."[106] The *extrême maquette* finds its literary parallel in the artist's personal language, in which he constructs with words rather than with paper.

Magiciens de la terre included six sculptures by Kingelez (fig. 14), a combination of works made in Kinshasa and Paris, as he had been commissioned by the curators on behalf of the Grande Halle de la Villette to make several sculptures on-site.[107] The curatorial team supplied him with materials, assistants, and a studio space in the exhibition hall. Two of these works were reproduced in the catalogue.

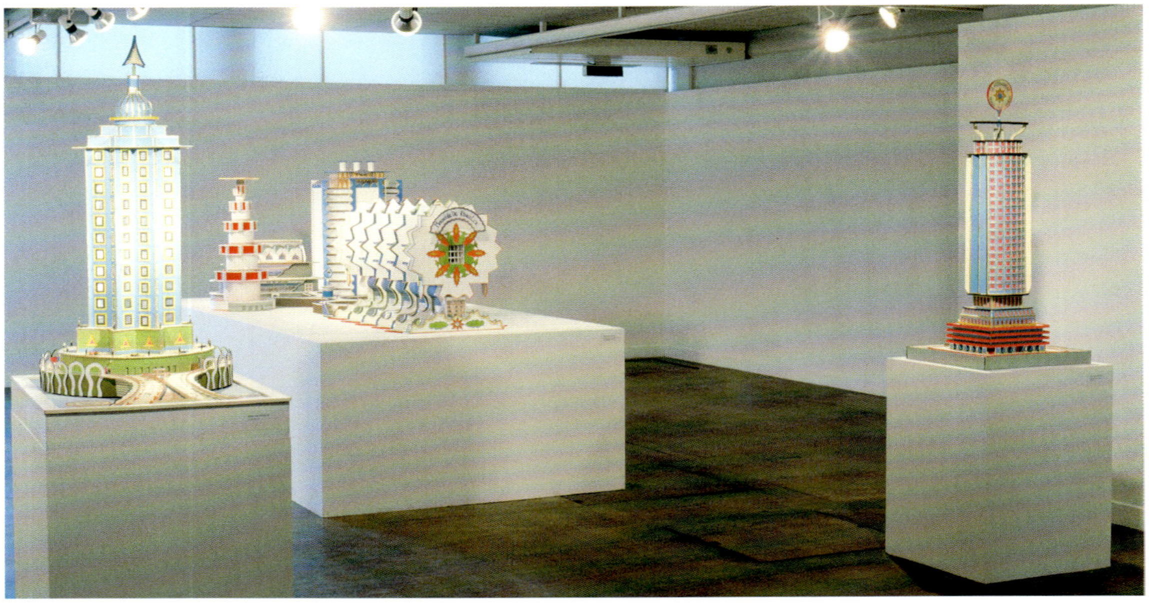

14. View of Kingelez's sculptures in the exhibition *Magiciens de la terre* at the Grande Halle de la Villette, Paris, 1989. From left: *La Croix du Ciel*, *Mausolée de Kingelez*, and *La Mitterannéenne Française* (all 1989)

La Croix du Ciel, a sky-blue tower more than eleven (miniature) stories tall and clad in a fitting azure, takes the form of an eight-pointed star (see fig. 14, left). The work is marked by no fewer than four assertions of the maker's identity: a round emblem with a fluted border that proudly announces in penciled block letters "BODYS ISEK-INGELEZ Kinshasa ZAÏRE ARCHITECTE MAQUETTISTE" (fig. 15); "Bodys isek-Kingelez L'Architecte," in red marker; and "Bodys-Isek-Ingelez" and "Bodys Isek Ingelez" in graphite. *La Mitterannéenne Française* (fig. 16), the other work reproduced in the catalogue, also reflects the artist's concerns with symmetry, regularity, and repetition, with nesting and layering, and with verticality and elevation, as it too reaches skyward, topped by a finial bedecked with an eight-pointed star. The title of the work introduces Kingelez's signature punning wordplay, in this case referring to François Mitterrand, then president of France. But while Mitterrand is referred to only once, the name of the maker ("Bodys," "Bodys-Isek-Ingelez," "Bodys-Ingelez-Isek") appears multiple times. These repetitions suggest the central position of the work's author. Unlike the anonymous objects Kingelez repaired at the IMNZ, these sculptures were not made by an invisible hand: the artist demands acknowledgement.

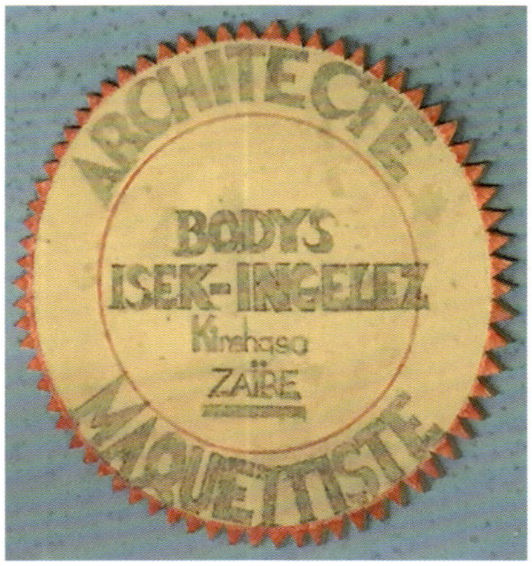

15. Bodys Isek Kingelez. *La Croix du Ciel* (detail), 1989. Musée du quai Branly–Jacques Chirac, Paris

Another work Kingelez made in Paris is *Mausolée de Kingelez* (see fig. 14, center, and p. 35, fig. 3), a sculpture of imposing scale and a horizontality new to his oeuvre. It takes the form of a multipointed, star-shaped tube, like one of his towers turned on its side and inflated. Video footage of the artist at work shows him hovering over the all-white skeleton of the unfinished work, placing and then re-placing elements with long tweezers and testing and adjusting the curve of the roof elements.[108] Constructed primarily of white foamcore and blue cardstock and decorated with marker, the central form has open grids at its ends that suggest large divided windows. They are lined with cotton mesh (presumably a newly acquired material), suggesting a screen or scrim. Perhaps most extraordinary are the tiny plastic figurines, the kind used to populate architectural models, arrayed inside like visitors to a tourist attraction (fig. 17).

Kingelez's participation in *Magiciens de la terre* was a turning point in his career, as it was the first significant

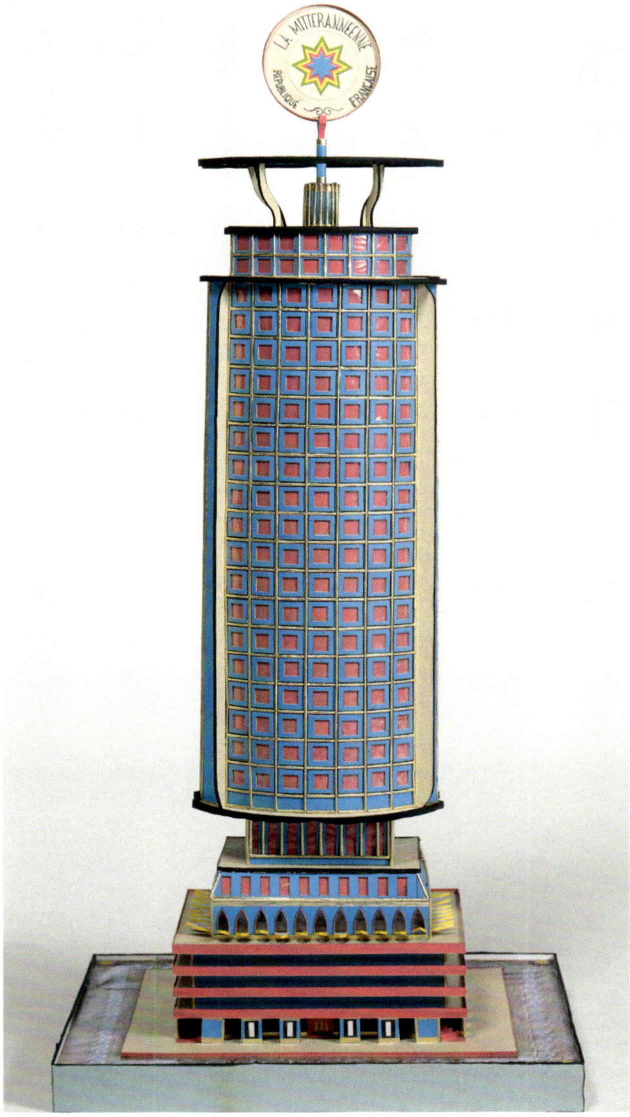

16. Bodys Isek Kingelez. *La Mitterannéenne Française.* 1989. 33 ½ x 17 ¾ x 17 ¾" (85 x 45 x 45 cm). Groninger Museum, Groningen, Netherlands

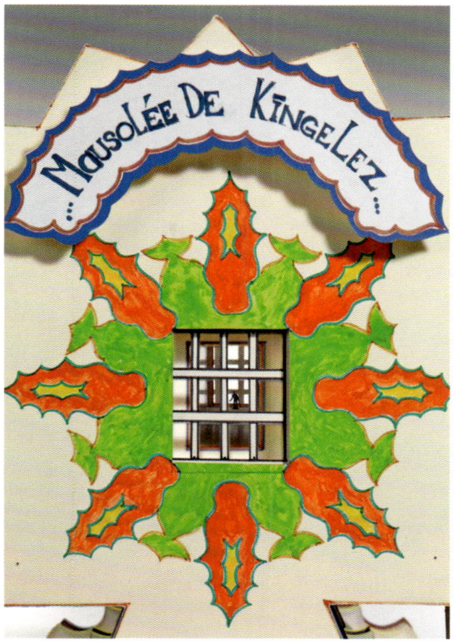

17. Bodys Isek Kingelez. *Mausolée de Kingelez* (detail). 1989. Musée du quai Branly–Jacques Chirac, Paris

exposure of his work to curators, scholars, and collectors. Prior to the exhibition, Kingelez had not been well known even in his hometown. A headline in the March 23, 1988, issue of the Kinshasa-based daily *Salongo*—"*Chéri Samba à Paris*"—heralds another local artist's inclusion in the first exhibition of "artists from the whole world," touting Samba's singular genius and his exceptional contribution to *Magiciens de la terre*, as described by Magnin.[109] The last sentence of the article reports that "*Bodis* [sic] *Kingelez maquettiste architecte autodidacte*" would also be included. Kingelez wrote to Magnin to request that the spelling of his name be corrected in the article, which suggests that he himself did not have the necessary contact at the newspaper to do so.[110] Soulillou has reported that when he located Kingelez in advance of the show, "he was living far from the center. . . . He had not many prospects to earn any [money] from his work in . . . Kinshasa."[111] A 1999 painting by Moké, *Kingelez à ses débuts* (Kingelez in his early days, fig. 18), depicts the young artist at work in a modest setting, slicing a sheet of colored paper. He is surrounded by sculptures (including 1981's *Approche de l'Échangeur de Limete Kin*) but isolated and ignored by those around him.

In addition to the works he made for *Magiciens de la terre*, Kingelez produced several other sculptures during his six months in Paris, including *Bel Atlas* and *Stars Palme Bouygues* (pls. 8 and 9).[112] These two sculptures directly reflect the artist's experience in Paris. Kingelez was in the city on July 14, 1989, the bicentennial of the French Revolution, when the Grande Arche de la Défense, a distinctive, massive hollow cube of a building (fig. 19), was inaugurated with a military parade. Part of Mitterrand's Grands Projets program of transformative new civic buildings, the monument was designed by a Danish team and engineered and built by the France-based multinational developer Bouygues. Its inauguration likely appeared on the front page of every newspaper in the city. Kingelez completed *Bel Atlas* two weeks later; it features a triangular form in lieu of the cube, floating within an open three-sided

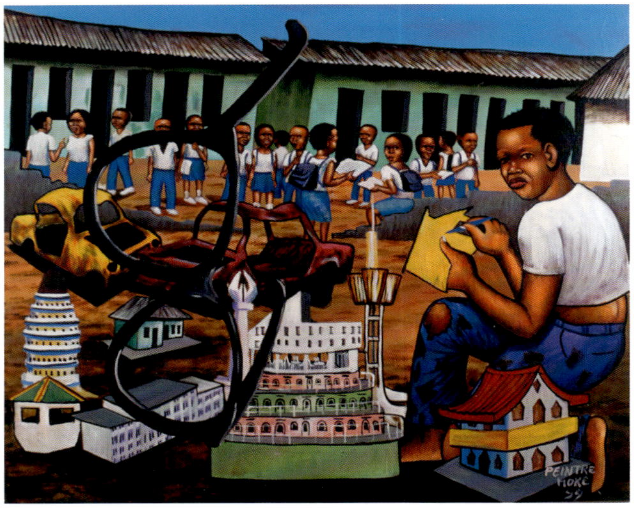

18. Moké (Congolese, 1950–2001). *Kingelez à ses débuts* (Kingelez in his early days). 1999. Acrylic on canvas, 54 ¾ x 66 ⅛" (139 x 168 cm). CAAC—The Pigozzi Collection, Geneva

frame. *Stars Palme Bouygues* followed shortly after; its remarkable inverted-triangle form was a tacit challenge issued to the company's founder, Francis Bouygues, by the artist.[113] Kingelez again worked with the blue, white, and red of the French flag, creating a sense of intricacy through repetition—in the open grid of the sculpture's two wings, the checkerboard of the base, the barbershop stripes of the entry arch, and the tricolor planters, benches, and barriers. The repetition also imposes a sense of structure and control, despite the seeming illogic of the overall form. If he were envisioning this as a built site, Kingelez thought of everything, from the parking to the bar. The sculpture is celebratory and joyful but also an assertion of confidence and prowess: Anything you can do, I can do better.

The photographer, collector, and businessman Jean Pigozzi was enraptured by *Magiciens de la terre*, particularly the works by African artists. He later recalled, "The great shock for me was that African art wasn't just what I had seen at the Musée du quai Branly in Paris or The Metropolitan Museum of Art in New York. It was Samba, [Frédéric Bruly] Bouabré, Kingelez, who had been completely unknown to me. When I saw Kingelez, I thought, 'Wow! I want to meet this guy. I want to take him to Las Vegas and help him build the most amazing casino ever!'"[114] Pigozzi quickly engaged Magnin to help him create what is now an unmatched collection of art from sub-Saharan Africa: the Contemporary African Art Collection (CAAC—The Pigozzi Collection). Of the twenty-one African artists in *Magiciens de la terre*, ten are represented in the CAAC—some, including Kingelez, in great depth.[115] After six months in Paris, Kingelez returned to Kinshasa, and one of Magnin's first trips as curator of the CAAC was to that city, where he reunited with the artist and began commissioning new works from him.[116] This relationship would last until the artist's death, and in time the collection grew to include more than thirty of his sculptures, by far the greatest concentration of Kingelez's work anywhere.

EXTRÊMES MAQUETTES AROUND THE WORLD

Since 1989, Kingelez's work has been shown in nearly thirty countries on six continents. In the years immediately following *Magiciens de la terre*, he was included in numerous important exhibitions, the first of which was *África hoy: Obras de la Contemporary African Art Collection*, the CAAC's initial major show, which opened in Las Palmas de Gran Canaria, Spain, in 1991, before traveling to the Groninger Museum, in the Netherlands, and Mexico City's Centro Cultural Arte Contemporáneo. Kingelez was the subject of monographic shows in Berlin, at the Haus der Kulturen der Welt in 1992, and in Paris, at the Fondation Cartier pour l'Art Contemporain in 1995. He traveled extensively, often visiting the cities where his work was on view (fig. 20). In 1997 he participated in the second Johannesburg Biennale, his first opportunity to exhibit in Africa. Titled *Trade Routes: History and Geography*, the biennial was overseen by artistic director Okwui Enwezor, who in the following years would have a critical role in making Kingelez's work visible to a broader public. The biennial addressed the general theme of historical cultural exchange; it comprised six installations, each organized by a different curator. Kingelez was part of the installation *Hong Kong, etc*, curated by Hou Hanru, which took the titular locale as emblematic of a postcolonial hybrid city, primed for the collision of the forces of globalization: unstable and ambiguous, on the verge of transformation, congested and soaring, bridging north, south, east, and west. Featuring a number of Asian and Asian-diaspora artists, including Huang Yong Ping and Fiona Tan, it created a framework in which the future-facing orientation of Kingelez's work was deeply resonant.

His sculptures were presented in a specifically African context in *The Short Century: Independence and Liberation Movements in Africa, 1945–1994*, a landmark 2001 exhibition organized by Enwezor, which examined a dynamic and politically charged half-century through the lens of liberation and art movements. Kingelez's work was presented in a section devoted to modern and contemporary art, which included paintings and drawings by Ibrahim El-Salahi, photographs by Seydou Keïta and Malick Sidibé, and sculpture by Yinka Shonibare. Together these works

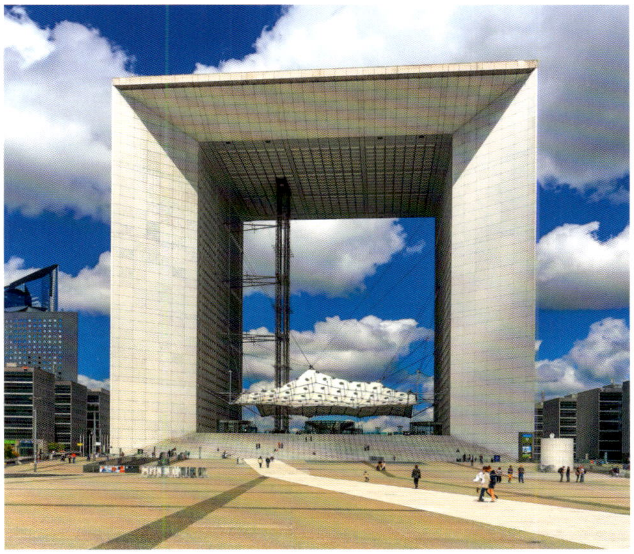

19. Grande Arche de la Défense (completed 1989), Paris, 2012

exemplified African artists' systematization, deployment, and use of modern forms, values, and structures rather than presenting modernism as a model imposed by the West. In the twenty-fifth São Paulo biennial, *Iconografias metropolitanas*, curator Alfons Hug positioned Kingelez's work not in an ethnographic or geographic framework but rather in a thematic one. It was included in a section devoted to utopia, a so-called "12th City" of focus in addition to the eleven real-world metropolises, including Caracas, Istanbul, and London, that structured the exhibition. His work appeared alongside that of artists including Carsten Höller (Germany), Los Carpinteros (Cuba), and Sarah Sze (USA).

Also in 2002, Kingelez's inclusion in documenta 11, the landmark quinquennial exhibition in Kassel, Germany, cemented his position as an artist of international significance. Deeply informed by the conditions of postcolonialism and globalism, Enwezor, the event's artistic director, aimed, he wrote, to create a space that rejected "normalization or uniformization of all artistic visions on their way to institutional beatification."[117] Kingelez was an ideal fit—an artist who had developed his own visual language and remained true to it, unswayed by broader currents in contemporary art, the demands of the market, or the influence of collecting and exhibiting institutions.

TOWARD UTOPIA: THE CITIES

In addition to the sculptures of individual buildings Kingelez made in those years, the 1990s saw him engaging at a new level with the broader urban landscape, combining multiple structures in single works as he had done much earlier in *Kinshasa: Cité du 24 Novembre de l'Authenticité Africaine*, the earliest known example. In *Magiciens de la terre*, Kingelez had installed *Mausolée de Kingelez* on the same pedestal as several other sculptures (designated simply as "immeubles," or buildings), which he connected with roadways and populated with tiny figurines (see fig. 14). But those structures lacked the characteristic attention to detail, layering, and repetition present in his work at the time, and they may have been constructed quickly in situ merely to provide the suggestion of a wider landscape. In 1992 Kingelez started amalgamating buildings in *Kimbembele Ihunga (Kimbembele Ville)* (pl. 22), a homage to his home village. Set on a tripartite base, the work comprises several distinct, fully realized buildings, noticeably smaller in scale than his earlier pieces. It also includes thoroughfares: the buildings are centered on the intersection of the boulevards Isek and Kingelez.

In 1993 he began another work named for his hometown, *Kimbembele Ihunga* (pl. 26), a massive sculpture that would take nearly two years to complete and that would mark a quantum leap forward in his thinking about multibuilding sculptures.[118] Filling a platform approximately six feet wide and ten feet long, it is a complex and comprehensive vision for the future of the community. At the "Gare Meridion," a high-speed train waits in the station beneath a roof with honeycomb cutouts. Buildings with grand, curving staircases and towers delineated with thin strips of gold metallic tape form a dizzying grid. They include a church, a grocery store, and numerous named structures: the "M'Boyo Building," the "Wa-ta-di" restaurant, and "Kingelez Stadium," with its soccer pitch. In his statement about the

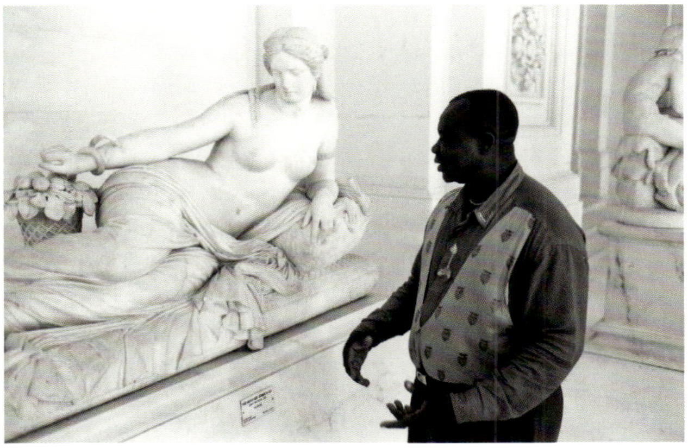

20. Kingelez at the Musée des Beaux-Arts de Nantes, France, at the time of the group exhibition *La grande vérité, les astres africains*, in which he was featured, 1993

work, the artist emphasized its futuristic aspect (as well as its connection to his own legacy):

> The monument of Kimbéville belongs to a genre of art which has attained its zenith presenting what already has the potential to become or is on the way to becoming a reality. Gradually the town of Kimbembele-Ihunga, abbreviated to Kimbéville by its creator-maker, the enlightened artist of new horizons, Bodys Isek Kingelez, should glorify the times rather than exist merely to further my own success and prosperity, in view of my fame and international reputation as a highly talented artist. . . . Kimbéville with its dazzling array of forms and colors is a 21st-century environment which has fired my artistic imagination.[119]

The text goes on to state that the community he created is a “real bridge between world civilizations of the past, the present, and the future”and cites its potential, if realized, to become a tourist attraction.[120] It describes the town’s sectors and sections, its leading clans, and how they are connected to him. A public sculpture in front of the town hall is a tribute to Kingelez’s father; striding forward, the figure bears some resemblance to *Le bouclier de la révolution* (The shield of the revolution), a monumental sculpture by Alfred Liyolo (born 1943) that replaced a likeness of Henry Morton Stanley on Mont Ngaliema in 1971 (fig. 21). Kingelez’s figure carries not a shield and spear but a book: “This statue carrying his body of knowledge in his hand, simply represents the intellectual heritage of common sense and good manners which belongs to multicultural people. This is the way my father has proudly risen above the meaning of a ceremonial life to practice art in praise of beauty and grace which will bring about a better world.”[121]

Kimbembele Ihunga is replete with formal self-references, evoking the cascading waves of *Stars Palme Bouygues* and the open geometries and fluted trees, now inflated to skyscraper height, of *Bel Atlas*. It is a summary of the artist’s formal invention up to that point in his career and a kind of self-portrait: a mapping of the people and places that shaped him. Of course, there was a local precedent for such a miraculous transformation, a dusty small town turned into an international metropolis: the (temporary) metamorphosis of Gbadolite into an utterly modern center for industry and government. Over the next several years, Kingelez immersed himself in the arduous creation of large-scale cities, making around eight altogether, including *Ville Fantôme* (pl. 28) and *Ville de Sète 3009* (pl. 30).

In the summer of 2000, Kingelez traveled to Sète, in southern France, for a residency at the boundary-crossing Musée International des Arts Modestes (MIAM), which was then just about to open its doors. Founded by artists Hervé Di Rosa and Bernard Belluc, the museum sought to elide distinctions between fine art, folk art, popular art, and the work of self-taught artists. MIAM commissioned a work from Kingelez, and during the weeks of his residency he created *Ville de Sète 3009*, a homage to his host city that he executed with an emerging formal looseness.

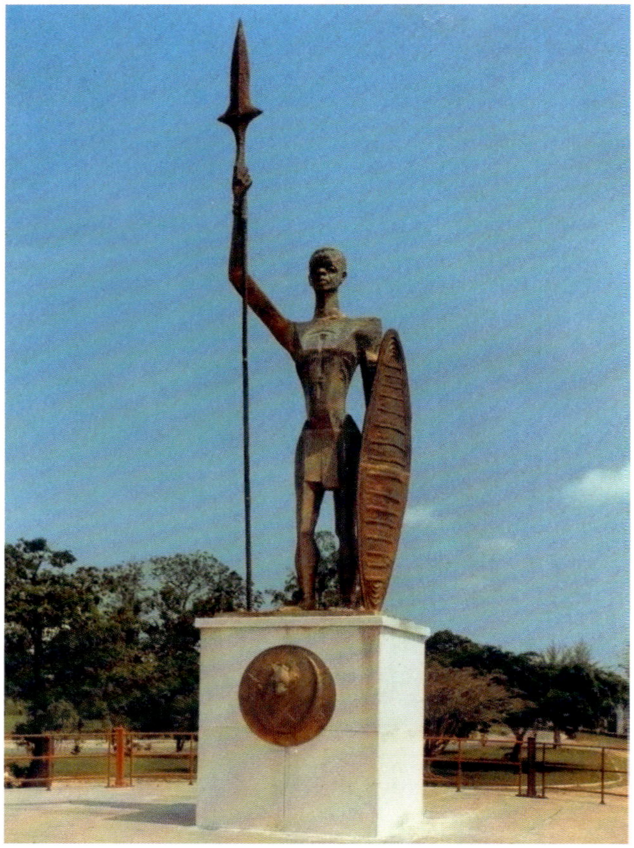

21. Alfred Liyolo (Congolese, born 1943). *Le bouclier de la révolution* (The shield of the revolution). Kinshasa, 1971. Bronze, 17′ 11⁄16″ (5.2 m) high

Traversed by canals and ringed with a blue that suggests the sea, *Ville de Sète 3009* makes concrete references to the maritime city in which it was made. There are numerous references to Paul Boyé, the textile and uniform manufacturer founded in Sète in 1904; to the Hôtel Azur, where Kingelez stayed, just down the quai de Bosc from MIAM; and even to the city’s summer water-jousting tournament, a tradition since the seventeenth century. None of the buildings bear any resemblance to their prosiac real-world counterparts, however; instead, they glow with translucent hues, sparkle with dustings of glitter, flash from a sea of metallic gold stars, and twinkle with the electric lights Kingelez installed along the work's central axis.

There is, notably, a hospital anchoring one corner of the sculpture. While a medical facility is the focus of *The Scientific Center of Hospitalisation the SIDA*, it is a rarer occurrence in Kingelez's work than a bank, an office, or a stadium. It was during this period in Sète that the artist experienced the symptoms that would shortly result in a cancer diagnosis. Pigozzi arranged for Kingelez to be treated in Paris, and the radical surgery that saved his life also sapped his energy, necessitating changes in his day-to-day behavior. Even before his treatment, however, Kingelez knew that all was not lost. He positioned the hospital in *Ville de Sète 3009* not far from the "*baie d'Espoir*," or Bay of Hope.

Kingelez's most productive period was now behind him, and his artistic output slowed. In October 2001 he told a visitor, "I'm so tired. It's so hot, it's the start of the rainy season. I just had cancer. . . . At the moment, I don't need more work."[122] The following year, however, Kingelez made another ambitious project: *New Manhattan (Manhattan City 3021)* (fig. 22), a response to the shattering terrorist attack on the World Trade Center towers in New York on September 11, 2001. The work, a city sculpture, reflected both his sympathy for the grieving city and a proposal for amelioration: "I have an idea to replace the two towers. I want to build three towers. The third tower is a defense against bombs. The third tower is filled with water, and its cooling effect will prevent any bomb from exploding. I want to prevent the current towers from being destroyed in a cruel manner. I think it's good. Thanks to my solution, the Americans will find an appropriate solution that will help dry their tears and heal their wounds."[123]

Success was double-edged for Kingelez. He achieved his dream of getting into "the realm of real estate," as he had joked, and toward the end of his life he reportedly owned as many as thirty houses dotted across Kinshasa.[124] Although he never made his home anywhere else, he occasionally expressed frustration with the city, which he considered to be at odds with his own ambitions—the call of "Work, work, work" that "resonated like an echo" in his head.[125] "I stay in Kinshasa to work," he said, "even though the climate is disastrous for my oeuvre and for me, because this is where I have the moral support of my family. But I am like a stranger in Congo, where I have never been recognized. It's mostly foreigners who commission my work."[126] By many accounts, Kingelez responded to his material success by becoming more reclusive, staying at home with his extended family, his wives, and his children, venturing outside only rarely.[127] Perhaps as a result, he wasn't as well known in his own country as Samba, for example, nor idolized internationally like the sapeur and pop star Papa Wemba, the "King of Rumba Rock," whose death in 2016 sparked outpourings of grief and public tributes from Paris to Nairobi.[128] In 2013, two years before his death, Kingelez said to a reporter, "Here in Kinshasa, I've never done any exhibition. Let me tell you, no one knows who I am or what I do. Two weeks ago, I was very sick, and I was about to die in front of my wife. No one in Kinshasa would have known. Nothing on the radio or the TV or the newspapers. That's the way it goes in the Congo."[129]

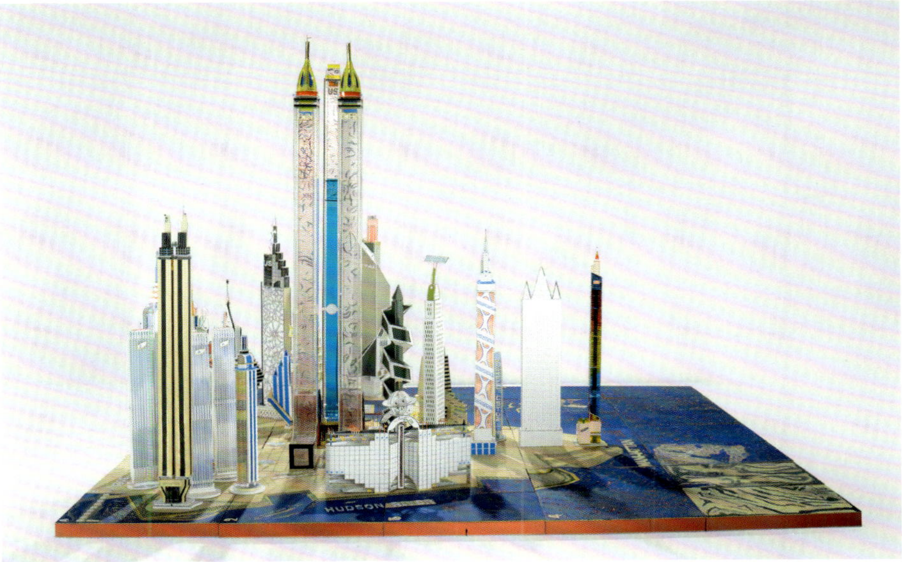

22. Bodys Isek Kingelez. *New Manhattan (Manhattan City 3021).* 2002. 6' 8" x 9' 10 ⅛" x 9' 2" (205 x 300 x 280 cm). CAAC—The Pigozzi Collection, Geneva

Kingelez died on March 14, 2015. Three days later, the notice of his death in the French newspaper *Le monde* hailed him as a "monument of Congolese art" and aptly identified both the utopian underpinnings of his oeuvre and the implicit social critique in his "chimerical architecture . . . without police or cemetery, traffic or congestion."[130]

In 2000 the artist claimed to have produced 3,014 works over the preceding twenty-five years.[131] While that is almost surely an overestimate, it is also certain that sculptures have been lost to floods and shipping accidents, to the effects of time on paper and glue, to oversight and human error. In researching this project, I have seen just over one hundred or so single works and eight cities by Kingelez in collections around the world. Yet even in this relatively modest number, his oeuvre is a towering achievement, a body of sculpture with tremendous visual allure and enduring social resonance.

Kingelez anchored his work in the present and the recent past and in the fabric of the city around him, inspired equally by colonial architecture, the ambitious buildings of post-Independence Zaire, and idioms that typify national building styles. But his work was always future facing. In an era in which cities, including Kinshasa, were (and continue to be) under pressure to accommodate unprecedented rates of growth and the attendant challenges to civic life, Kingelez pointed a way forward, offering models of beauty, harmony, and functionality. His work addressed the great challenges of the twentieth century—decolonization, health crises, the quest for nationhood and national identity—but it is infused with potential, both philosophical and formal. In his hands, new, cooperative ways of living and working were possible, and the most mundane of materials could become technically precise, inventive, and elegant objects. He declared himself "a designer, an architect, a sculptor, engineer, artist." His dazzling sculptures, manifestations of a future that perhaps only he could see, suggest one additional role: "A visionary," he said, "is someone who dreams of what doesn't exist yet."[132]

Title and epigraph: The phrase "*Kingelez visionnaire*" is inscribed throughout the artist's work *Kimbembele Ihunga* (pl. 26). For the epigraph, see Bodys Isek Kingelez, "Artist's Statement," in *Perspectives 145: Bodys Isek Kingelez* (Houston: Contemporary Arts Museum, 2005), 9. This extraordinary autobiographical statement was adapted from an interview in French between Kingelez and André Magnin in Paris and Kinshasa in 2000.

Notes

1 Kingelez, "Artist's Statement," 5.
2 Kingelez in the film *Kingelez: Kinshasa, une ville repensée*, directed by Dirk Dumon (Brussels: Piksa, 2004), 5:16 min.
3 Kingelez, quoted in Robert Draper, "Kinshasa: Urban Pulse of the Congo," *National Geographic* 224, no. 3 (September 2013): 118.
4 Ibid., 123. Sapeurs are members of a regional urban subculture of nattily dressed adherents of "La Sape," an abbreviation for the Société des Ambianceurs et des Personnes Élégantes, or "Society of tastemakers and elegant people."
5 Traditionally, art in the region often took the form of wooden sculpture with figurative references. Later, in the contemporary period, *peinture populaire*, or "popular painting," would become a dominant idiom.
6 Okwui Enwezor and Chika Okeke-Agulu, "Situating Contemporary African Art: Introduction," in *Contemporary African Art since 1980* (Bologna: Damiani, 2009), 12.
7 Enwezor, "Between Localism and Worldliness," *Art Journal* 57, no. 4 (Winter 1998): 32–33.
8 Stuart Hall, "Black Diaspora Artists in Britain: Three 'Moments' in Postwar History," *History Workshop Journal* 61, no. 1 (2006): 23.
9 John Picton, "In Vogue, or the Flavor of the Month: The New Way to Wear Black," in *Reading the Contemporary: African Art from Theory to the Marketplace*, ed. Olu Oguibe and Enwezor (London: Institute of International Visual Arts, 1999), 120.
10 Though the exact date of his birth is rarely cited, it can be found concealed in at least one of his midcareer works, *Pacific Art* of 1989 (now in a private collection, Paris). There, amid looping graphite lines that equally suggest gravel paths circumscribing the central structure and automatic writing, is nestled a stylized "Bodys 27 8 1948." Kingelez dedicated a 2000 sculpture to his mother; titled *Maman Isek Mabo Bendele,* the work is in the collection of the Fondation Cartier pour l'Art Contemporain, Paris.
11 Kingelez relates this information in unpublished video footage by Marco di Castri and Gianfranco Barberi, shot during preparation for the exhibition *Magiciens de la terre*, Paris, May 1989.
12 Marc Leo Felix and C. C. Lu Henry, *Kongo Kingdom Art: From Ritual to Cutting Edge* (Taipei: National Taiwan Museum of Fine Arts, 2004), 249.
13 Kingelez, "The Essential Framework of the Structures Making Up the Town of Kimbembele-Ihunga (Kimbéville)," in this volume, 50.
14 Ibid., 51.
15 Kingelez, quoted in Guy Duplat, "Le maître des maquettes," *La libre belgique*, October 23, 2001. Trans. by the author. For the role of Belgian missionaries in the education system, see Barbara Yates, "White Views of Black Minds: Schooling in King Leopold's Congo," *History of Education Quarterly* 20, no. 1 (Spring 1980): 27.
16 For an example, see p. 50 in this volume.
17 Kingelez, "Artist's Statement," 2.
18 Ibid.
19 Kingelez in the film *Kingelez: Kinshasa, une ville repensée*, 14:44 min.
20 Enwezor, "A Conversation with Okwui Enwezor," interview by Carol Becker, *Art Journal* 61, no. 2 (Summer 2002): 12.
21 See, for example, Howard W. French, "Mobutu Sese Seko, Zairian Ruler, Is Dead in Exile in Morocco at 66," *New York Times*, September 8, 1997. A commonly used colloquial interpretation of his name is "The rooster that leaves no hen intact." Ghislaine C. Kabwit, "Zaïre: The Roots of the Continuing Crisis," *Journal of Modern African Studies* 17, no. 3 (September 1979): 382.
22 Kabwit, "Zaïre: The Roots of the Continuing Crisis," 390.
23 Sakombi Inongo, quoted in Kenneth Lee Adelman, "The Recourse to Authenticity and Negritude in Zaire," *Journal of Modern African Studies* 13, no. 1 (March 1975): 137.

24 Mobutu Sese Seko, quoted in Kabwit, "Zaïre: The Roots of the Continuing Crisis," 389.

25 The work is now in the collection of the Institut des Musées Nationaux du Congo, Kinshasa.

26 Johannes Fabian, *Remembering the Present: Painting and Popular History in Zaire* (Berkeley and Los Angeles: University of California Press, 1996), 157.

27 Kabwit, "Zaïre: The Roots of the Continuing Crisis," 390.

28 Adelman, "The Recourse to Authenticity and Negritude in Zaire," 135.

29 Kingelez, "The Essential Framework," 51.

30 Kingelez, "Maquettes of Post-Modes Art," in this volume, 49.

31 Kingelez, quoted in Marion Laval-Jeantet, Benoît Mangin, and Anaïd Demir, *Veilleurs du monde: Gbêdji kpontolè* (Paris: CQFD, 1998), 128.

32 *National AIDS Control Program Assistance Project (Credit 1953-ZR), Project Completion Report: Zaire (Report No. 14743)* (Washington, D.C.: World Bank, June 27, 1995), http://documents.worldbank.org/curated/en/135821468025758933/pdf/multi0page.pdf.

33 Kingelez, "Artist's Statement," 5.

34 Kingelez, quoted in Christine Salvadé, "Le zaïrois Kingelez n'a jamais voulu être artiste," *Le nouveau quotidien*, no. 1051 (July 4, 1995): 19. Trans. by the author. For the "university-trained technocrats," see Kabwit, "Zaïre: The Roots of the Continuing Crisis," 386.

35 Kingelez lists these areas of study in his "Artist's Statement," 4–5. He mentions his focus on economics in the video interview "Exposition de Bodys Isek Kingelez à la Fondation Cartier–Entretien avec l'artiste–1995," 34:02 min., posted on YouTube by Fondation Cartier pour l'art contemporain, Paris, April 28, 2014. The University of Lovanium was later absorbed into the Université Nationale du Zaïre (UNAZA). Its former campus is now the University of Kinshasa.

36 It is noted in an exploratory 1985 UNESCO study for a possible Musée National de Kinshasa that Kingelez speaks French, English, Kikongo, Lingala, and Swahili. See Alpha Oumar Konaré and Patrick O'Byrne, *Création du Musée national de Kinshasa* (Paris: Organisation des Nations Unies pour l'Éducation, la Science et la Culture and Programme des Nations Unies pour le Développement, 1985), n.p.

37 The other major centers were (and are) Lubumbashi and Kisangani.

38 For this history, see Joseph Ibongo, "First Chapter: Genèse et Développement," in *La peinture populaire et publicitaire de Kinshasa (République démocratique du Congo): Éléments d'histoire culturelle de la ville et analyse iconologique des œuvres représentatives* (Louvain-la-Neuve, Belgium: Université Catholique de Louvain, 1999), 14–27, and Grace Stanislaus, "Contemporary African Artists: Changing Tradition," in *Contemporary African Artists: Changing Tradition* (New York: Studio Museum in Harlem, 1990), 22.

39 Kojo Fosu, *20th Century Art of Africa* (Accra, Ghana: Artists Alliance, 1993), 41.

40 Thomas Bayet, "Le premier atelier," in *Beauté Congo: 1926–2015: Congo kitoko*, ed. Adeline Pelletier (Paris: Fondation Cartier pour l'Art Contemporain, 2015), 73.

41 Lema Kusa and Bamba Ndombasi, "L'enseignement des arts plastiques au Congo: Évolution et expériences," a paper presented at the UNESCO Regional Conference on Art Education in Africa, Port Elizabeth, South Africa, 2001, 4, http://www.unesco.org/fileadmin/MULTIMEDIA/HQ/CLT/pdf/Arts_Edu_Afr_Disp_lemakusa_en.pdf. The Académie was integrated into the Université Nationale du Zaïre (UNAZA) in 1981.

42 Fosu, *20th Century Art of Africa,* 123.

43 Kingelez, quoted in Duplat, "Le maître des maquettes."

44 Lye Mudaba Yoka, quoted in Draper, "Kinshasa: Urban Pulse of the Congo," 109.

45 Kingelez, "Artist's Statement," 5.

46 Ibid.

47 Kingelez in the film *Kingelez: Kinshasa, une ville repensée*, 24:21 min.

48 Madeleine Mupanga in ibid.

49 During his tenure, Cornet organized and participated in numerous field-research trips in Zaire, not only acquiring objects for the museum but making copious notes about regional customs, traditions, and languages. Today Cornet's *cahiers* are housed at the Special Collections & Archives, J. Edgar and Louise S. Monroe Library, Loyola University, New Orleans.

50 This is Kingelez's job title as listed in Konaré and O'Byrne, *Création du Musée national de Kinshasa*, n.p. Kingelez tells the story of this period in his "Artist's Statement," 5–6, and in the video interview "Exposition de Bodys Isek Kingelez à la Fondation Cartier–Entretien avec l'artiste–1995" (see note. 35 above). The current locations of both *Musée National* and *Commissariat Atomique* are unknown.

51 Sarah van Beurden, "Exhibition Review: Forty Years of IMNC," *African Arts* 45, no. 4 (Winter 2012): 90.

52 Kingelez, quoted in André Magnin, "Bodys Isek Kingelez," in *ARS 01: Unfolding Perspectives* (Helsinki: Kiasma—Museum of Contemporary Art, 2001), 121.

53 Kingelez, "Artist's Statement," 6.

54 In the 1980s, the few existing galleries tended to cater to European expatriates. Apparently, Kingelez did approach at least one of these galleries and was told that his wasn't the kind of art in which its clients were interested. Jean-Hubert Martin, conversation with the author, October 9, 2017.

55 Christian Girard, conversation with the author, October 10, 2017.

56 Brendan Gill, Jane Boutwell, and Louis P. Forster, "La République du Congo (Léopoldville)," *New Yorker,* June 9, 1962, 22–23.

57 See International Atomic Energy Agency, *Research Reactors in Africa* (Vienna: Vienna International Center, November 2011), https://www.iaea.org/OurWork/ST/NE/NEFW/Technical-Areas/RRS/documents/RR_in_Africa.pdf, 8, and Chris McGreal, "Missing Keys, Holes in Fence and a Single Padlock: Welcome to Congo's Nuclear Plant," *Guardian*, November 23, 2006.

58 Kingelez, "Artist's Statement," 9.

59 Girard's account can be found in his article "Les extrêmes architectures de Bodys Isek Kingelez," *Art Press* 136, no. 5 (1989): 47.

60 Shaje Tshiluila, "Institut des Musées Nationaux du Zaïre," in *Congo-Zaïre: Thango, de Brazza à Kin*. (Paris: Éditions ADEIAO, 1991), 30.

61 Jacques Soulillou and Girard, "Une internationale de l'art urbain," *autrement*, "Les capitales de la couleur," ed. Bruno Tilliette, special issue no. 9 (October 1984): 275–82. Trans. by the author. The current locations of *Le Ministère Belge de la Guerre* and *Le Palais Modeste d'Espagne de l'Antique Marine Commerciale* are unknown.

62 Ibid., 278. Brazzaville, the capital of the Republic of Congo, lies directly across the Congo River from Kinshasa.

63 Ibid., 282.

64 Girard, "Les extrêmes architectures de Bodys Isek Kingelez," 47.

65 Kingelez, "Artist's Statement," 6.

66 Muhammed Ali and George Foreman stayed in Nsele during the run-up to the famed 1974 Rumble in the Jungle boxing match.

67 V. S. Naipaul, "A New King for the Congo," *New York Review of Books*, June 26, 1975, 24.

68 See, for example, James Brooke, "Mobutu's Village Basks in His Glory," *New York Times*, September 29, 1988, and Reuters, "Legacy of Corrupt and Ruthless Dictator Who Built Versailles in the Jungle," *Independent*, May 4, 1997.

69 For an account of these features, see Brooke, "Mobutu's Village Basks in His Glory."

70 Olivier-Clément Cacoub, quoted in "Hommage à Olivier Clément Cacoub, 'l'architecte du soleil,'" harissa.com, January 28, 2016, http://www.harissa.com/news/article/hommage-olivier-cl%C3%A9ment-cacoub-%C2%AB-larchitecte-du-soleil-%C2%BB. Trans. by the author.

71 Cacoub, *Architecture de soleil* (Tunis: Ceres Productions, 1974), 21. Trans. by the author.

72 Pierre Goudiaby Atepa, "Pierre Goudiaby ATEPA, Bâtisseur du futur—Master-Builder of the Future," interview by Mathieu Ropitault, part of "Pierre Goudiaby: Senegalese Architect," *Unseen Art Scene* (blog), June 8, 2008, http://africanartists.blogspot.com/2008/06/pierre-goudiaby-atepa-senegalese.html.

73 Goudiaby, quoted in David Hecht, "BBC Report—Pierre Goudiaby Atepa Making Dreams Real!," Group Atepa, January 2, 2000, http://cristalagency.com/atepa/index.php/actualites/376-bbc-report-pierre-goudiaby-atepa-making-dreams-real.html.

74 This is one of the few instances I am aware of in which Kingelez recreated an existing built structure.

75 The building had inoperable windows, and after the air conditioning broke down, it was considered uninhabitable. The site has since been redeveloped as the Kempinski Hotel Fleuve Congo. Mwana Mbota, "Léopoldville 1960—Independence Changes the Architectural Equation," *Kinshasa Then and Now* (blog), August 20, 2011, http://kosubaawate.blogspot.com/2011/08/leopoldville-1960-independence-changes.html.

76 Ismail Serageldin, "Cultural Continuity and Cultural Authenticity," in *Home and the World: Architectural Sculpture by Two Contemporary African Artists: Aboudramane and Bodys Isek Kingelez* (New York: Museum for African Art; and Munich: Prestel, 1993), 23.

77 Marjorie Jongbloed, "Thomas Bayrle and Bodys Isek Kingelez: Architecture between Fantasy and Reality," in Jongbloed et al., *DC: Thomas Bayrle, Bodys Isek Kingelez* (Cologne: Museum Ludwig, 2001), 13.

78 Jean-Marc Patras, "Bodys Isek Kingelez—'Extreme Maquettes,'" in *Home and the World*, 58.

79 Dan Cameron, "Cocido y crudo," in Cameron et al., *Cocido y crudo* (Madrid: Museo Nacional Centro de Arte Reina Sofía, 1994), 325.

80 I am grateful to Mwana Mboka for an extraordinary blog post on this event: "Kinshasa 1969—FIKIN Puts Congo on a New Map," *Kinshasa Then and Now* (blog), March 20, 2015, http://kosubaawate.blogspot.com/2015/03.

81 Fernand Tala-Ngai later became the minister of finance for multiple governments in the Democratic Republic of the Congo.

82 Mboka, "Kinshasa 1969—FIKIN Puts Congo on a New Map."

83 By the mid-1970s, FIKIN was in decline.

84 Kingelez, unpublished text accompanying the work *Palais d'Hirochima*, 1991. Trans. by the author. The Japanese city of Hiroshima is, in fact, home to an imperial palace that featured the tiered, peaked-roof style that Kingelez quotes. Built at the end of the sixteenth century, it was destroyed during the atomic bombing of that city in 1945, during the Second World War, and then reconstructed in 1958.

85 "Lotissement de maisons dites hollandaises," Wikinshasa.org: Atlas de l'architecture et du paysages urbains, last modified May 26, 2011, http://www.wikinshasa.org/index.php/Lotissement_de_maisons_dites_hollandaises.

86 Artist Joan Rabascall recalls discussing the cold weather with Kingelez in Groningen. Rabascall, conversation with the author, October 4, 2017.

87 Robin Young, "Africa's Fabric Is Dutch," *New York Times*, November 14, 2012.

88 "United Nations Events for U.N. Organization's 50th Anniversary," United Nations Press Office, Geneva, November 24, 1994. The exhibition was organized by Adelina von Fürstenberg.

89 Kingelez in the film *Kingelez: Kinshasa, une ville repensée*, 25:25 min.

90 Ibid.

91 Kingelez, quoted in Salvadé, "Le zaïrois Kingelez n'a jamais voulu être artiste." The overall effect in *U.N.* is freer, less attached than earlier work to rigid, regular systems. Ironically, the actual Palace of Nations, planned in the 1920s and completed in Geneva in 1936, is an imposing, harmoniously symmetrical neoclassical structure that has much in common with Kingelez's slightly earlier work.

92 Cameron, "Cocido y crudo," 318. *Magiciens de la terre* was held May 18–August 14, 1989, at the Centre Georges Pompidou and the Grande Halle de la Villette, Paris. For more information, please see one of the several exhaustive, well-researched studies of the show, such as Lucy Steeds et al., *Making Art Global (Part 2): Magiciens de la terre, 1989* (London: Afterall, 2013).

93 Guy Brett, "Earth and Museum: Local and Global?," *Third Text* 3, no. 6 (Spring 1989): 91.

94 Martin, "The Whole Earth Show," interview by Benjamin H. D. Buchloh, *Art in America* (May 1989): 150–58; 211–13.

95 The team later sought advice from Chérif Khaznadar, the founding director of the Maison des Cultures du Monde, which since 1982 had been inviting keepers of "intangible cultural heritage" to Paris, for ways to help their visiting artists feel more at home. Martin, conversation with the author, October 9, 2017.

96 Ibid.

97 Soulillou, correspondence with the author, October 15, 2017.

98 Martin, conversation with the author, October 10, 2017. For Magnin's first encounter with Kingelez and the long relationship between the two, see the interview with Magnin in this volume.

99 Kingelez in di Castri and Barberi, unpublished video footage.

100 Jonathan Jones, "Bodys Isek Kingelez: Kimbéville—City of Tomorrow," *Art & Design* 11, no. 9–10 (September–October 1996): 32–35.

101 Susan Vogel, "Fanciful Dreams of Africa's Past and Future," *New York Times*, August 15, 1993.

102 Draper, "Kinshasa: Urban Pulse of the Congo," 123.

103 Kingelez in di Castri and Barberi, unpublished video footage.

104 Kingelez in "Atlas des 100 artistes exposés," in Mark Francis et al., *Magiciens de la terre* (Paris: Éditions du Centre Pompidou, 1989): 167. Trans. by Charlotte Barat.

105 Girard, conversation with the artist, October 9, 2017.

106 Marie Lemeltier and Céline Soutif, "Bodys Isek Kingelez: 'Un homme nouveau pour un habitat nouveau,'" in Elvan Zabunyan, Valérie Mavridorakis, and David Perreau, *Fantasmapolis: La ville contemporaine et ses imaginaires* (Rennes, France: Presses Universitaires de Rennes, 2005), 87. Trans. by the author.

107 Kingelez's work was installed in a gallery themed "*Cicatrices et origines*" (Scars and origins), which also included works by John Fundi, Henry Munyaradzi, Jangarh Singh Shyam, and Twins Seven Seven.

108 Di Castri and Barberi, unpublished video footage.

109 Kmbl., "Chéri Samba à Paris," *Salongo*, March 23, 1988, 5. Trans. by the author.

110 He wrote, "N.B. My name is written in the manner below and not in the way that you have said in the newspaper *Salongo* in Zaire. *Rectify this please.*" Letter from Kingelez to Magnin, April 16, 1988, Centre Pompidou Archives, Paris. Emphasis in the original. Trans. by the author.

111 Soulillou, correspondence with the author, October 15, 2017.

112 Patras, conversation with the author, August 1, 2017.

113 Ibid.

114 Jean Pigozzi, conversation with the author, January 25, 2018.

115 These ten artists are Frédéric Bruly Bouabré, Seni Camara, Jean-Jacques Efiaimbelo, John Fundi, Samuel Kane Kwei, Kingelez, Agbagli Kossi, Esther Mahlangu, Samba, and Cyprien Tokudagba.

116 Magnin, conversation with the author, October 9, 2017. As a cultural attaché, Soulillou had been able to help Kingelez obtain a six-month visa. Soulillou, correspondence with the author, October 10, 2017.

117 Enwezor, "The Black Box," *documenta 11_Platform 5: Exhibition* (Ostfildern-Ruit, Germany: Hatje Cantz, 2002), 43.

118 Magnin, "Kingelez et ses extrêmes maquettes," *Jeune Afrique*, no. 1803 (July–August 1995): 64.

119 Kingelez, "The Essential Framework," 49–50.

120 Ibid., 51.

121 Ibid.

122 Kingelez, quoted in Duplat, "Le maître des maquettes."

123 Kingelez in the film *Kingelez: Kinshasa, une ville repensée*, 26:59 min.

124 Draper, "Kinshasa: Urban Pulse of the Congo," 123. For the joke about real estate, see Kingelez, "Artist's Statement," 6.

125 Kingelez, "Artist's Statement," 5.

126 Kingelez, quoted in Duplat, "Le maître des maquettes."

127 Kingelez himself noted that his neighbors wondered why he and his family "never went out into the streets." Draper, "Kinshasa: Urban Pulse of the Congo," 123.

128 Amos Ngaire, "Plans Underway to Fly Papa Wemba's Body to Kinshasa," *Nation*, April 26, 2016, http://www.nation.co.ke/lifestyle/showbiz/Papa-Wemba-body-to-be-flown-home/-/1950810/3176808/-/t07hviz/-/index.html.

129 Draper, "Kinshasa: Urban Pulse of the Congo," 123.

130 Roxana Azimi, "L'artiste congolais Bodys Isek Kingelez est mort," *Le monde*, March 17, 2015. Trans. by the author.

131 Kingelez, "Artist's Statement," 9. In the French version of this statement, the number 3,017 is given. See "Interview de Bodys Isek Kingelez," in *Bodys Isek Kingelez* (Brussels: La Médiatine, Centre Culturel Wolu-Culture, 2003), 12.

132 Kingelez in the film *Kingelez: Kinshasa, une ville repensée*, 19:35 min.

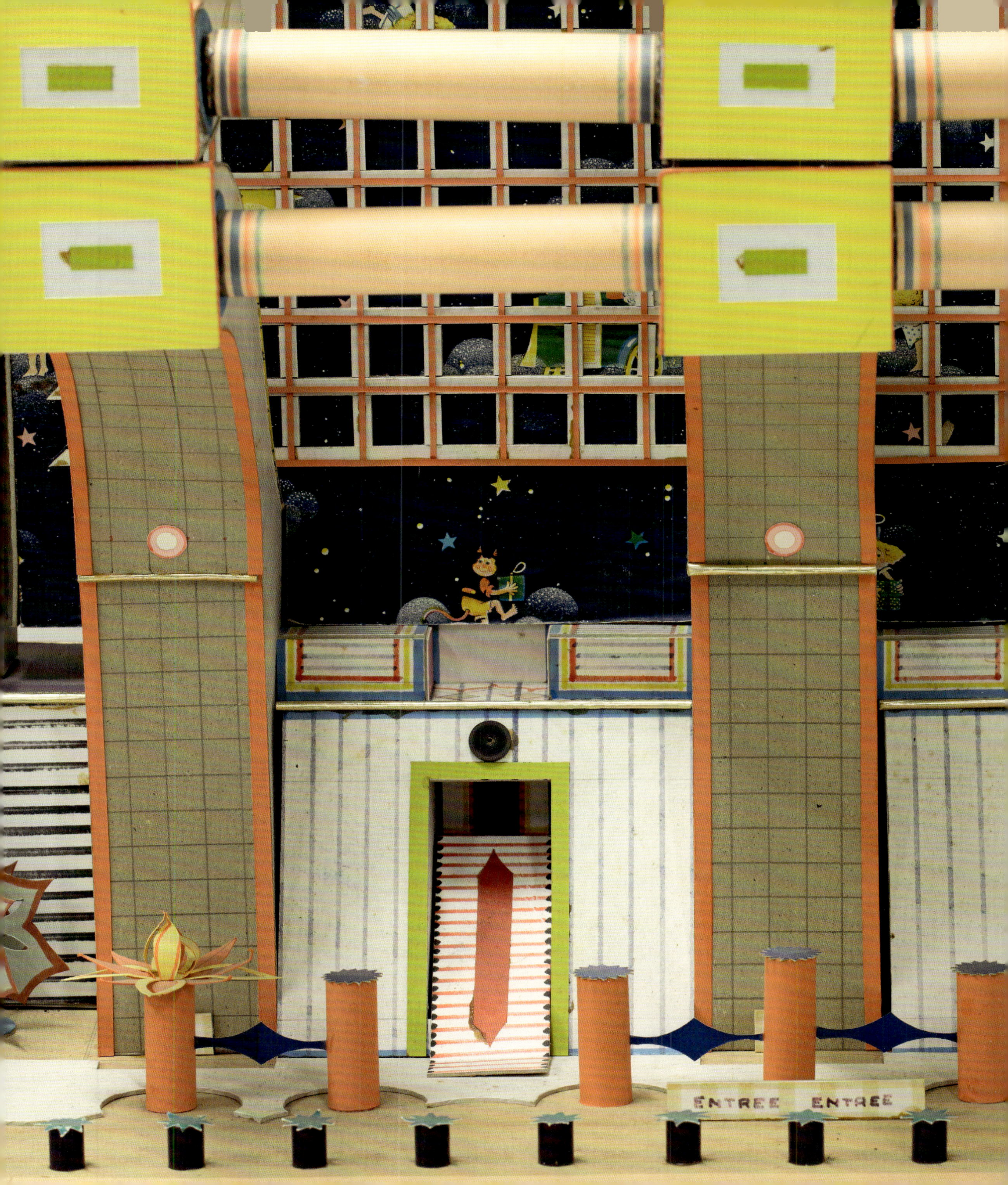
ENTREE ENTREE

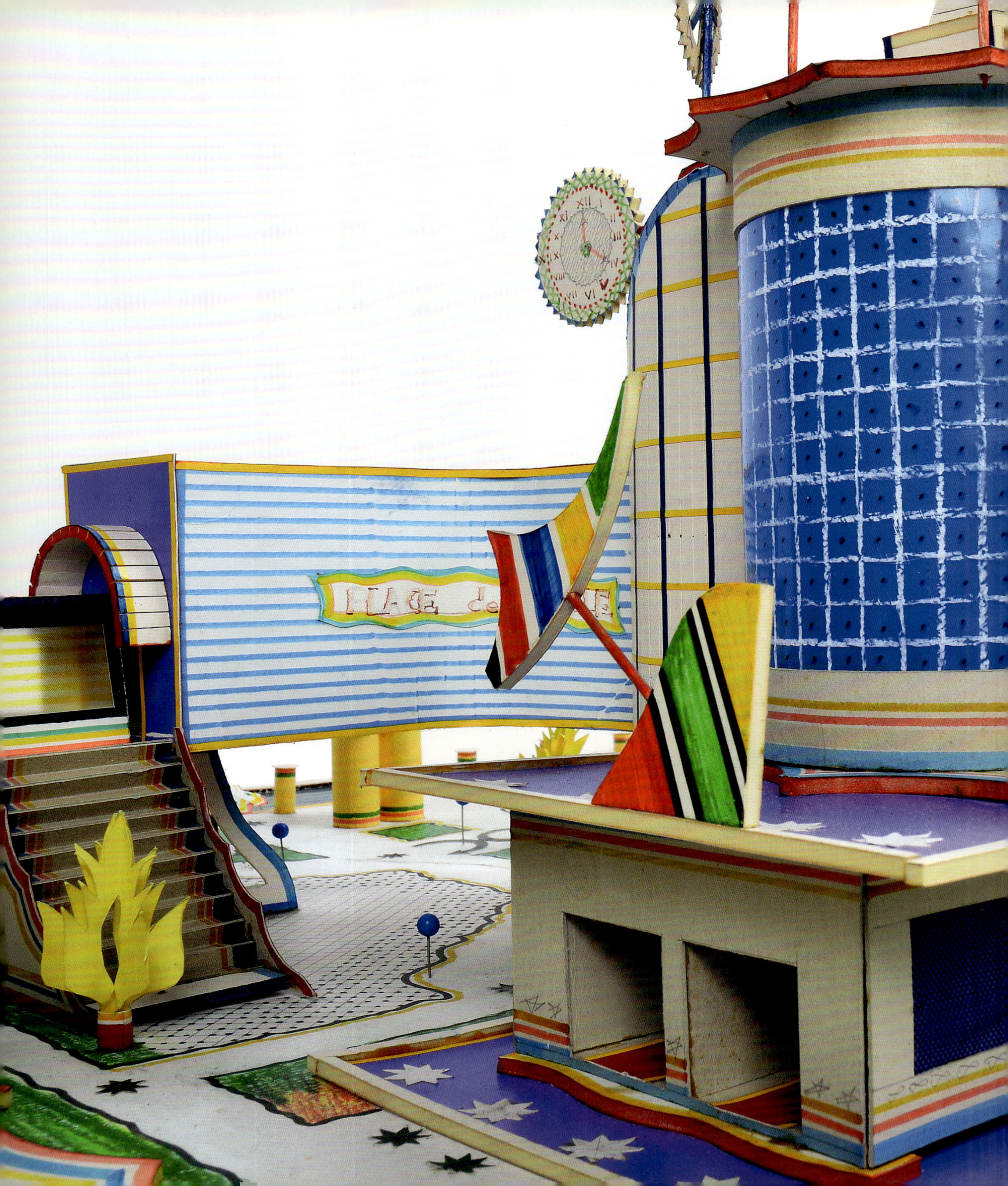
PLACE de

ON KINGELEZ'S AUDACIOUS OBJECTS

Chika Okeke-Agulu

I created these cities so there would be lasting peace, justice and universal freedom. They will function like small secular states with their own political structure, and will not need policemen or an army.

—Bodys Isek Kingelez

Of the many claims Bodys Isek Kingelez made about his art and life, among the most intriguing and crucial is this statement: "Contrary to what I've often heard said, I was a sculptor before being a restorer. And I insist on this point."[1] The artist's emphasis is on the word "before," and his aim was to rewrite what he saw as an errant narrative in the literature on his life and work.

The story went like this: In the late 1970s, Kingelez was hired by the Institut des Musées Nationaux du Zaïre (the national ethnographic museum in Kinshasa) as a restorer of the objects in its collection, and, as Jean-Marc Patras has claimed, it was this "constant contact with the 'old stuff' he was restoring (which the whites admired so much) that prompted him to create his own powerful, modern work."[2] The implication was that Kingelez's status as a modern artist was underwritten and guaranteed by his reconnection to traditional art as a restorer of Congolese artifacts. Kingelez, however, insisted that it was his early success with sculpture that led to his appointment at the museum, seeming to suggest that traditional art had no place in his emergence as a modern artist. He struggled against the forces that sought to identify him as merely a restorer of masks—a craftsman who would never attain the creative accomplishment of the traditional artists on whose work the institution and the state placed so much value. His treatment of his six years of employment at the museum as peripheral or incidental, rather than formative, was also a reclamation of his story and practice from a narrative that depicted him as a mimic of the European modernists whose work was famously inspired by encounters with the art of Kingelez's ancestors.

But what was at stake in this assertion? I suggest that Kingelez might have been motivated by a deep suspicion of the prevailing tendencies at the time to define modern African artists by a supposed unconditional attachment to their ancestral arts, or to see them as conduits through whom ancient, native creativity found new expression—attitudes that have a long history in the Congo and elsewhere on the continent.[3] Insisting on this point was thus a declaration of his imaginative agency, but it also affirmed his desire for self-narration, given the history of near-total dependence by artists like him on the interpretive frameworks and narrative agenda of their Western interlocutors.

Kingelez was not always clear about the status of his objects, despite what seems to have been an irrepressible urge to expatiate through writing on each individual work and on his oeuvre as a whole. Consider, for instance, his use of the term *extrême maquette* to describe his constructions.[4] A maquette is a sketch, scale model, or preparatory study; does this mean that Kingelez imagined his objects as part of a creative and constructional process that could someday culminate in a building? The answer might be a partial affirmative, for he seemed to have thought of some, if not all, of his sculptures as architectural models. His *Stars Palme Bouygues*, of 1989 (pl. 9)—a pinnate design in which a central column with suspension cables bears the weight of its two fan-shaped wings—was apparently designed as a dare-to-build challenge to Bouygues, a French construction and real estate conglomerate that has had vast interests across Africa since the late colonial period.[5] And he spoke of his *Kimbembele Ihunga*, of 1994 (pl. 26), as "the blueprint for a real town," a "large-scale architectural act," and a "maquette [that] is a promise of something real."[6]

The design and construction of Kingelez's works do suggest an interest in the relationship of building materials to spatial organization and architectonics, and there is no question that he was a committed student—or, better, a freewheeling sampler—of modern architecture. Without regard for modernist conventions or styles, he combined and juxtaposed diverse elements of twentieth-century Western architecture, his palette so promiscuous that it seems as if his goal were sensory thrill, an unapologetic display of what his ecstatic imagination could do. It is not enough to call his mode postmodern—Jonathan Jones once described it as "African postmodernism"[7]—for he mostly eschewed older architectures (whether Western or African) as well as the histrionics of postmodernism; and he did not seem to put any limit on the array of modern forms, spaces, patterns, colors, and materials he brought to bear on his single- and multi-structure compositions. Although he frequently referred to himself as a (modern) architect, his sensibility was that of an artist—a sculptor of stupendous, eclectic sensibilities, who used modern architectural forms as compositional elements. The works are not maquettes in the normal sense of the term, and Kingelez apparently came to this conclusion as well. By qualifying them as *extreme* maquettes, he indicated that they are objects that simultaneously approximate and exceed the functional, conceptual, and objective conditions of the sculptor's or architect's model.

This is evident in his detailed discussion of *Kimbembele Ihunga*, which he described as depicting his place of birth in both its past, present, and future manifestations—that is, as simultaneously a rural, "traditional" village and a futuristic city with wide boulevards and skyscrapers, in the center of which is a sculptural monument to his father as bearer of "the intellectual heritage of common sense."[8] The work is not merely a futuristic fantasy; it is also a meditation on a past that never was or on a reality that the artist has placed in perpetual doubt. It conflates temporalities: the work is a reflection neither on Congolese architectural heritage nor on its present urban realities, and we are not even sure that Kingelez was prognosticating about an architecture of the future. His writings and commentaries about his sculptures ensure that we cannot settle on any specific connection between things that existed in his mind and in time and place. Combined, therefore, Kingelez's objects and texts formally and conceptually test our power of comprehension and our ability to imagine. They are at once products of a fertile, ecstatic imagination and architectonic manifestations through which the artist explored the terrains and boundaries of the real and the fantastical, the social and the political, the metaphysical and the beautiful.

The works exceed the bounds of both sculpture and architecture; they are symbolic texts on the state of our global, postcolonial world. Not only do Kingelez's sculptures and writing reify each other, but the sculptures, by themselves, play with visual and textual syntax in such a way that they become hybrid image-texts—a conflation at once confounding, compelling, complicated, and alluringly inarticulate. Yet if Kingelez's works are to be read in this way—and here I am thinking specifically of Achille Mbembe's description of the image as "always a conventional comment, the transcription of a reality, a word, a vision, or an idea into a visible code that becomes, in turn, a manner of speaking of the world and inhabiting it"[9]—what do they reveal? What does he communicate through them? A full understanding must await a more extensive analysis. In the meantime, we see him deploying his works as coded texts that run the gamut of political commentary, philosophical rumination, environmental ethics, architectural critique, and more. Let's consider what might be the least obvious of these: the political.

Among the works Kingelez contributed to the 1989 exhibition *Magiciens de la terre*, which brought him to international attention, is *La Croix du Ciel* (see p. 22, fig. 14), a blue high-rise structure with square windows framed in yellow and black. It is laid out in a multipoint, star-shaped plan and sits on a high, similarly star-shaped olive-green base on which are large yellow triangular shapes with red cores. The color scheme of this base is a transmogrification of the flag of Zaire (fig. 1) devised for the newly renamed country by its despotic president, Mobutu Sese Seko, in 1971, at the onset of his indigenization campaign (officially known as *authenticité*). That green Mobutu flag, retired after his ouster in 1997, had at its center a powerful dark-brown arm and hand, set within a yellow circle, bearing a torch of red tongues of flame—the latter likely connected to Mobutu's self-styling as a warrior whose victories leave

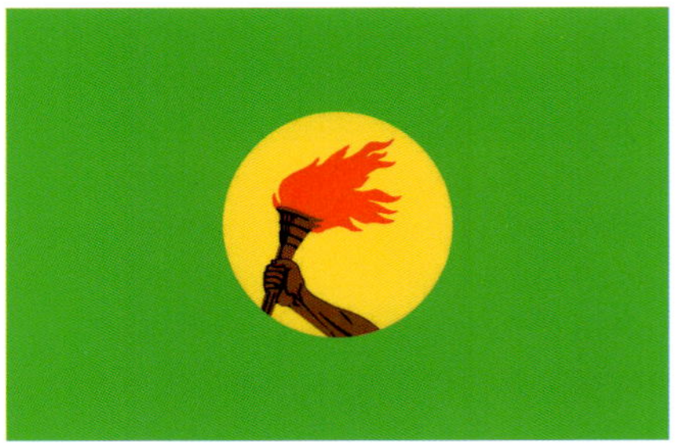

1. Flag of Zaire, 1971–97

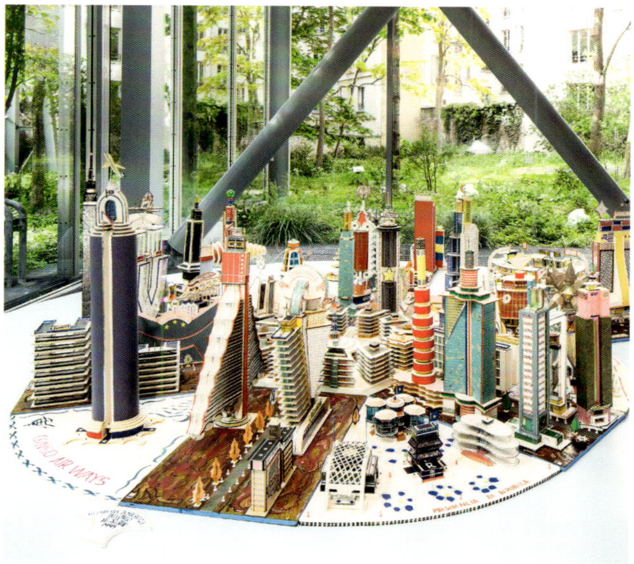

2. Bodys Isek Kingelez. *Projet pour le Kinshasa du Troisième Millénaire*. 1997. 39 ⅜" high x 10' 10 ¹¹⁄₁₆" diam. (100 x 332 cm). Fondation Cartier pour l'Art Contemporain, Paris

fire in their wake.[10] Kingelez, like many of his compatriots under a despotic regime, might not have been vocal about his political convictions, yet it is impossible to miss the sentiment conveyed in a structure with a base wrapped with the national flag yet missing the boastful symbol of its ruler. There is a similar transgression of the Mobutu-era flag in 1993's *Place de la Ville* (pl. 23), in which the complete motif appears but with the hand and torch merely outlined in red. Moreover, Kingelez's penchant for placing star-bearing flags or star-shaped motifs—a key feature in colonial and postcolonial Congolese flags, before and after Mobutu—atop his structures (see *Industria da Pharmacia*, of 1992 [pl. 21], for example) seems to be a wicked play with or surreptitious disavowal of the national imaginaries promoted by a regime to which visual and cultural symbolism meant everything.

Another aspect of the political in Kingelez's practice is his deployment of spectacular architectural form as a counter-narrative to the dystopian realities of Kinshasa, the structural chaos of the Congolese state, and, ultimately, the anomie of the global-postcolonial epoch. In 1997, as rebel forces were mounting a successful violent coup against the Mobutu dictatorship, Kingelez made *Projet pour le Kinshasa du Troisième Millénaire* (fig. 2), a sculpture which imagines third-millennium Kinshasa as "a free, peaceful city . . . where delinquents, police and prisons do not exist."[11] In this work, the clean, safe, marvelously designed and ordered metropolis is a powerful, if symbolic, rejection of a city, nation, and body politic ravaged by decades of oppressive, state-sanctioned disorder and official mismanagement.

This practice of coded utterance through the art of buildings, in its expansive references to global sites and phenomena (see, for example, *Palais d'Hirochima* [1991, pl. 15] and *Centrale Palestinienne* [1993, pl. 24]), its mystical and philosophical resonances, its formal exuberance, its ethical concerns (for example, in *The Scientific Center of Hospitalisation the SIDA* [1991, pl. 17]), and, finally, its insistent self-glorification (most notably in *Mausolée de Kingelez* [1989, fig. 3]), mirrors his writings about his art and life. In the artist's hands, image and text, deployed as much for their ability to both produce meaning and keep it in abeyance as for their surplus and colorful theatricality, were tools for exploring and engaging with contemporary life in the Congo and the wider world.

As singular as Kingelez's creative sensibility might be, it finds echoes in the broader field of cultural and artistic production in Kinshasa, the Congo, and elsewhere in Africa. The formal drama of his art, the bombast and tropical color of his writing, his supreme sense of self-importance, and his own sartorial style (fig. 4) are unmistakably reminiscent of the sapeurs, members of the cult of high fashion known as the Société des Ambianceurs et des Personnes Élégantes, or "Society of tastemakers and elegant people";[12] they show

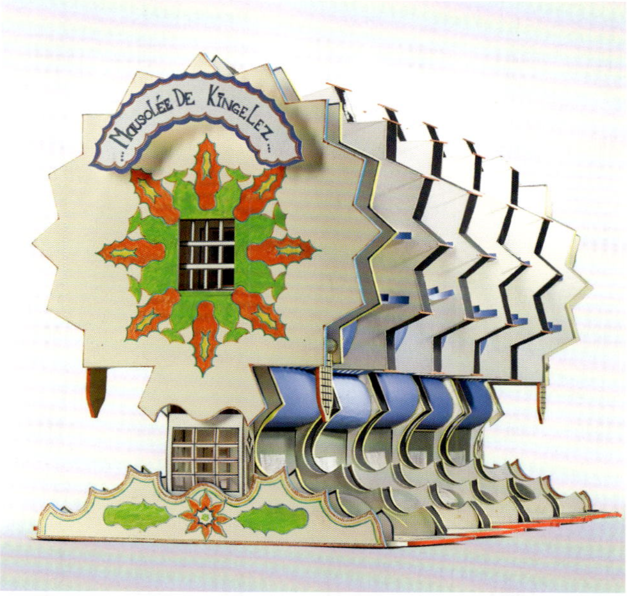

3. Bodys Isek Kingelez. *Mausolée de Kingelez*. 1989. 25 ⅜ x 24 ⁷⁄₁₆ x 44 ⅞" (64.5 x 62 x 114 cm). Musée du quai Branly–Jacques Chirac, Paris

the same will to excess and material-visual flamboyance. More pertinently, given the vaunted emphasis on a national culture revivified by indigenous Congolese traditions (and Maoist fashion) during Mobutu's *authenticité* program, Kingelez's work and the style of the sapeurs—in their insistent refusal to "go native," instead miming spectacular European aesthetic codes—constitute a form of symbolic resistance to official ideology and rhetoric. In other words, the marked efflorescence of the decades-old sape culture and the increasing formal complexity of Kingelez's work by the mid-1980s constitute imaginative coping mechanisms, invocations of alternative realities at a time when the regime, having bankrupted the economy and been all but abandoned by the Western powers that had supported it for years, was unleashing terror and misery on the population.[13] As Bob W. White has noted, the lyrics and hypnotic dance movements invented by soukous music stars, with their veiled social criticism, similarly served the populace as symbolic shelters from the depredations of the regime.[14]

The intense, chaotic urban milieu of Kinshasa and the perpetually fraught political landscape of the Congo catalyzed Kingelez's artistic imagination, and his deployment of form, text, and image find resonances in Kinois visual and expressive cultures and in the political and social histories of the Congo. In search of his own formal language, he also playfully stomped all over the landscape of modern architecture. His fantastical, colorful, and audacious objects leave no one in doubt about their status as an artist's imaginative contribution to the ever-necessary task of envisioning the present and future world.

Epigraph: The artist is quoted in his biography on the website of CAAC—The Pigozzi Collection, http://www.caacart.com/html/kingelez_bio_english.html.

Notes

1 Bodys Isek Kingelez, "Artist's Statement," in *Perspectives 145: Bodys Isek Kingelez* (Houston: Contemporary Arts Museum, 2000), 6.

2 Jean-Marc Patras, "Die Vision eines Visionärs," in *Architekturvisionen aus Zaire* (Berlin: Haus der Kulturen der Welt; Stuttgart: Edition Cantz, 1992), 8. Trans. Fiona Elliott.

3 In the Congo, at the end of the Second World War, the Frenchman Pierre Romain-Desfossés, whose work remains influential, established the workshop "Le Hangar" in today's Lubumbashi, convinced that unschooled African artists were unconsciously endowed with what he called a "Nilotic etiquette." For a discussion of Romain-Desfossés's art teaching and influence in the Congo, see V. Y. Mudimbe's "*Reprendre*: Enunciations and Strategies in Contemporary African Arts," in *Reading the Contemporary: African Art from Theory to the Marketplace*, ed. Olu Oguibe and Okwui Enwezor (London: Institute of International Visual Arts, 1998), 31–47.

4 See Jacques Soulillou and Christian Girard, "Une internationale de l'art urbain," *autrement*,"Les capitales de la couleur," ed. Bruno Tilliette, special issue no. 9 (October 1984): 275–81.

5 Jonathan Jones, "Bodys Isek Kingelez: Kimbéville—City of Tomorrow," *Art & Design* 11, no. 9–10 (September–October 1996): 33–35.

6 Kingelez, "The Essential Framework of the Structures Making Up the Town of Kimbembele-Ihunga (Kimbéville)," in this volume, 51.

7 Jones, "Kimbéville—City of Tomorrow," 33.

8 Kingelez, "The Essential Framework," 51.

9 Achille Mbembe, "The Thing and Its Double," in *On the Postcolony* (Berkeley, Calif.: University of California Press, 2001), 142.

10 Born Joseph-Désiré Mobutu in 1930, he renamed himself Mobutu Sese Seko Kuku Ngbendu wa Za Banga, which is often loosely translated as "The all-powerful warrior who, because of his endurance and inflexible will to win, will go from conquest to conquest leaving fire in his wake." See p. 28, note 21, in this volume.

11 Kingelez, "Artist's Statement," 9.

12 See for instance, Robert Draper's description of the artist as "a bantamlike, middle-aged Kinois dressed entirely in red, from his sunglasses to his leather shoes." Draper, "Kinshasa: Urban Pulse of the Congo," *National Geographic* 224, no. 3 (September 2013): 118.

13 For a good account of the United States' Cold War–era policies toward the Mobutu regime, see Osita G. Afoaku, "The U.S. and Mobutu Sese Seko: Waiting on Disaster," *Journal of Third World Studies* 14, no. 1 (Spring 1997): 65–90.

14 Bob W. White, "Listening Together, Thinking Out Loud: Popular Music and Political Consciousness in Congo-Zaire," *MUSICultures* 41, no. 2 (2014): 54–74.

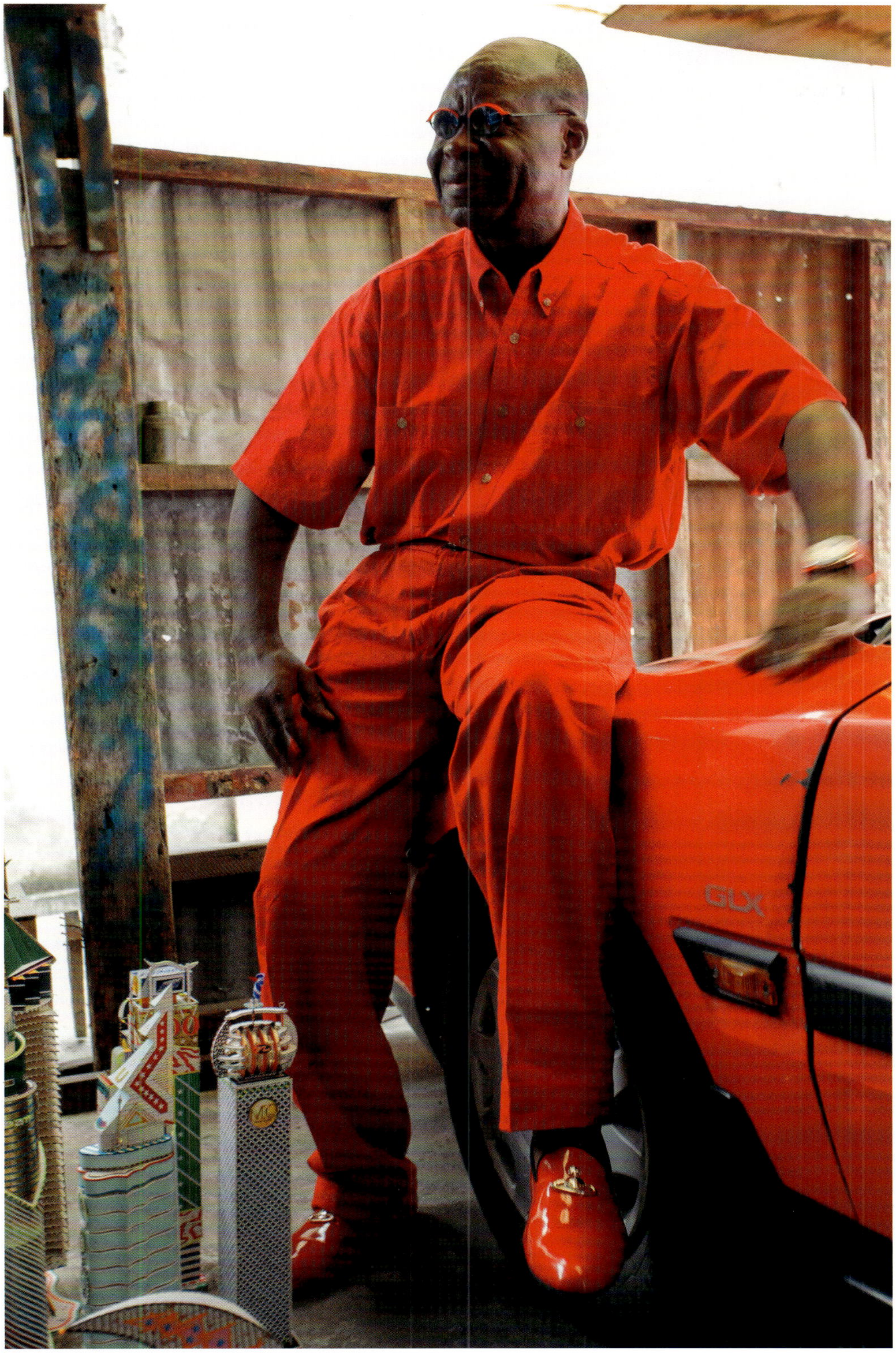
4. Kingelez in Kinshasa, 2012

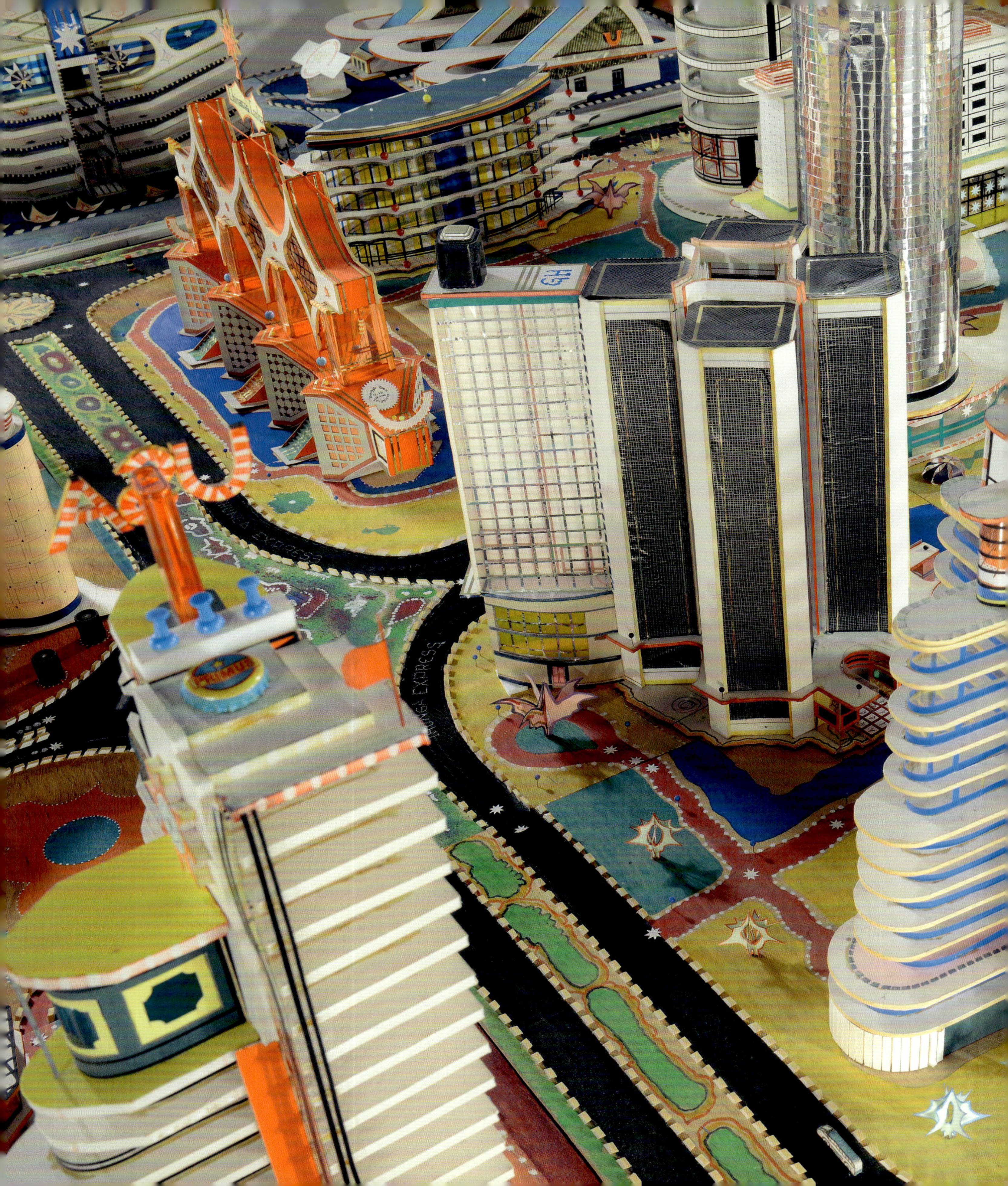
PRIMUS

REPLAYING AFRICAN ABSTRACTION: KINGELEZ'S IMAGES OF ARCHITECTURE

David Adjaye

Bodys Isek Kingelez's work features the signifiers of architecture, but he is not a proto-architect. As I see it, he is more of a mental-mapping phenomenon, and his sculptures represent a dogged mining of the contemporary African psyche. The power of his work comes from his ability to aggregate his observations in fantastical scenarios. The single-mindedness of the project is illuminating.

Many Africans have a vivid image of the future of the continent and of their cities, a vision that grew from the incredible promise of the independence movements of the twentieth century. But instead of the hoped-for growth of nations, there was a crash: many newly independent countries suffered coups and other retrograde denigrations of their democracies. While Africans lived amid the aesthetics of poverty, they were also keenly aware of the larger world, and this relationship has impacted the collective psyche. It is in this context that Kingelez is interesting: as the boy from a Congolese village with a futuristic vision not just for the place where he lives but for the world—a vision spurred by his lack of experience with the conditions he envisions. This is the fascination: a young African visualizing the future.

Arriving in Kinshasa in 1970, Kingelez might have found its sheer density overwhelming. The city is horizontal, organized in twenty-four communes with grand boulevards and dignified buildings, many in a Belgian Art Deco style. The lack of investment in infrastructure is obvious, but the major monuments give the impression that the city is more developed than it really is. From the waterfront, you can see Brazzaville and the silhouette of the Nabemba Tower, also known as Elf Tower, on the opposite bank of the Congo River (fig. 1). Kingelez would have noticed the tower's distinctive profile as it was being constructed, between 1983 and 1986, but he probably never went there, as the river is as powerful a barrier as the Berlin Wall before its fall. Keenly aware of the benefits of education, he attended the University of Lovanium (now the University of Kinshasa), whose campus—a tropical paradise devoted to study—is set on a low hill to the south of the city center. The original buildings are designed in a similar style to the monuments that punctuate the city's boulevards. As a newcomer to Kinshasa, Kingelez was one of an increasing number of people from other regions and other countries establishing new lives there. Having seen city people come to his village, he himself went to the city, inhabiting the multiple identities—rural and urban—that have been a part of the African experience since the inception of colonialism.

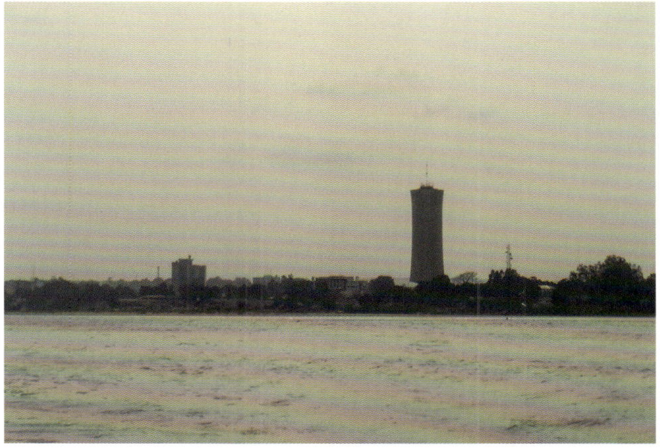

1. View from Kinshasa of the Nabemba Tower in the Brazzaville skyline, 2009

There is a deliberate naïveté in Kingelez's sculptures, because he wasn't trying to represent things as they were. Taking a sideways step, he imbued the works with the immediacy of thought—but they don't have the perfection that thoughts have. Rather, they reflect distortions in the way the mind deals with images. Mental images are not precise: they are fleeting systems, with only *sparks* of thought. There is a looseness in the way the works are assembled—a mismatch between the parts—that allows us to approach them as concepts or images rather than depictions of reality. If they were more precise, I would worry that the artist believed they were actual buildings. Using the skills he honed as a restorer of historical artifacts, Kingelez made objects that constantly hint at reality but always stop you believing in it—a powerful combination.

The connection Kingelez made between geometric form and decoration is an important theme in postwar tropical architecture. Kinshasa is located in the continent's forest region, an area of high rainfall and humidity that covers West Africa and the Congo basin. Overhanging roofs and covered verandas are common responses to this environment, together with brise-soleils and other shading devices (fig. 2). Colonial versions of this architecture were rigorous and formal, but in the hands of local builders, screening systems proliferated and became increasingly ornamental. This particular combination of pure form and applied decoration is a widespread phenomenon in the forest region and likely made a strong impression on Kingelez when he arrived in Kinshasa. His awareness may have been intuitive, but he seems to have understood that the buildings have a layered presence and make use of exaggerated systems (fig. 3). This is very much a forest language: the use of exaggerated systems to deal with extremity. Whether Kingelez understood this as a response to climate or just absorbed it, he seemed to see all architecture as forest architecture. Even when he went to Paris, this influence persisted.

Kingelez combined the mechanisms of cosmopolitan culture into a hyper-African view of the future. Looking at his *U.N.* and *Sports Internationaux* monuments, from 1995 and '97 (pls. 27 and 29), it is evident that he was an internationalist; his sculptures are a fusion of concepts that might be equally at home in Tokyo, New York, or downtown Kinshasa, and he was clearly looking at models beyond his immediate environment. He was drawn to nodes of culture, respite, entertainment, and commerce—to concentrations of human activity that result in built form. He stated that he was interested in "working systems."[1] This is a beautiful way to describe his project, as it expresses the idea that each work is part of a larger system to which the artist made additions and adjustments. It implies that his imagination

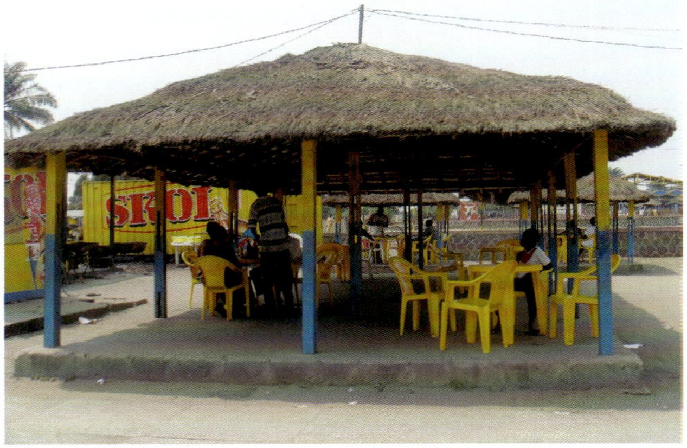

2. Bar with protection from sun and rain, Kinshasa, 2009

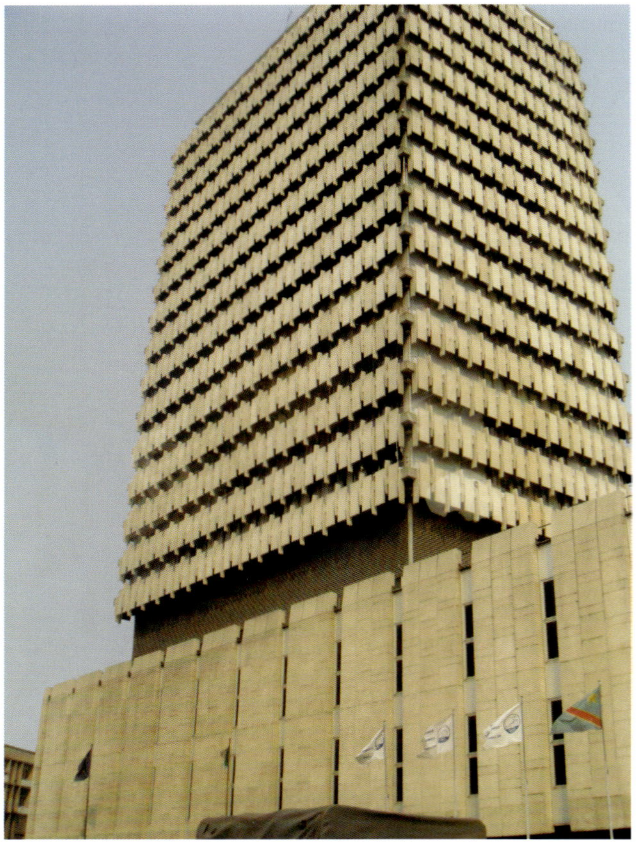

3. Banque Commerciale du Congo, Kinshasa (c. late 1970s), with layered presence and exaggerated facade system, 2009

was a fully realized reality, and that each work represents one facet of a larger project.

The sculptures that show parts of cities seem remarkably similar to those depicting individual buildings, even though they include roads and pavements, public buildings, and places of entertainment. *Kimbembele Ihunga*, made in 1994 (pl. 26), celebrates Kingelez's home village, but rather than picturing it developed into a city, he shows us the city that might grow up after the village disappears. He is talking about millennia—he is a big thinker! *Ville Fantôme*, of 1996 (pl. 28), is less a city than a representation of a hyper-condition that, if it were to become a reality, would drive us mad. Kingelez was warning us about our increasing levels of construction and consumption; he created an image that puts a mirror to our excess. *Ville Fantôme* is prophetic, a call to understand—not necessarily to restrain—our impact on the built environment.

In Kingelez's later works, there is a reduction in complexity and a more singular sculptural power. In 2007's *Dorothe* (pl. 33), for example, there is no longer any suggestion of utilitarian architectural purpose, and this increases the effectiveness of the sculptural form. Kingelez is a trickster: he uses the image of architecture, but he is actually a sculptor. His works have more in common with those of forest tribes, and if he had carved them out of timber they would not be seen as buildings. It is speculation on my part, but I think he is replaying the development of abstraction in African art, but with new materials and through his own particular vision of the world.

Kingelez identified with the contemporariness of his built surroundings, whether ugly or beautiful, and he tried neither to beautify nor downgrade what he saw. He told us what the facts were, how they had impacted him, and what effect they might have on other people. He is the first artist to understand the psychic space of the continent.

Notes

1 Bodys Isek Kingelez, "Artist's Statement," in *Perspectives 145: Bodys Isek Kingelez* (Houston: Contemporary Arts Museum, 2005), 5.

IN SEARCH OF POSSIBILITIES

Sammy Baloji

It's May 2015. The anthropologist Filip De Boeck and I are analyzing Kinshasa's urban topography, attempting to understand how this colonial city, originally conceived for 400,000 inhabitants and today home to more than eleven million, has evolved over the years.[1] Fed continuously by a massive exodus from the interior of the country, which is ravaged by unemployment and war, Kinshasa has not stopped growing. The last attempt at a planned expansion was the development of the commune of Nsele: inaugurated in 1966 by President Mobutu, it was only partially completed. As the city suffocated under a demographic influx, new architectural projects arose spontaneously, often in the form of gated communities for the affluent and the (hypothetical) middle class. Like the colonial *cordon sanitaire*, which defined the physical separation between white and black, a hierarchy of social class was imposed. High walls began to encircle the expatriate community, among whom a few well-to-do Congolese were also housed. Next to this, other urban residents—often the eventual occupants—conceived and constructed their own private architectural projects.

One such project is the enigmatic home of "the Doctor" in an industrial zone of Limete, a commune of Kinshasa, which De Boeck and I have been invited to visit. The building is twelve stories high, defying the clouds, and it takes center stage next to a few half-finished attempts at low buildings. The Doctor—a self-declared specialist in aerospace medicine—decided to construct a sort of Noah's Ark in which to float above the chaos of the city. The building is meant to include a medical clinic, a private residence, various professional offices, a restaurant with housing for a chef and family, and a school of aviation with lodging for its teachers. The top floors will accommodate an air traffic control tower that could assist the main tower at the airport in N'djili in case of a terrorist attack; it will also offer a permanent vantage point from which to contemplate the city and the Congo River and a place for tourists to take photographs far from police officers in search of bribes. The building's twelve stories, built of metal-reinforced concrete, are connected by "ergonomic" stairways without railings. At each level, a concrete platform embedded in the wall serves as a bench for those who might need to rest, and the concrete roof is conceived to support solar panels—as yet absent—that could supply the neighborhood with electricity during power outages. Some of the building's interior walls feature white and colored tile, meticulously combined. We film the Doctor as he shows us around his unfinished masterpiece, emanating an energy at once excessive and controlled.

The Doctor's outsized architectural proposition recalls the political and poetic artworks of Bodys Isek Kingelez. Faced with the chaos of the early 1990s and the impending demise of Mobutu's dictatorial regime, Kingelez responded in his work to an urgent need to transform urban reality. In *Kinshasa la Belle* (1991, pl. 14) as in *Ville Fantôme* (1996, pl. 28), he found his sculptural materials in the cast-offs of a society born of Léopoldian colonial conquest, marked by racial and social inequity, and in collapse under an increasingly brutal extractive capitalism. From this emerged a series of three-dimensional visual propositions, imaginary cities in which global stability is nourished by justice and liberty. Cities—as in the 2008 sculpture *La cité touristique* (The tourist city, fig. 1), by Pume Bylex (born 1968)—where self-realization regarding identity, the material, and the spiritual, long ignored, is possible.[2] Cities—as in the paintings of Turbo Lusavuvu Makaya (born 1969)—that fuse the old colonial authority and its former colony into a futuristic projection, examining a colonial memory, not yet fully

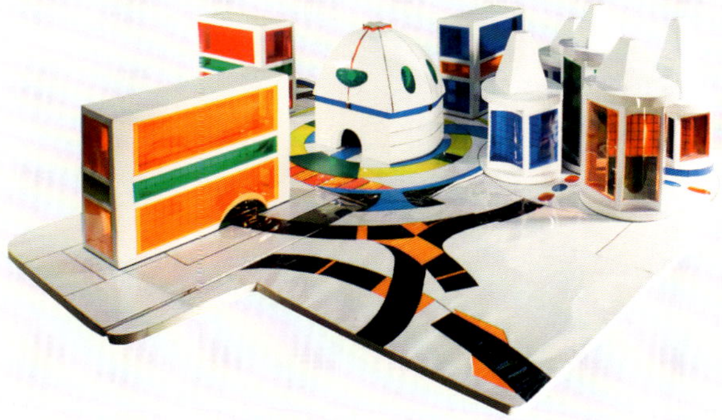

1. Pume Bylex (Congolese, born 1968). *La cité touristique* (The tourist city). 2008. Chromolux color papers pasted on wood and polystyrene, 25 9/16" x 8' 10 11/16" x 8' 10 11/16" (65 x 271 x 271 cm). Collection REVUE NOIRE, Paris

explored, whose vestiges continue to afflict society today.[3] Elsewhere, the vagaries of a working-class Katangese society left behind by the reorganization of the mining sector are conveyed by Jean Katambayi (born 1974) in artworks on cardboard covered with mathematics and physics equations, vectors of a future yet to be invented.[4] From the legacy of Kingelez and his contemporaries, inspired by the uncertainty of the moment, a new generation of Congolese artists emerges, ready to write the future.

Notes

1 For more on this photographic/anthropological project, see Filip De Boeck and Sammy Baloji, *Suturing the City: Living Together in Congo's Urban Worlds* (London: Autograph ABP, 2016).

2 For the work of Pume Bylex, see Jean-Loup Pivin and Pascal Martin Saint Leon, *Pourquoi pas Bylex? Pume* (Paris: Revue Noire, 2012).

3 For more on Turbo Lusavuvu Makaya, see Bambi Ceuppens and Baloji, *Congo Art Works: Peinture populaire* (Tervuren, Belgium: Musée Royal de l'Afrique Central; Brussels: Racine, 2016).

4 The work of Jean Katambayi was included in *A Temporary Futures Institute*, an exhibition co-organized by Anders Kreuger and Maya Van Leemput for M HKA, Antwerp, in 2017.

EARLY ENCOUNTERS WITH KINGELEZ: AN INTERVIEW

André Magnin and Sarah Suzuki

Sarah Suzuki: Your efforts, André, were instrumental in bringing Kingelez's work to a wider audience, and you also had a close personal relationship with him over a long period of time. But let's begin at the beginning: What do you recall about your first meeting with Kingelez?

André Magnin: I met Kingelez in 1987 when I was doing research for the exhibition *Magiciens de la terre*, on my first trip to Kinshasa. That's also when I met Chéri Samba. I visited all the artists at the Académie des Beaux-Arts, all the *peintres populaires*, and many others.[1] But the two most important artists I met at that time were Samba and Kingelez. Samba was already famous, because there were a lot of Belgians and French in Kinshasa who bought his work in the 1970s and '80s. But very few people knew Kingelez's work.

SS: And so you visited him at his house?

AM: Yes, at his house. In Kinshasa there were no galleries, no venues for art, except the Goethe-Institut and the Centre Culturel Français. At that time he was living near the airport, in one of the poorer neighborhoods of Kinshasa.

SS: Did he already have his confidence, his sense of purpose?

AM: Yes, yes. You could see it immediately. He was living in a modest neighborhood but his house was immaculate, and it was the only one like that. There was a little garden. It was neat; it was a tiny house with little curtains. So he already had—how can I say—a high opinion of himself; you could see that through the way they were living, the organization of the little house. I took many, many slides. I don't remember the date, but he had an American flag—

SS: Oh, the outfit [fig. 1], his top and pants!

AM: He made it himself.

SS: That's amazing! Why do you think he chose the American flag?

AM: Because, I think, he believed that the Americans had plundered all his ideas, all the great American architects had plundered all his ideas. [*Laughs*] He told me a hundred times, "Bloody America, they stole all my ideas!" It is not true. It was impossible because nobody had seen his work before *Magiciens de la terre*.

SS: Did you know from the first time you met him that you would include his work in *Magiciens de la terre*?

AM: Well, I think in a way it had already been decided. When we made our research trips, we usually had leads, and in this case we had seen a little reproduction [p. 15, fig. 4]. After each trip, Jean-Hubert Martin, Aline Luque, and I (Mark Francis was not yet there at the time) would convene to share and discuss what we had seen. And little by little we made choices, selected artists, and made changes over the course of two or three years.

SS: There are some letters from Kingelez in the archives at the Centre Pompidou about which works he was preparing to send to Paris. At one point he changed his proposal, and he needed a bit more money to make the new works he was planning. Do you know where he was able to buy supplies in Kinshasa?

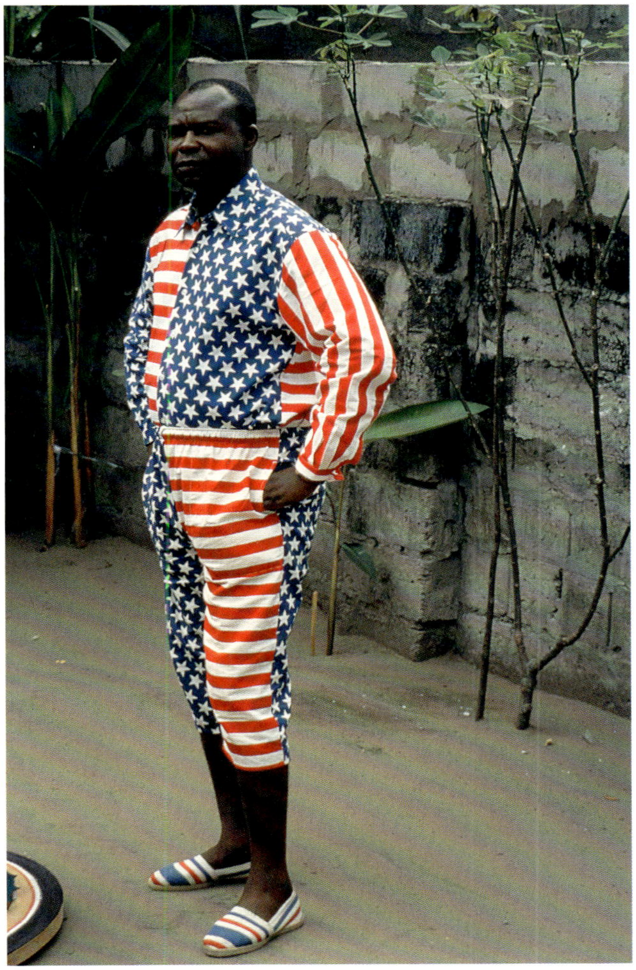

1. Kingelez in Kinshasa, 1990

AM: In the beginning he was using only waste materials.

SS: Truly?

AM: Yes, for all the maquettes. It was impossible to find affordable materials in Kinshasa at that time. The situation was very difficult, and Kingelez had no money. Almost everything he used was salvaged. There were UHU glue stick boxes, shoeboxes. He reused everything, all the cardboard, all the plastic, the stuff from the city center's stores. It was in Paris that he had access to artists' materials. Immediately upon his arrival in Paris he made a list of the things he needed, including two or three assistants.

SS: Where in Paris did he work?

AM: At the Grande Halle de la Villette. We asked Kingelez to come one month early, I think. On the right side of the Grande Halle de la Villette, when you entered, there was a big space, full of light, and that's where he worked. The first big sculpture he made was his mausoleum [p. 35, fig. 3].

SS: Do you think that when he was in Paris he went to Les Invalides and saw Napoleon's tomb?

AM: I don't know. It's not impossible. The artists worked all day at La Villette. A friend of mine drove them there in the morning and then back to their hotel in the evening. On the weekend, tours of Paris were organized for the artists that had come from faraway countries. There was a bus that took them to different monuments, and even a boat ride down the Seine.

SS: Did Kingelez bring any family with him?

AM: No, the family didn't come. He was alone. He asked for three assistants, but they didn't last long. After a week, it was either he who didn't want them anymore, or the assistants couldn't take it. So we had to replace them often.

SS: A complicated installation! What impact do you think this experience in Paris had on him after he went back to Kinshasa? Certainly he had new materials.

AM: Yes, he brought a lot of materials home. On the last day of the show, or one day after it closed, I met Jean Pigozzi, who had become totally focused on African contemporary art. I started working with him immediately [as curator of Pigozzi's Contemporary African Art Collection, now known as CAAC—The Pigozzi Collection]. And one of the first trips I made, to begin the collection, was to Kinshasa, because there were a lot of artists there—not only Samba and Kingelez but also Cheik Ledy, Moké, Pierre Bodo, etc. I commissioned pieces from Kingelez for the CAAC.

SS: Was this an easy process or a complicated one?

AM: In the beginning it was easy, because we were the only ones buying.

SS: Do you think he was frustrated because people in Kinshasa didn't know what he was doing or who he was?

AM: No, because he was very private. He never received people at home. Never. But I went many times to his house. There was his first wife, then his second and his third, the children. Then he bought two or three houses in the city center of Kinshasa. There was a very, very high wall around his home, with wire mesh on top. When he went out, it was extremely discreet. Nobody was allowed to see what he was doing at his home or take any photographs, not even his wives! He stored all his works in one place, and he covered them with sheets so nobody could see them. Even I, when I was visiting him—before he'd show me anything, he wanted to make sure that I hadn't visited any other artist before him. That was very important.

If I went to see Samba before him, he would refuse to see me. He'd say, "What are you doing with these artists? I am the only one, so you have to start with me!" Kingelez rented out some of his houses, but sometimes he would use them himself—he would work in several different places at once, in order, he said, not to be followed. Kingelez would tell me to meet him *there*, and when I would go *there*, his wives would tell me that he was somewhere else. And so I had to track him down. It was on purpose; he wanted to be hard to find. [*Laughs*]

SS: So he wasn't, or didn't want to be, a known figure in Kinshasa? He didn't socialize publicly with friends in government, or with other artists?

AM: Over the years, I've often gotten people together for dinners and parties in Kinshasa. At some point in the 1990s I organized a dinner for all the artists I was working with, plus some friends. I invited everybody, and Kingelez came for the first time. He asked to be right at the center of the table.

SS: Of course, where else would he go?

AM: He accepted my invitation just that once. After that he refused to join us. You see, to him, all the others weren't artists.

SS: When did you first find out about Kingelez's writings?

AM: When I talked with him about the work, he was extremely difficult to understand, because he invented words, you know? He would give me a very long explanation for each building, and eventually I asked him to write all the stories down on paper. I don't know if he was writing before that.

SS: He had beautiful penmanship.

AM: He had very beautiful handwriting. Very precise. He wrote in front of me sometimes. He would just start writing—without stopping, without correction, with no crossing out. Even though he was inventing words! It's incredible. It was very precise and also completely chaotic.[2] The writing has a personal logic through which one has to find one's way. It can be highly confusing, but in the end it makes sense.

SS: Did he ever talk to you about his time working at the Institut des Musées Nationaux du Zaïre?

AM: Yes, yes. Do you know how he made his first artwork? What he explained to me was that one night he had a dream, a vision, then he stood up and he started working. He became extremely nervous, he was sweating, and he had to make an architecture, he felt compelled. He wouldn't stop, day and night, until he was done. And his neighbor—that is what Kingelez told me—his close neighbor saw this first maquette. He worked as a guard at the museum, and he was so impressed that he offered to bring the sculpture to work and show it to the director. At the museum, nobody believed that Kingelez had made it. So they invited him to come in, to prove that he could do it again. He didn't replicate the work, he made a different one. The museum was stunned by his creations, and they hired him. They offered him a job as a restorer. But his salary was smaller than what he had made as a teacher, and after some time he decided to leave. He devoted himself to model making. He decided to start working, building—

SS: As an artist.

AM: As an artist. He made a work for the architect Christian Girard. Before that, he had made maybe one or two sculptures for the museum, but nobody knows where they are now. After that, *Magiciens de la terre*, and after that—

SS: And after that, history.

AM: Exactly.

SS: Do you have any recollections about anything Kingelez said about the works you commissioned for the CAAC?

AM: He was completely free in making his creations. If my memory is correct, on their first meeting Pigozzi suggested to him that he make a whole city, but, in fact, it was the artist's dream as well. He realized his first major city, *Kimbembele Ihunga* [pl. 26], in 1994; it is named after his native village. He made *U.N.* [pl. 27] the following year, for the fiftieth anniversary of the United Nations. For me the best buildings were those in which he combined bought and

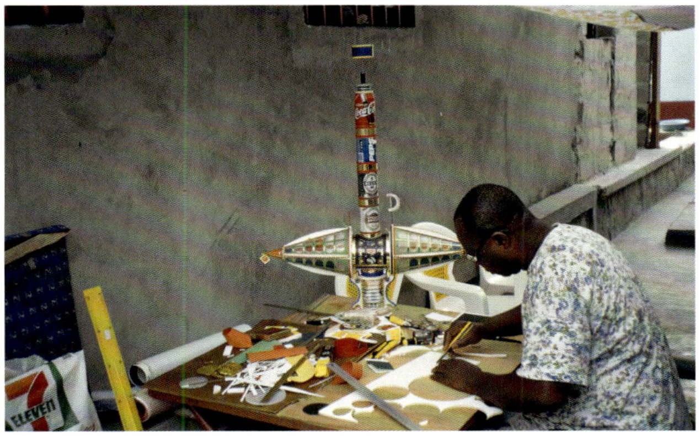

2. Kingelez in Kinshasa, with *Sports Internationaux* (pl. 29), 1998

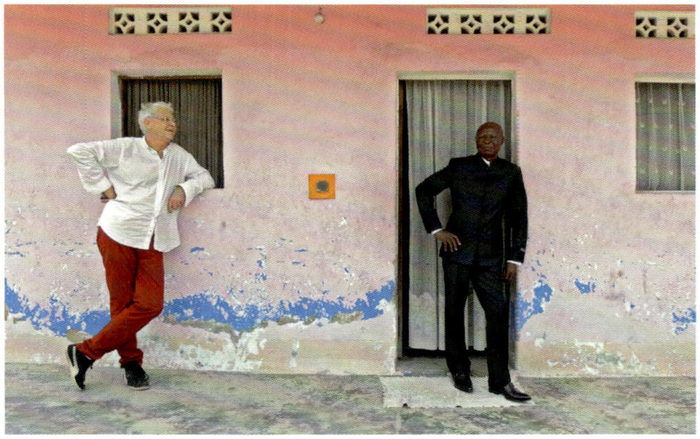

3. André Magnin and Kingelez outside the artist's home, Kinshasa, 2014

found materials—printed paper, corrugated cardboard, thumbtacks, bottle caps, electrical parts, straws, soda cans [fig. 2]. I helped many others commission works too: the Fondation Cartier pour l'Art Contemporain; Kasper König for the Museum Ludwig; agnès b; the Musée International des Arts Modestes, in Sète [pl. 30], where he made the artwork on-site.

SS: In 2000 he spent a month in Sète, in southern France, and that's when he realized he was ill.

AM: Yes, exactly. After his diagnosis he stayed in Paris for a long time. We rented an apartment for him and got him into Tenon hospital. Pigozzi was incredibly supportive of the CAAC artists when it came to their health. If he hadn't been, Kingelez would have died. Eventually he returned to Kinshasa, and I continued to visit him there [fig. 3].

SS: Kingelez had a vision for Kinshasa and for the world, but did he ever want his sculptures to be built as architecture?

AM: I think he hoped that people would be sensitive to his dreams, and that politicians might conceive of a city that *could* have been designed by Kingelez. But I think he knew that they would never be built. It was a utopia, an alternative to the real Kinshasa in which he lived. I think that's also why he refused to let people see what he was making—because he knew nobody would understand or care. They would say he was crazy. But he was not crazy. He was a visionary, and his work was a dream—his dream.

Notes

1 *Peintres populaires* are makers of the "popular painting" that first emerged in the Congo in the years after independence from Belgian rule. They work in a colorful vernacular style and with imagery based on contemporary reality, local history, and everyday subjects.

2 For examples of the artist's writings, see p. 49 in this volume.

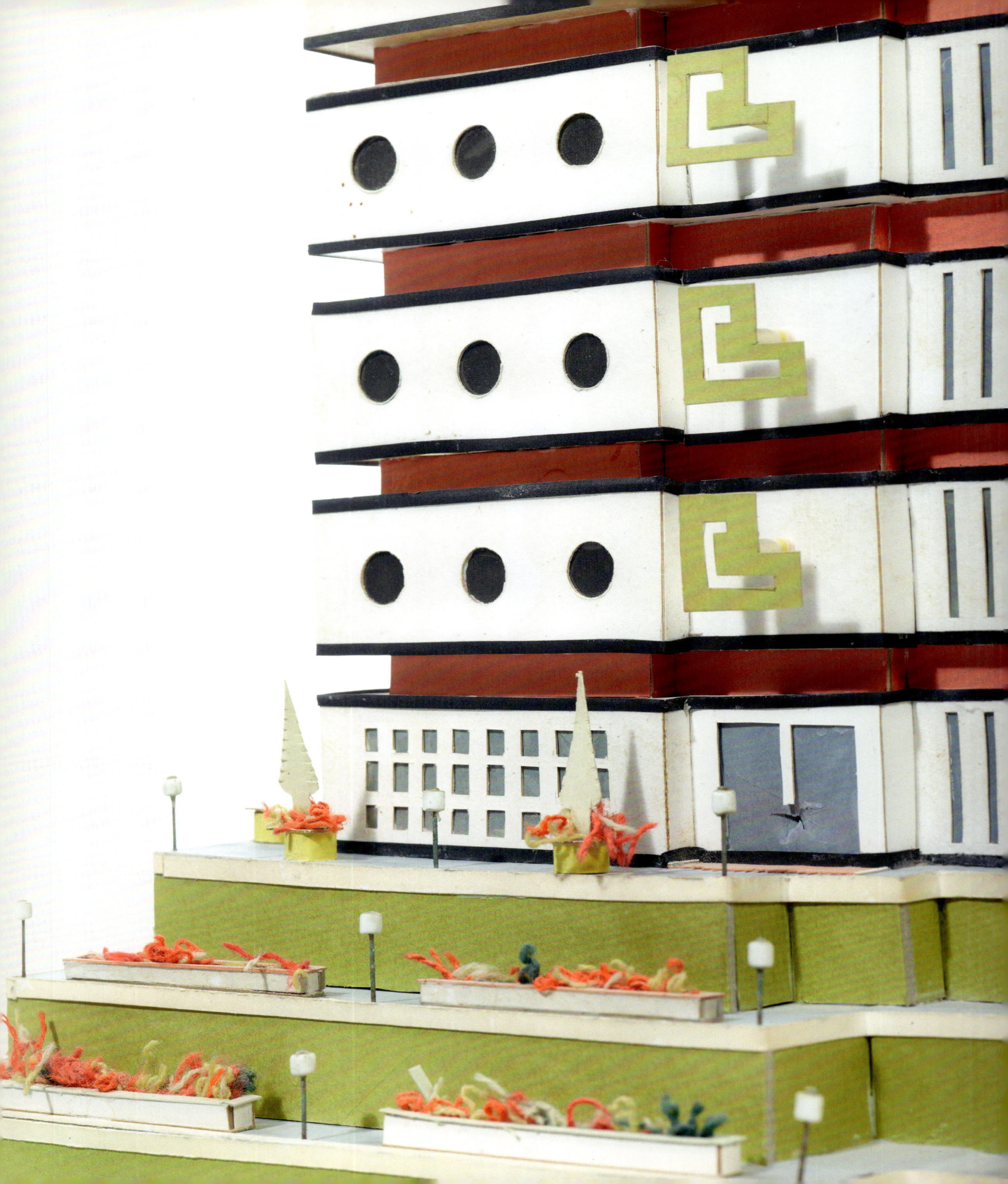

WRITINGS BY KINGELEZ

Very early in his career, Kingelez began producing texts to accompany his sculptures. A parallel artistic practice of sorts, these writings, which vary in length from just a few sentences to elaborate paragraphs covering many pages, feature grandiloquent language organized in highly inventive grammatical structures, composed in French in Kingelez's distinctive, cursive penmanship. They generally address some aspect of the artist's intentions, explaining the connotations of particular symbols or colors in the work, for example, or describing the interior life of the sculpture in question.

In the undated manuscript "Maquettes of Post-Modes Art" (fig.1), Kingelez briefly describes four recent sculptures, two of which—*Reveillon Fédéral* (pl. 20) and *Kimbembele Ihunga (Kimbembele Ville)* (pl. 22), both completed in 1992—are discussed in the excerpt printed here. It was first published in English in the artist's magazine *Gagarin* in 2003 as "Scale Models of Post-Modes Art."

"The Essential Framework of the Structures Making Up the Town of Kimbembele-Ihunga (Kimbéville)" relates to the 1994 work *Kimbembele Ihunga* (pl. 26), which was included in the show *Big City: Artists from Africa* at the Serpentine Gallery, London, in 1995, and the text was published in English in the exhibition's catalogue. *Kimbembele Ihunga*, the first of the artist's major city sculptures, is a reimagining of his place of birth, and in the text Kingelez weaves biographical details and a chronicle of the community together with detailed descriptions of the role of the work in his fantasies of the village's past, present, and future.

MAQUETTES OF POST-MODES ART

[. . .]

III Kimbembele-Ihunga/City

"This extra modern model incarnates in my subconscious especially a village that some day would become an ultra-modern and original city with a famous 'Roundabout' over which a guardian angel will be suspended, as the symbol of victory after a period of agitation and compassion . . . "

IV Reveillon Fédéral (Democratia)

"Really amazing and impressive, this fever of democracy that compromises the world, has made me conceive this maquette, where the red and yellow symbolizes victory and absolutely reminds us of 'the Martyrs' blood' that ran through the meanders of this fight for pure freedom . . . "

THE ESSENTIAL FRAMEWORK OF THE STRUCTURES MAKING UP THE TOWN OF KIMBEMBELE-IHUNGA (KIMBÉVILLE)

Historical Background to Kimbéville

The monument of Kimbéville belongs to a genre of art which has attained its zenith presenting what already has the potential to become or is on the way to becoming a reality. Gradually the town of Kimbembele-Ihunga, abbreviated to Kimbéville by its creator-maker, the enlightened artist of new horizons, Bodys Isek Kingelez, should glorify the times rather than exist merely to further my own success and prosperity, in view of my fame and international reputation as a highly talented artist. This town, a natural product of my thought processes, represents the shape of my

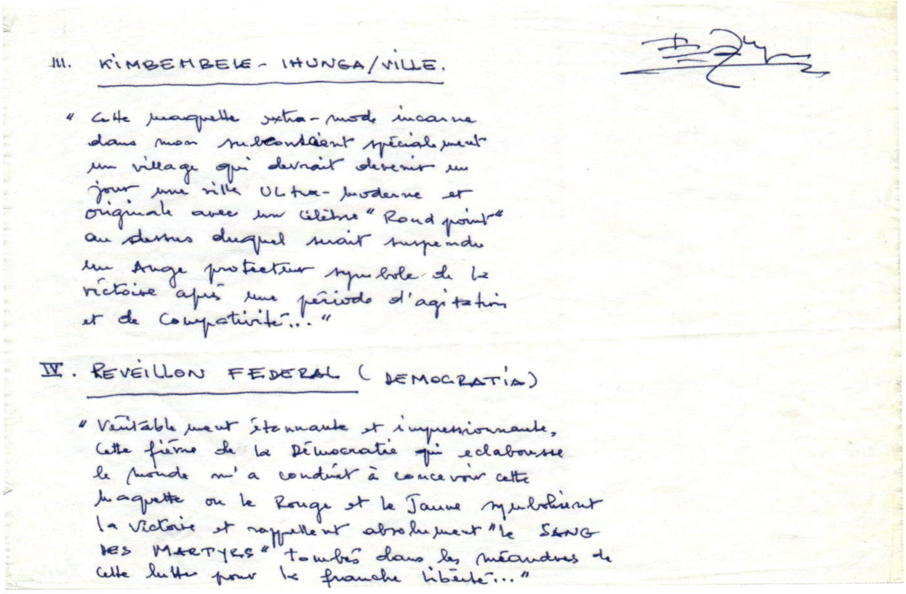

III. KIMBEMBELE-IHUNGA/VILLE.

" Cette maquette extra-mode incarne dans mon subconscient spécialement un village qui devrait devenir un jour une ville ULtra-moderne et originale avec un célèbre " Rond point " au dessus duquel serait suspendu un Ange protecteur symbole de la victoire après une période d'agitation et de compétitivité..."

IV. REVEILLON FEDERAL (DEMOCRATIA)

" Véritablement étonnante et impressionnante, cette fièvre de la Démocratie qui éclabousse le monde m'a conduit à concevoir cette maquette où le Rouge et le Jaune symbolisent la victoire et rappellent absolument " le SANG DES MARTYRS " tombés dans les méandres de cette lutte pour la franche liberté..."

1. Excerpt from Kingelez's manuscript "Maquettes d'art post-modes" (Maquettes of Post-Modes Art), c. 1992. Courtesy André Magnin, Paris

imagination; it is the very image of my ability to create a new world as well as being a gauntlet thrown down to professional artists in the arena of inventive references for beauty and grace. Kimbéville with its dazzling array of forms and colors is a 21st-century environment which has fired my artistic imagination. It is a town where Kingelez, the enlightened artist, was born on 27 August 1948. Every artist on earth achieves self-expression through the most deep-rooted origins of their nature. Kingelez of Kimbéville is no longer merely an artist from his native town, he is the favored poet of his traditional sources. The town's glittering vista radiates along countless boulevards which lead in all directions, thereby preserving the originality of Kimbéville's diamond-like divisions; parallelism is a thing of the past.

The overall concept of the town, the very problem of quality architecture, ranks it among the high-caliber, super-multisystem phenomena of futurist architecture. The landscape design and the concrete styles used in shaping the buildings systematically combine to represent and reflect the different cosmopolitan cultures which surround the town's unquestionable unity. Kimbéville will be responsible for the rapid creation of a tourist trade, as people will flock to see the town's many sights, the lifestyle of its inhabitants, and the ways in which it differs from what has gone before: its avenues, its emphasis on form, its overall appearance, its artistic landscape displaying the magnificent intermingling outlines of the differently shaped buildings, which give the TOP place of honor to the leading cultures of the world.

So the town of Kimbéville is similar to an extremely realistic prototype gem which should in fact exist in all its glory in accordance with the issues and requirements of housing standards. A town which symbolizes my sources, found geographically in what could be called:

–the traditional village of KIMBEMBELE-IHUNGA
–in Belo sector
–in the IDIOFA territory/the Kwilu region
–province of Bandundu
–in the Republic of Zaire
–in the heart of the African continent

Conclusion
Still talking about accelerated civilizations, the town of Kimbéville acts as a mechanism for development with a myriad of distinctive features applying as much to the buildings as to the varied elements of its clearly defined landscape which blatantly demonstrates why this town was created. Its creator, the artist Kingelez, a man of high moral fiber, will keep his future promises with this work of art which will accompany him into the 21st century. Kimbéville is a real town which, given time, will exist; it is not an effigy made up of well-known brand names which is doomed to remain a maquette.

Inextricably linked to its historical past, put down on paper within the context of its delirious, uncommon structures, its ideas have gained a lot of ground which will guarantee its future reputation—there is no going back.

Kingelez's art, through the medium of this image-maquette which invokes an ancient traditional village, i.e. Kimbembele-Ihunga, situated within the south-west borders of the Province of Bandundu, is a concrete imaginative leap built with the careful equanimity that comes from knowledge. It has created a real bridge between world civilizations of the past, the present and the future.

Kingelez's art, which provides the blueprint for a real town, is a large-scale architectural act which champions what is most important to the artist: the time-honored traditions of his village.

The vista of Kimbéville, the sight of which sometimes beggars description, is larger than life, making it an image which contains all the major universal values, providing countless resonant references.

These highly diverse model buildings have a certain imperative quality since this highly stylized landscape demands admiration as much for its eye-catching appearance as for the far-reaching compass of the genre. Its visual extravagance acts as a universal focus of attention.

And, all the while, conspicuous, well-known landmarks form part of a logical system of architecture which is not opposed to revealing the ambitions of the artist, who would not want the real existence of the town of Ihunga to be undermined by its true nature.

In line with this large-scale investiture, certain curious names can be seen on the buildings which form the town of Kimbéville; names which have taken on a clannish quality.

In the same way as the traditional village of Ihunga is comprised of five groups, there are also five clans, namely:

the LODI clan (my mother's clan)
the BAYETE clan (my father's clan)
the BOLOUMBOU clan (neighboring clan)
the MISSAMOU clan
the KIMBEMBELE clan

These clans form the entity of Kimbéville, which has been modernized in view of its recreated nature.

Planned in this way, Kimbéville is still basically traditional despite the fact that its former appearance has altered with the passing years. This concern has caused the artist Kingelez to devote a great deal of attention to ensuring that the existence of these various civilizations is charted.

If you examine this town's specificity closely, you get the feeling that, due to its eye catching and extremely demanding effects, you could go on admiring it endlessly. Frankly, it would take me a lifetime to relate even half its history.

Nevertheless, in terms of its architectural autonomy, its distinctive features so full of promise, this town should appear on a definitive list of the greatest towns on earth.

Kimbéville is not far from being fêted as a potential tourist town, with regard to which its critics have not played a significant part in its history because Kingelez himself has given a meaning to the town's existence.

The gigantic, carefully erected, statue which represents the wisdom of my father, Maluba Kingelez, who died on 27 March 1968, is dedicated to him and should be situated right in the administrative center of the town of Ihunga.

In other words, this statue carrying his body of knowledge in his hand, simply represents the intellectual heritage of common sense and good manners which belongs to multicultural people. This is the way my father has proudly risen above the meaning of a ceremonial life to practice an art in praise of beauty and grace which will bring about a better world.

Opposite this Kingelez monument, a superb communal building mirrors itself, doubly interesting in the fascinating and obscure way that both foundation and form are constructed.

The partial view of the Monde-Vision building, with its superlative details, effortlessly substantiates the incomparable, highly elaborate modern achievement of the town. This collection of realist buildings, unaffected by the dictates of fashion, represents an unparalleled devotional vision. The aim of these buildings is to promote this new image throughout the world. These boulevards, these lanes with their spotless pavements, hardly ever become congested, blocking freedom of movement. On the contrary, they provide people with pleasant, easy access to all parts of the town.

The town of Kimbéville flourishes. People flock here because the wind blows in off the sea and the mountains, refreshing its complex beauty in which all the heightened colors join forces constantly to create an environment where everyone can feel at home.

This maquette is a promise of something real. The attractions of this town include a plethora of services, hotels and restaurants. Sometimes with an American flavor, sometimes Japanese, Chinese or European, not to mention African fare.

The town has it all, from sun-up to sun-down, and for forever and a day. The artist, Kingelez, prophet of African art, is striding towards a new world which is more modern, more prosperous and a better place to live.

This lengthy resumé about the town was written by someone who devotes his daily life to excellence.

PLATES

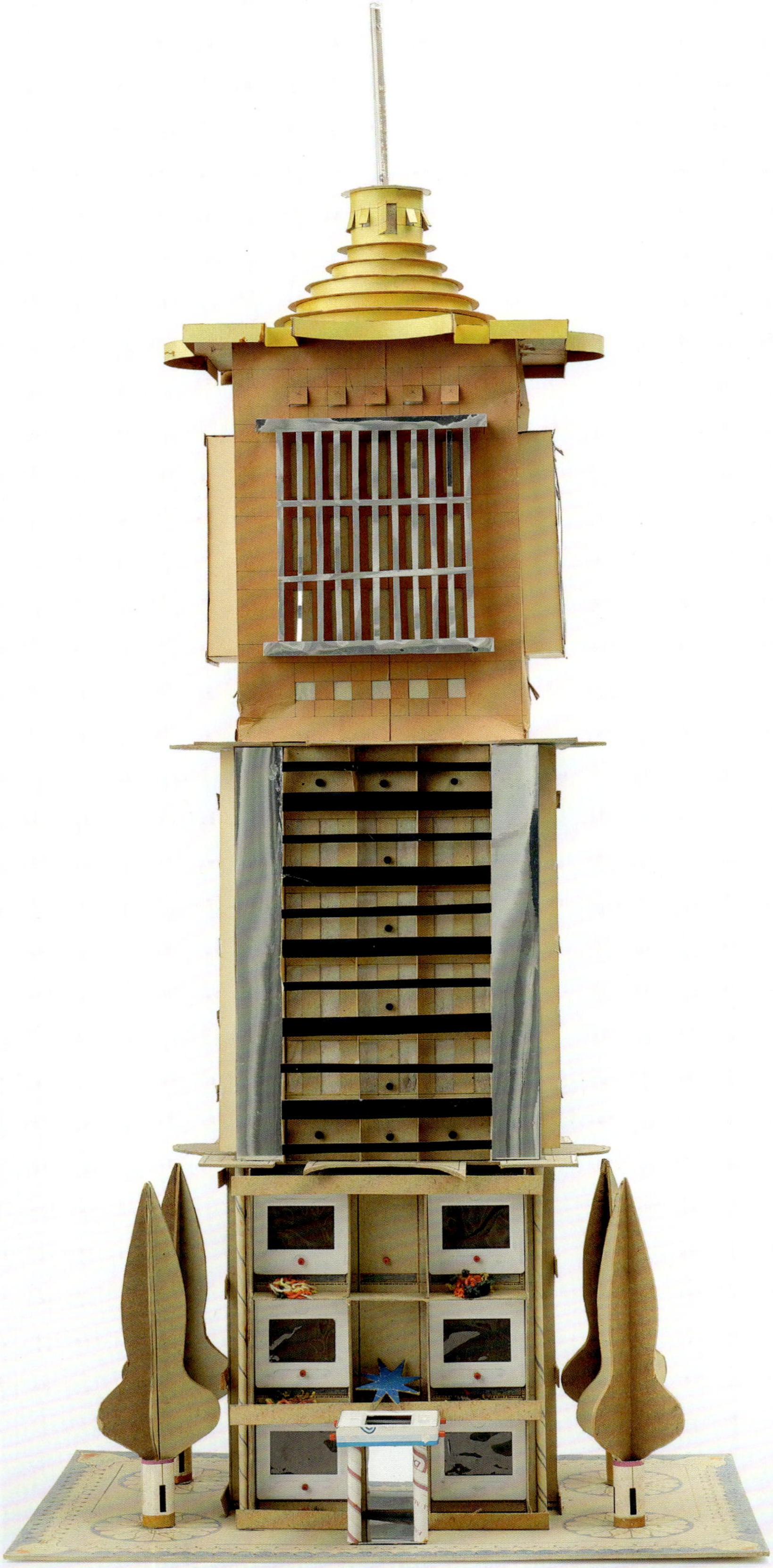

1

Untitled. c. 1980
32 15/16 x 14 7/8 x 9 5/8"
(83.6 x 37.8 x 24.5 cm)
Private collection, Paris

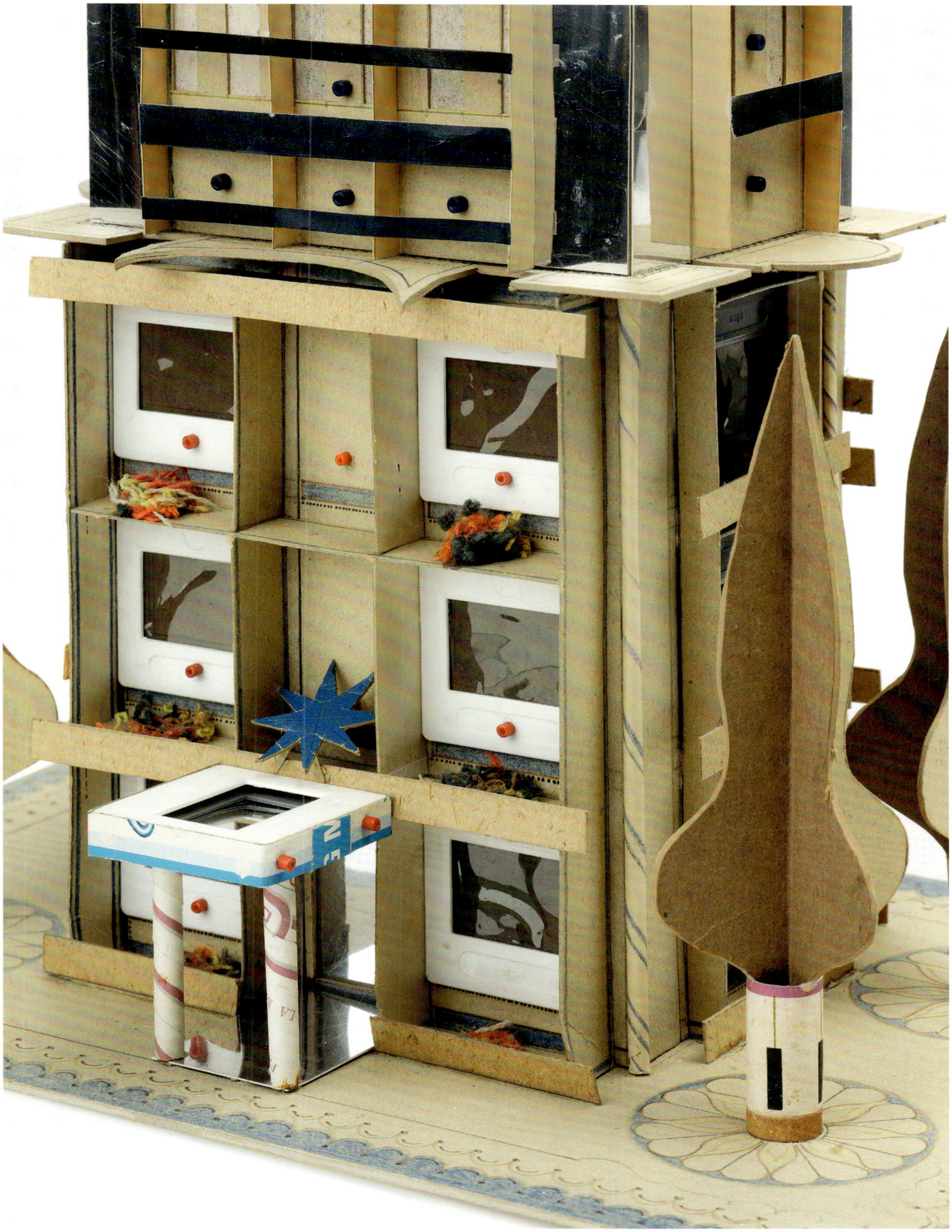

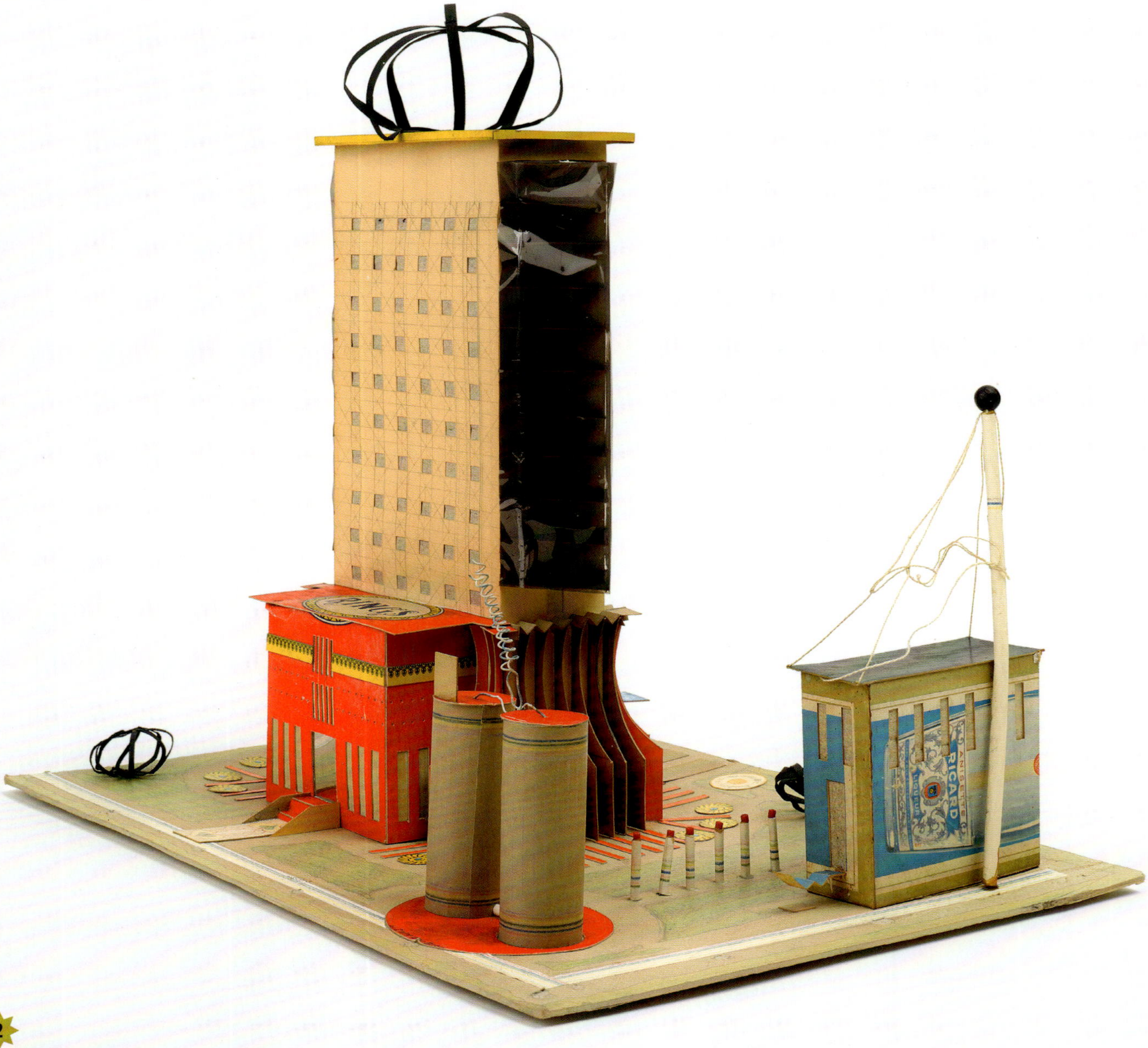

2

Untitled. 1980
15 3/8 x 17 3/8 x 12 3/8" (39 x 44.2 x 31.5 cm)
Private collection, Paris

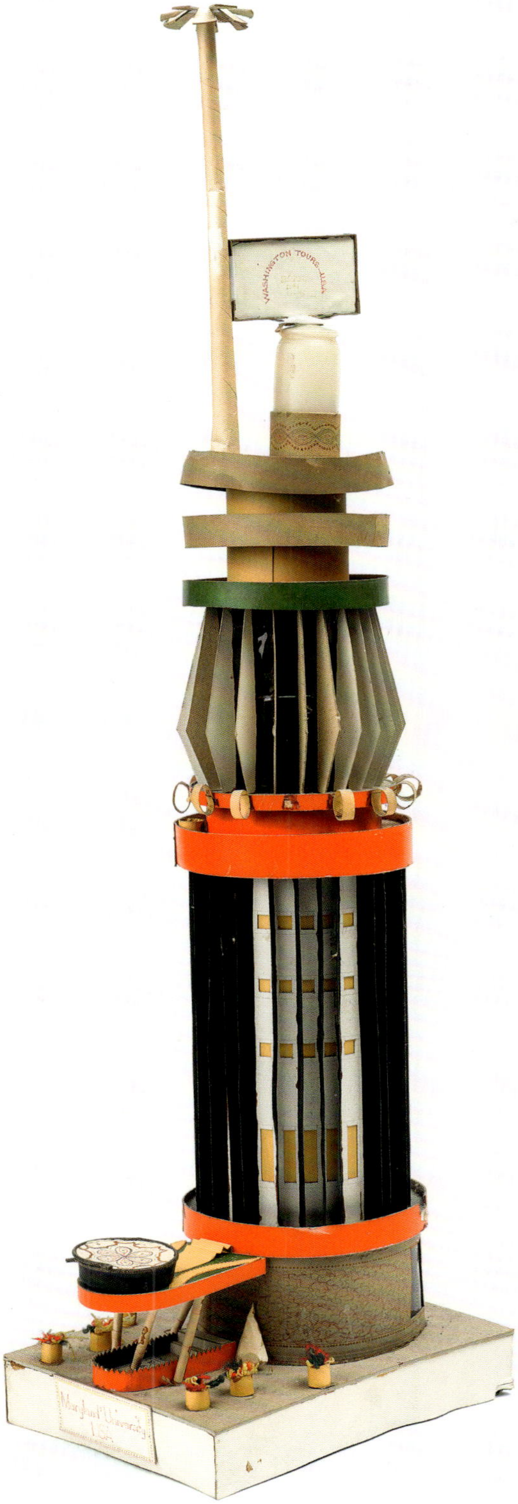

3

Maryland University USA. 1981
26 x 5 9⁄16 x 7 ½" (66 x 14.2 x 19.1 cm)
Private collection, Paris

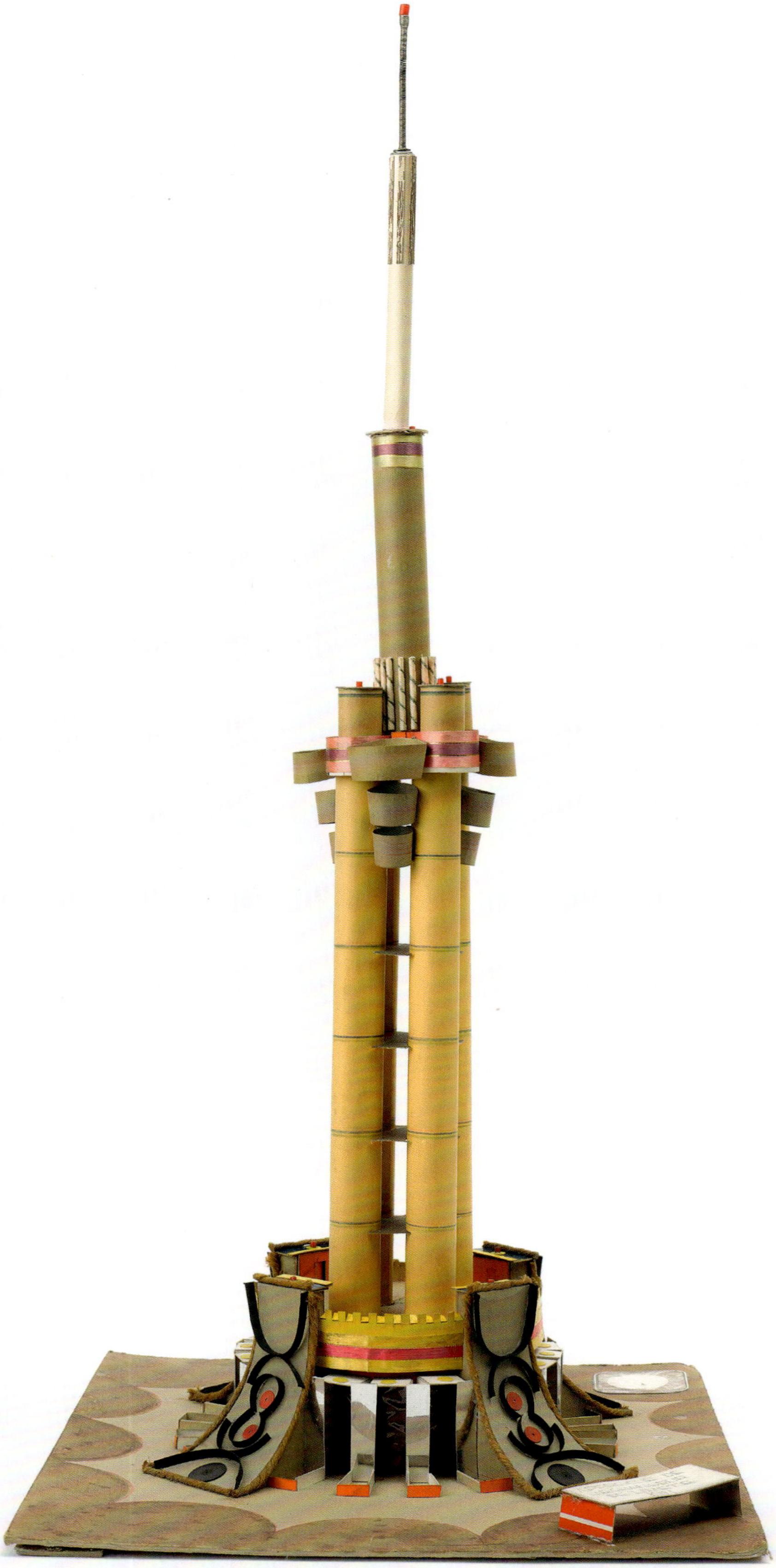

4

Approche de l'Échangeur de Limete Kin. 1981
32 5⁄16 x 13 7⁄8 x 16 3⁄4"
(82 x 35.2 x 42.6 cm)
Private collection, Paris

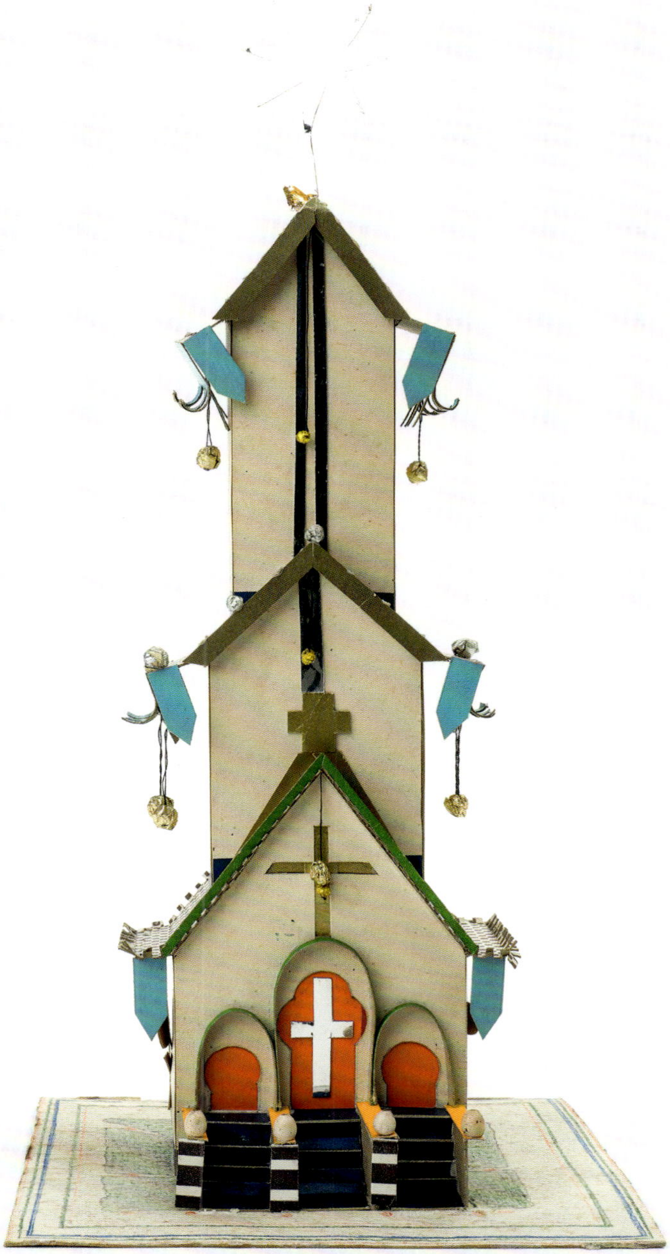

5

Untitled. 1982
12 3⁄8 x 7 1⁄16 x 7 3⁄16" (31.4 x 18 x 18.2 cm)
Private collection, Paris

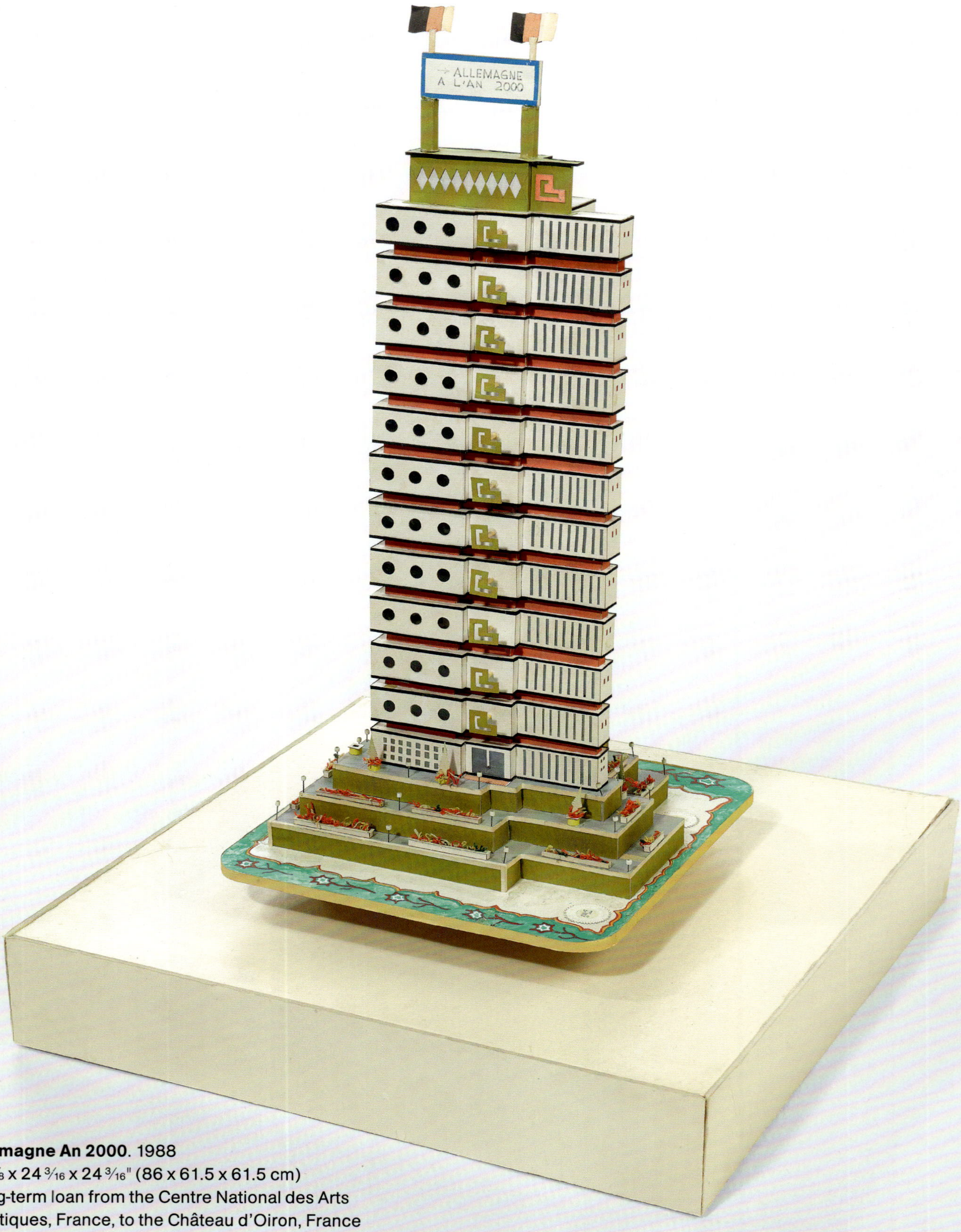

6

Allemagne An 2000. 1988
33 7⁄8 x 24 3⁄16 x 24 3⁄16" (86 x 61.5 x 61.5 cm)
Long-term loan from the Centre National des Arts Plastiques, France, to the Château d'Oiron, France

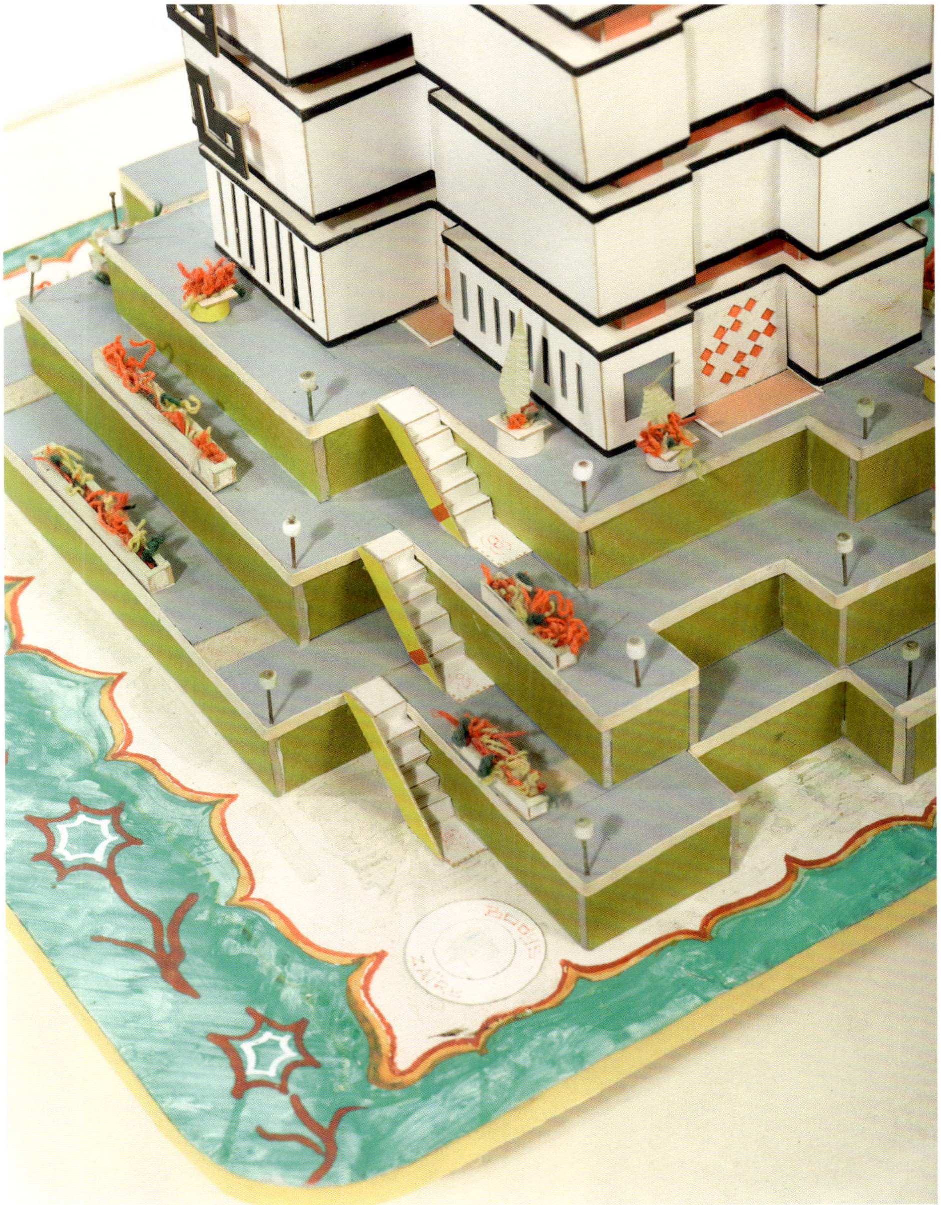

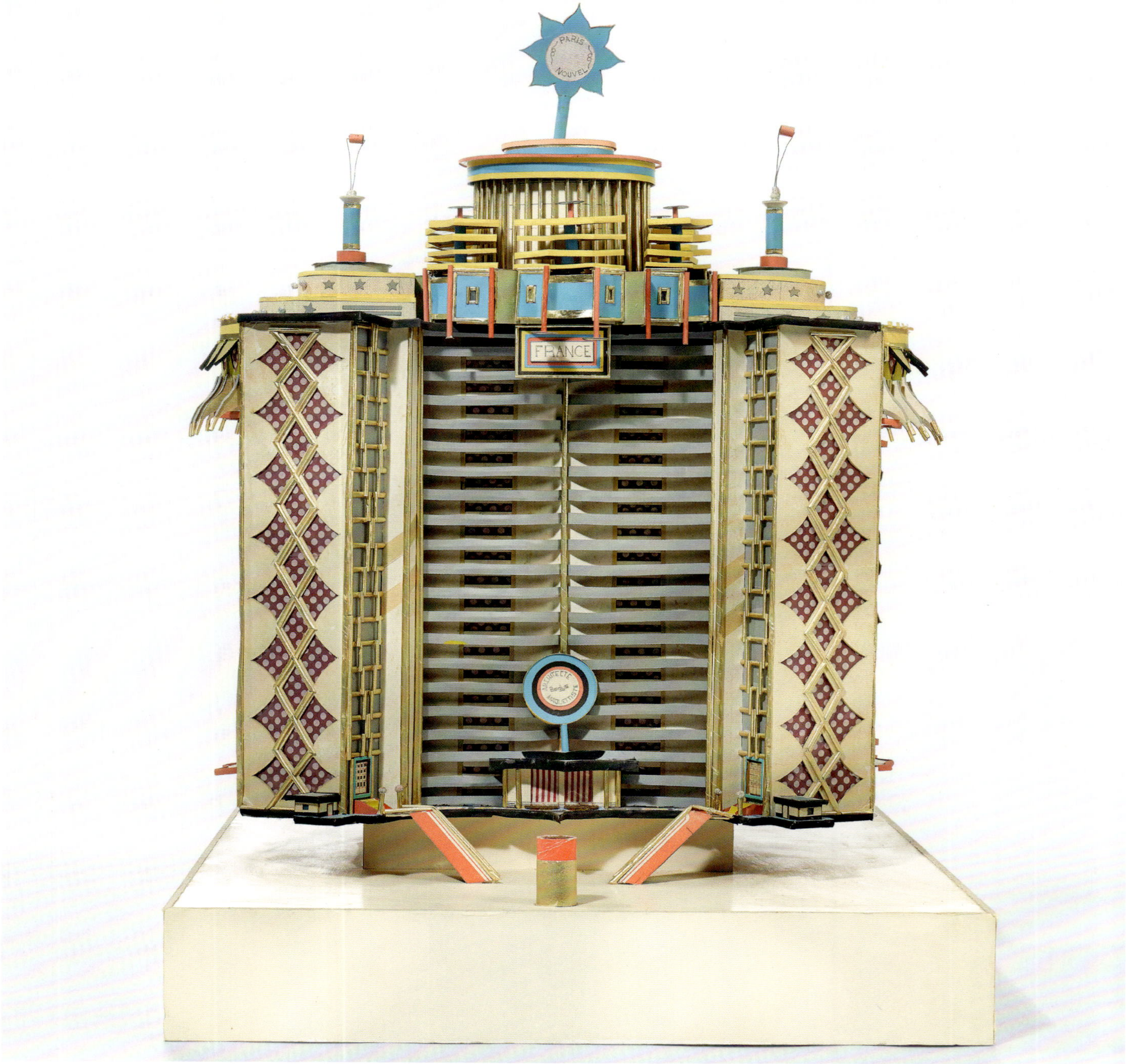

7

Paris Nouvel. 1989
$33\,^{7}/_{16}$ x 24 x $27\,^{9}/_{16}$" (85 x 61 x 70 cm)
Long-term loan from the Centre National des Arts Plastiques, France, to the Château d'Oiron, France

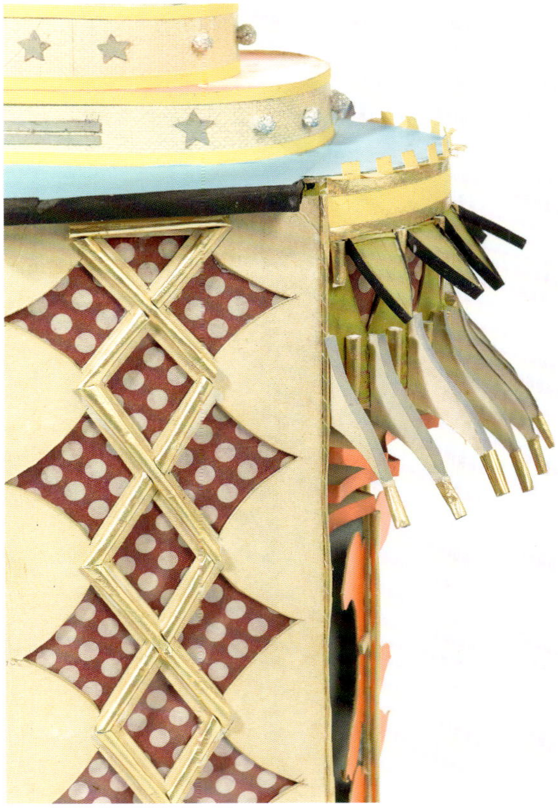

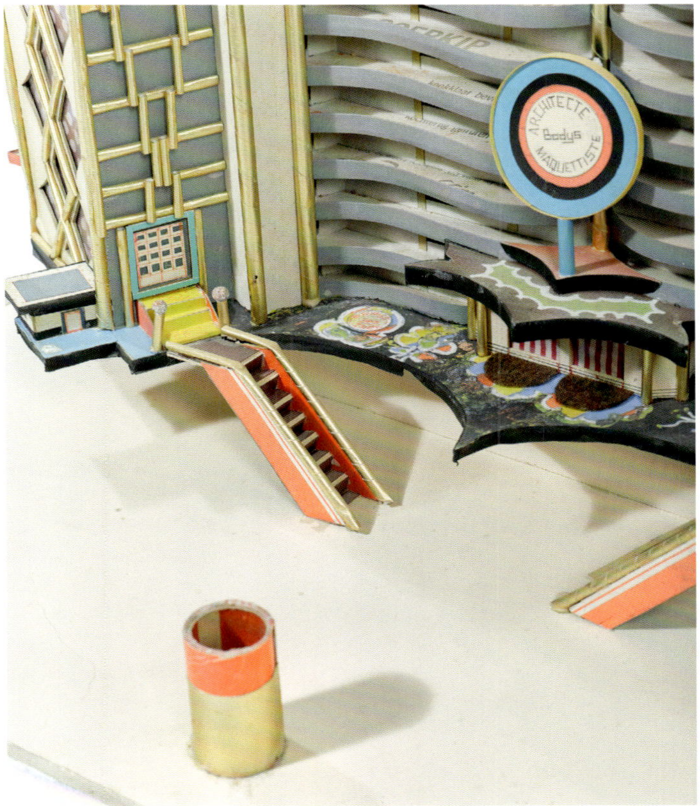
ARCHITECTE
Bodys
MAQUETTISTE

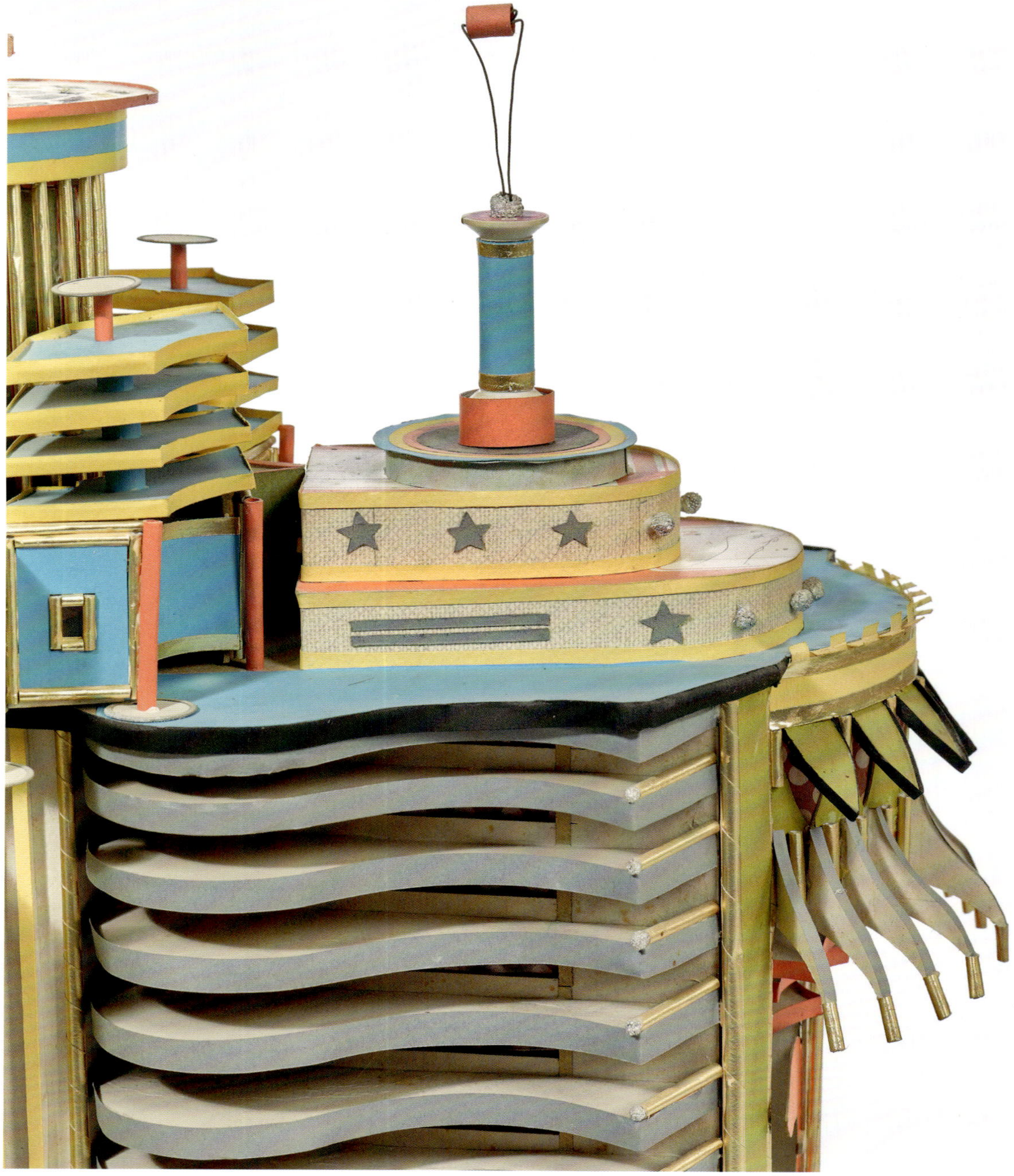

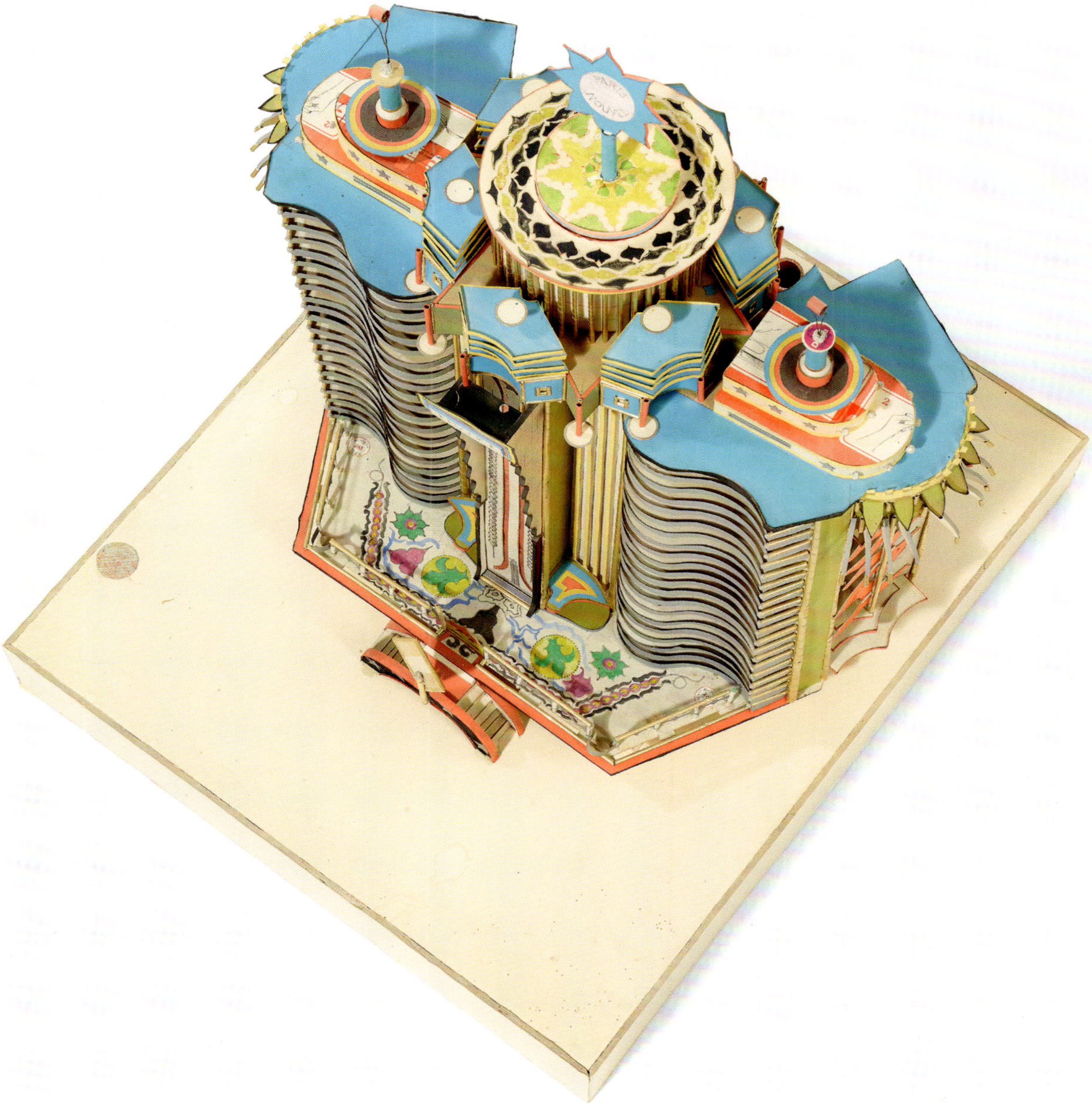

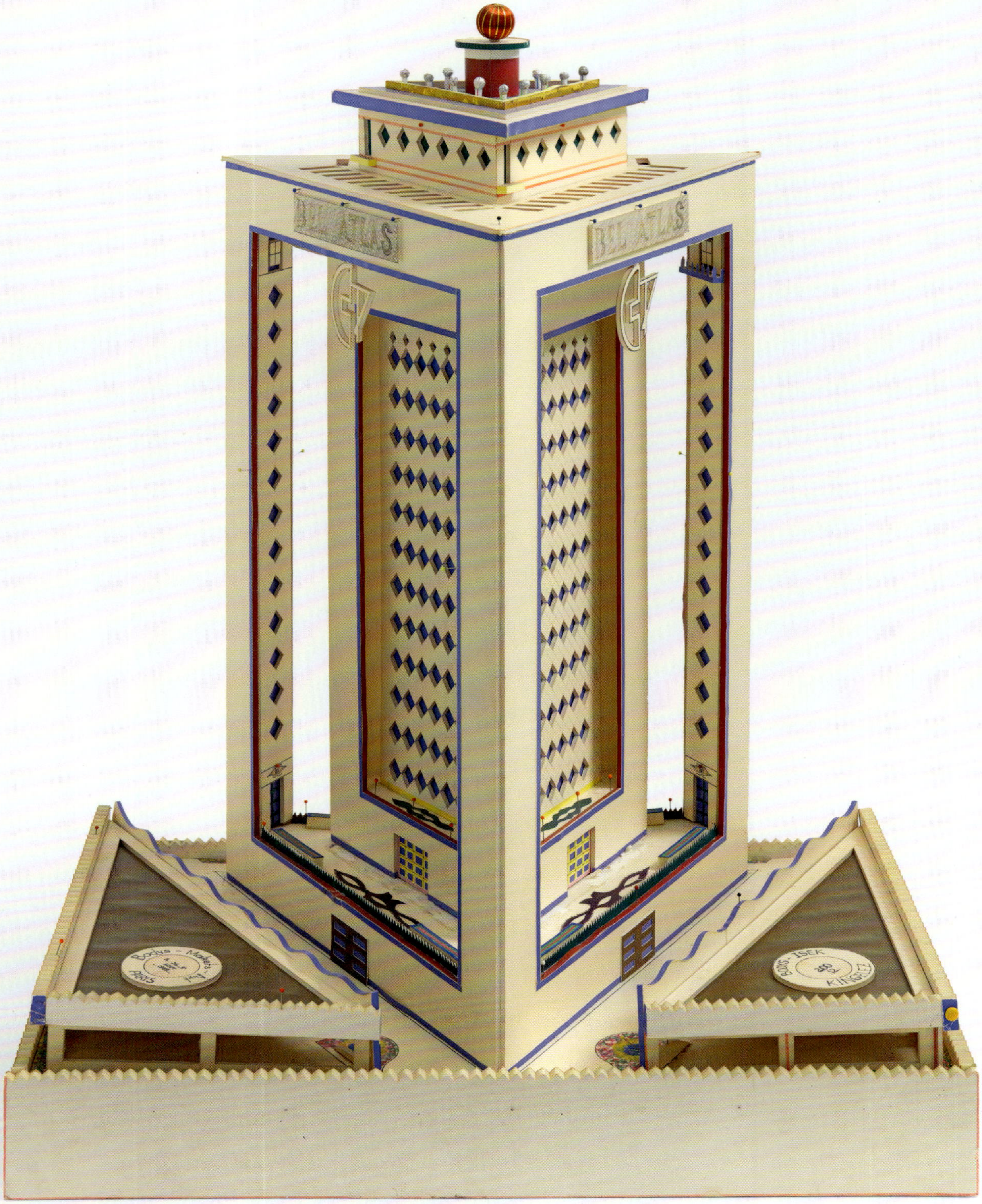

8

Bel Atlas. 1989
33 7/16 x 26 x 17 5/16" (85 x 66 x 44 cm)
Sandro De Sanctis/African Collection

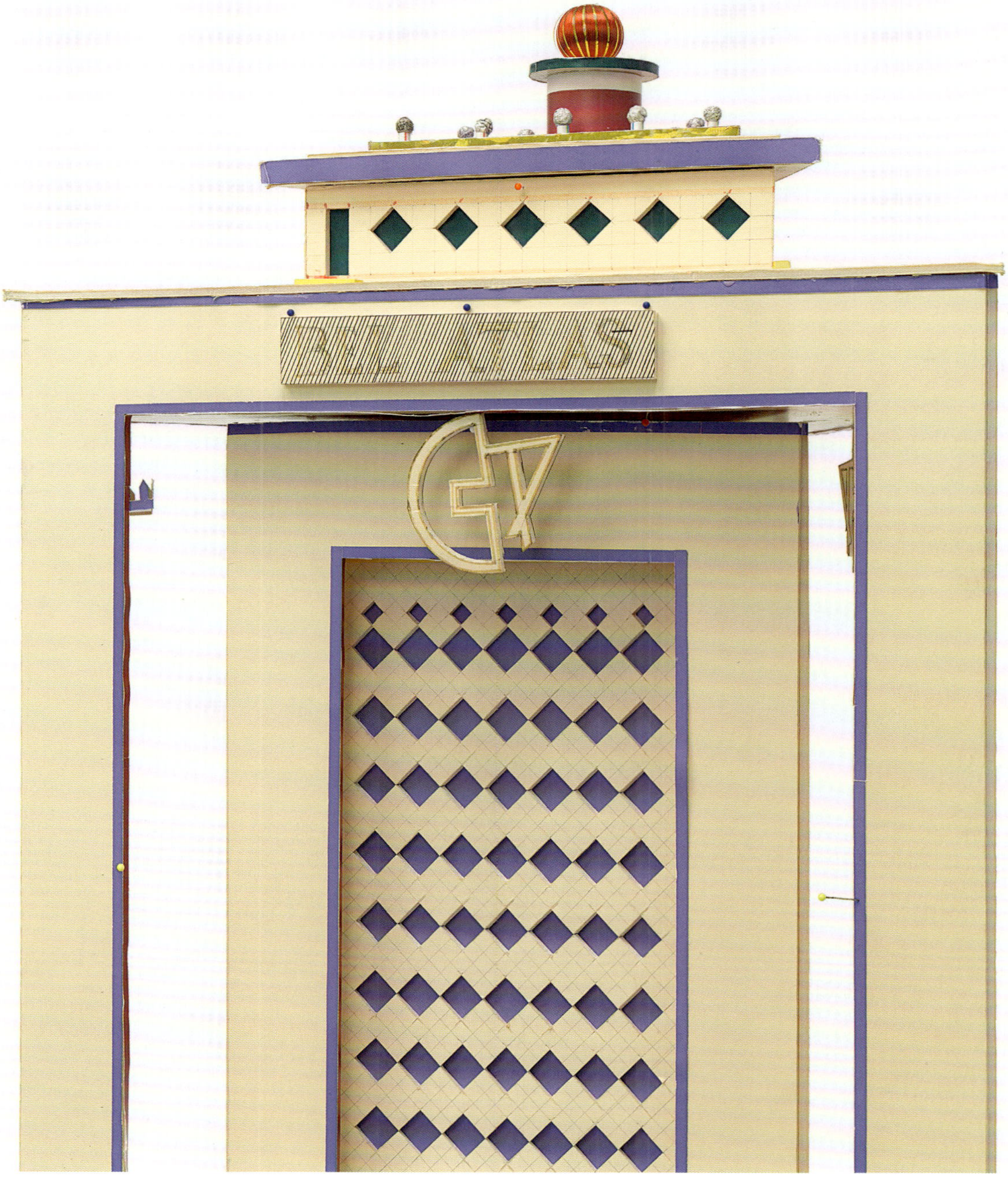
BEL ATLAS

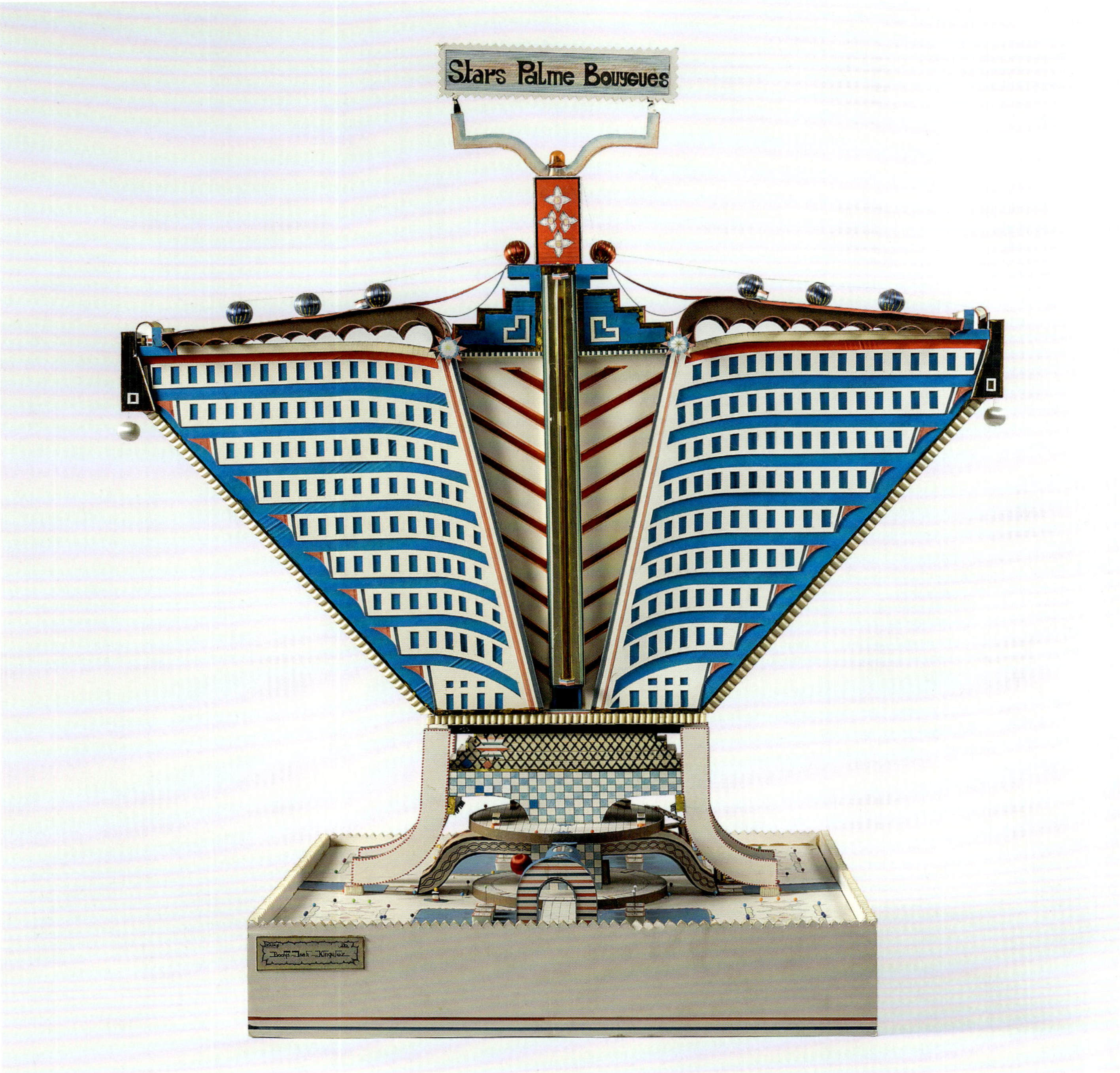

9

Stars Palme Bouygues. 1989
39 3/8 x 15 3/4 x 15 3/4" (100 x 40 x 40 cm)
van Lierde collection, Brussels

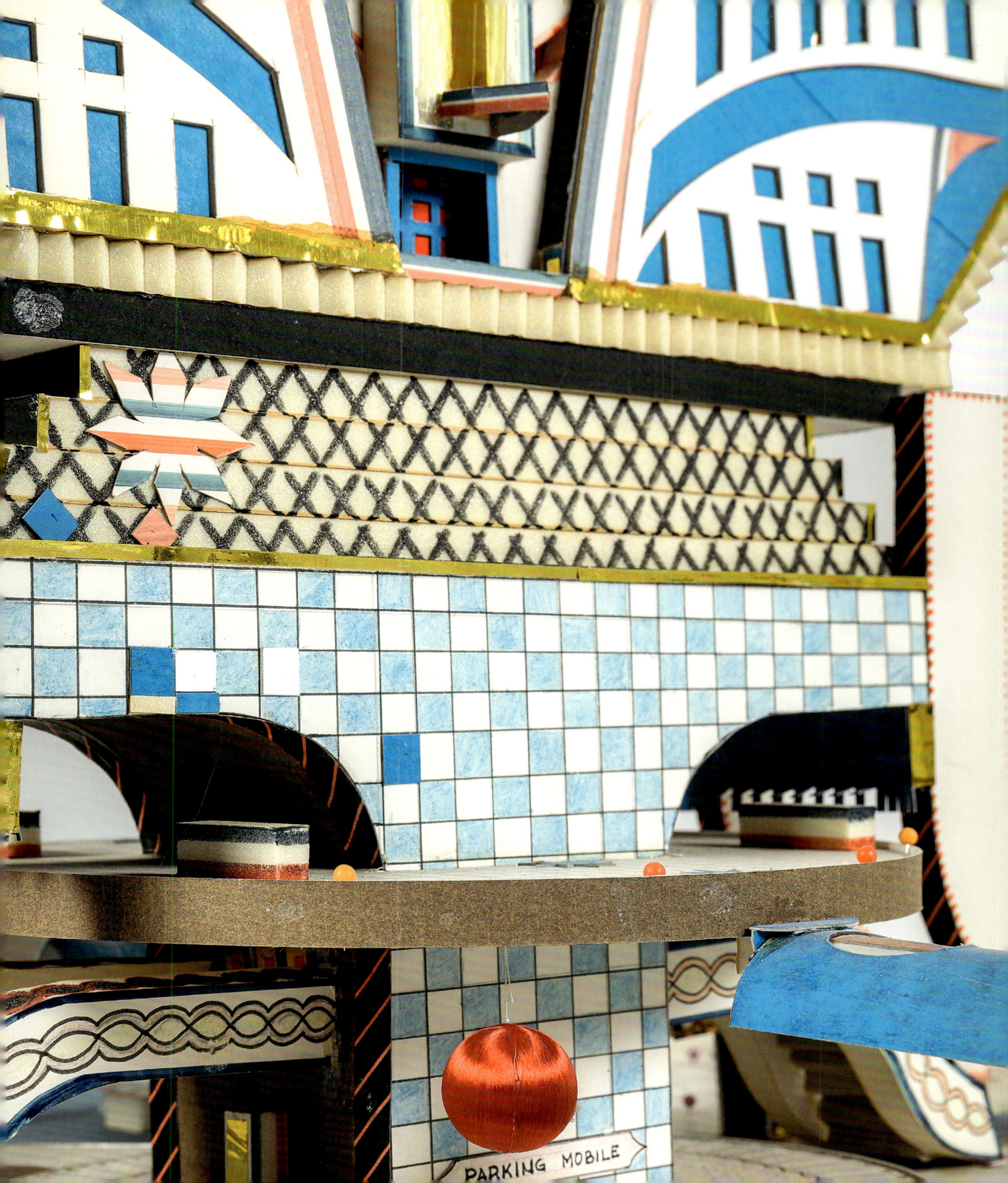
PARKING MOBILE

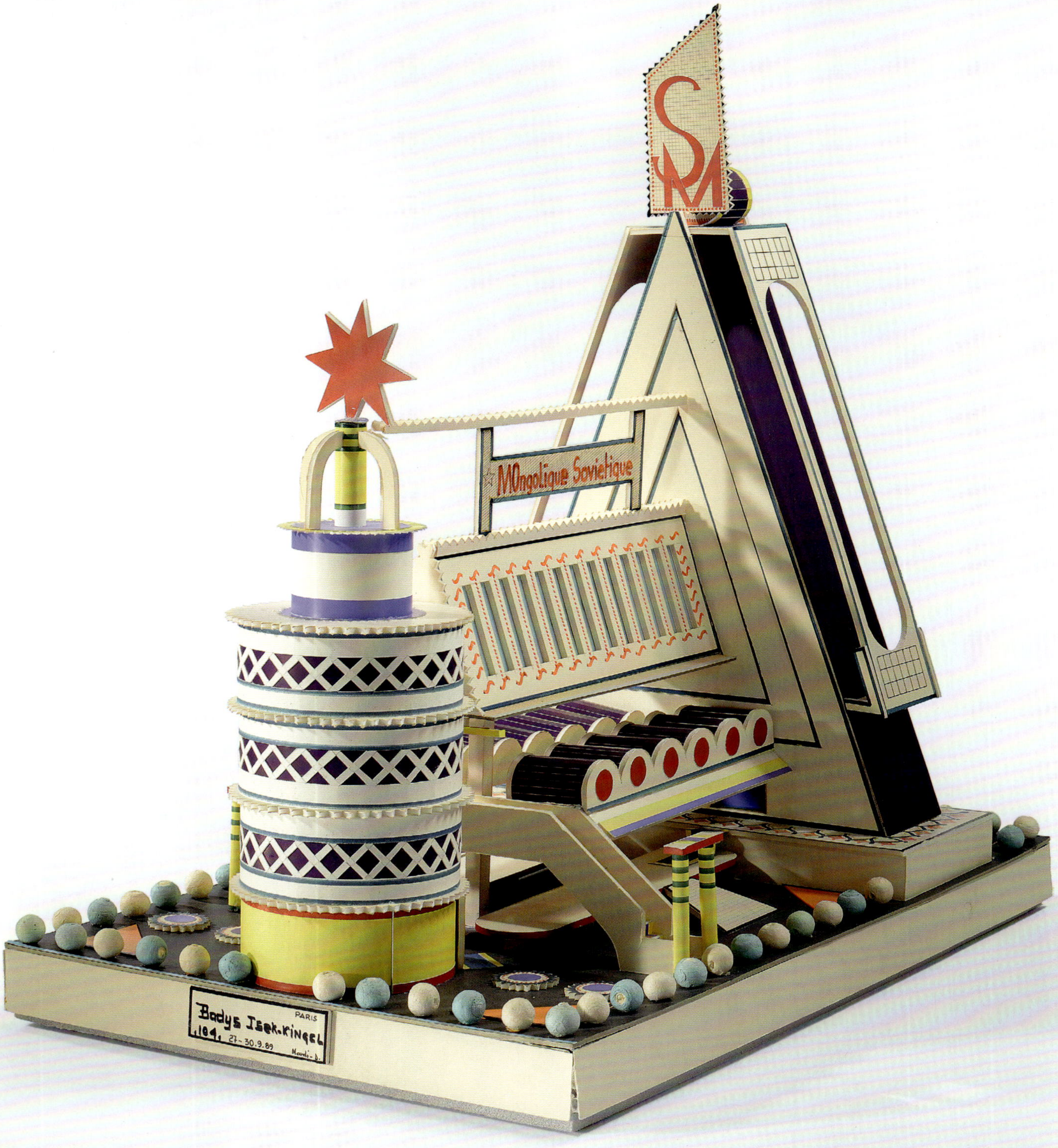

10

Mongolique Sovietique. 1989
24 7⁄16 x 15 3⁄4 x 24 7⁄16" (62 x 40 x 62 cm)
CAAC—The Pigozzi Collection, Geneva

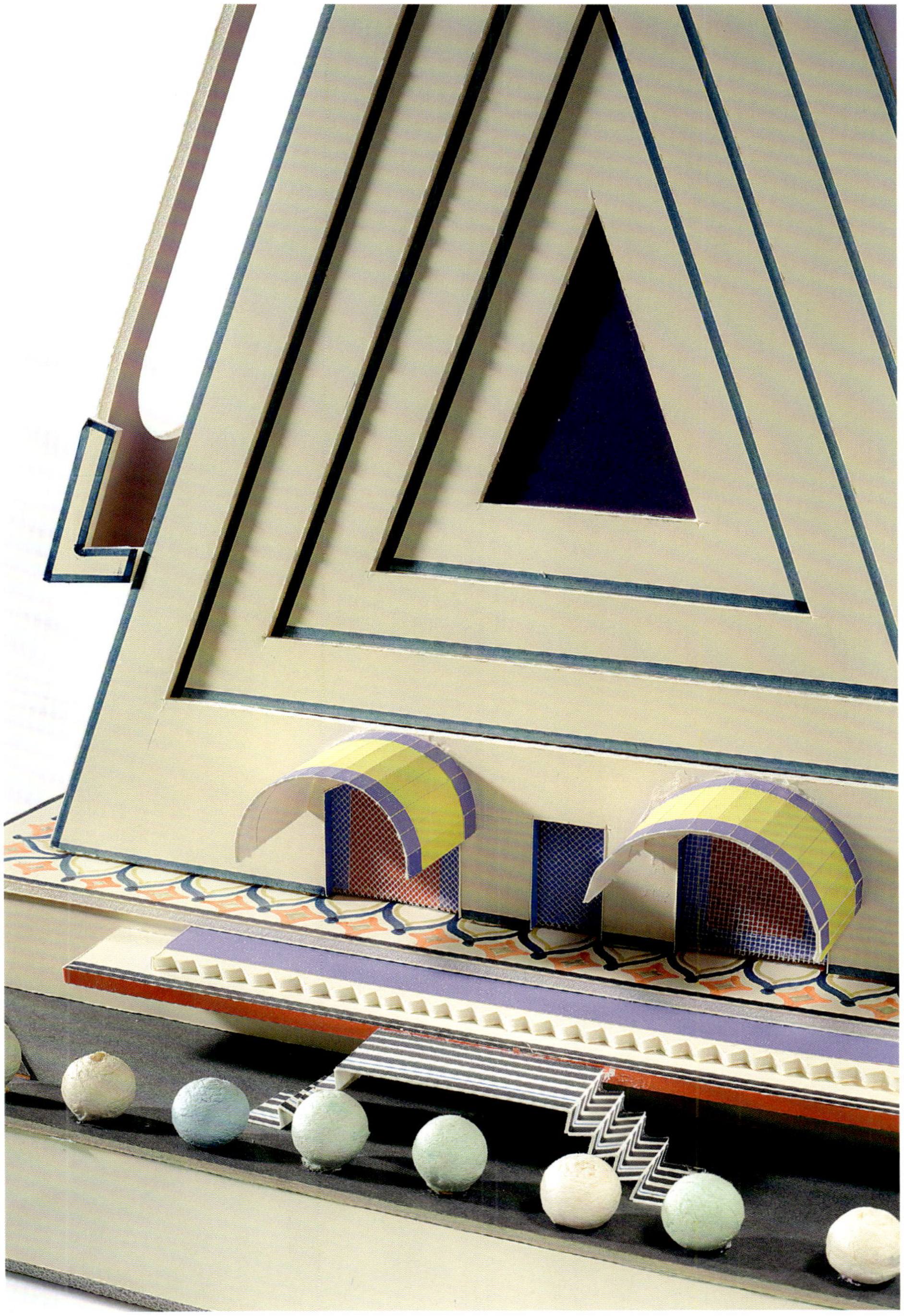

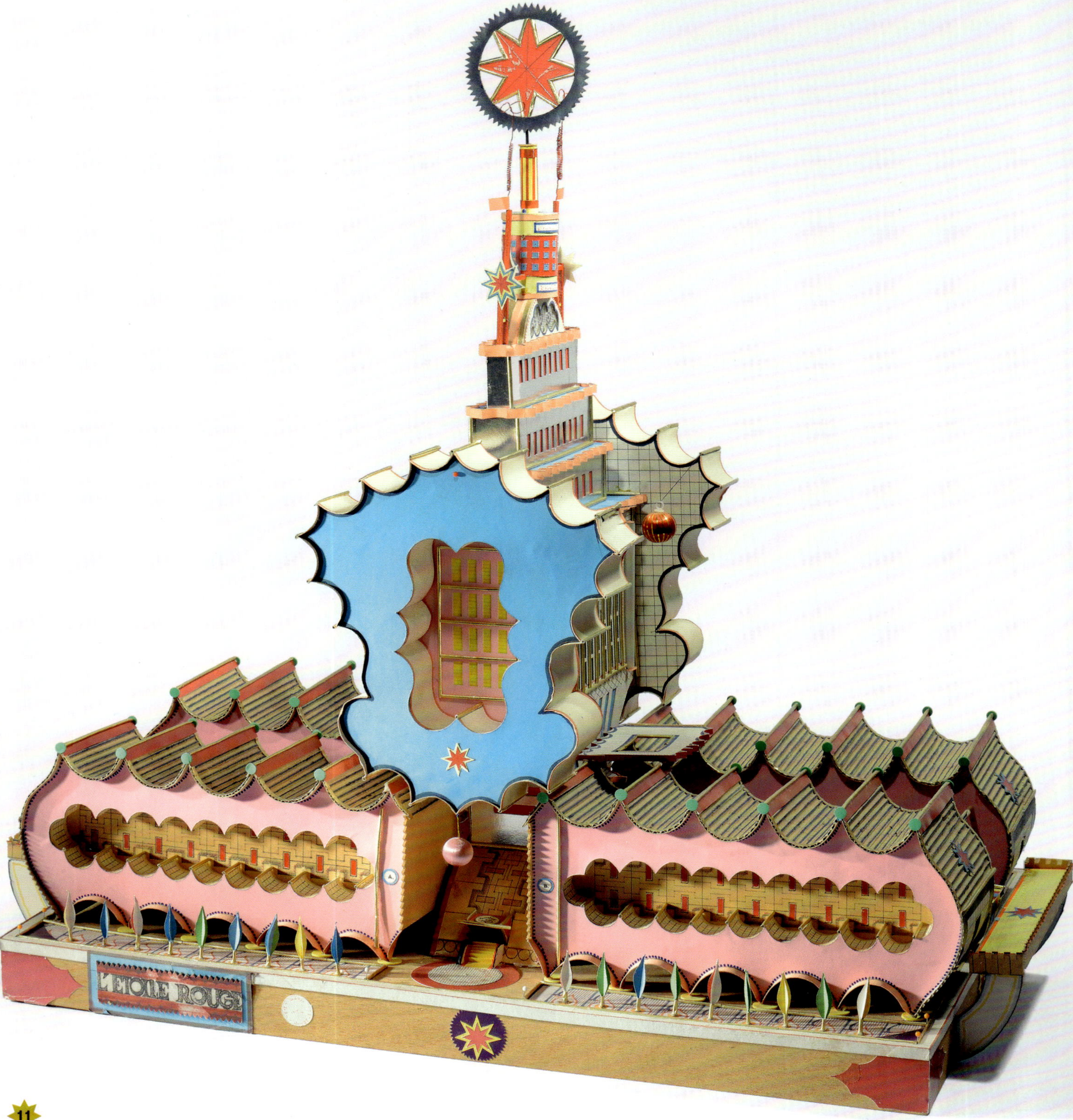

11

Étoile Rouge Congolaise. 1990
33 7/16 x 36 1/4 x 19 11/16" (85 x 92 x 50 cm)
CAAC—The Pigozzi Collection, Geneva

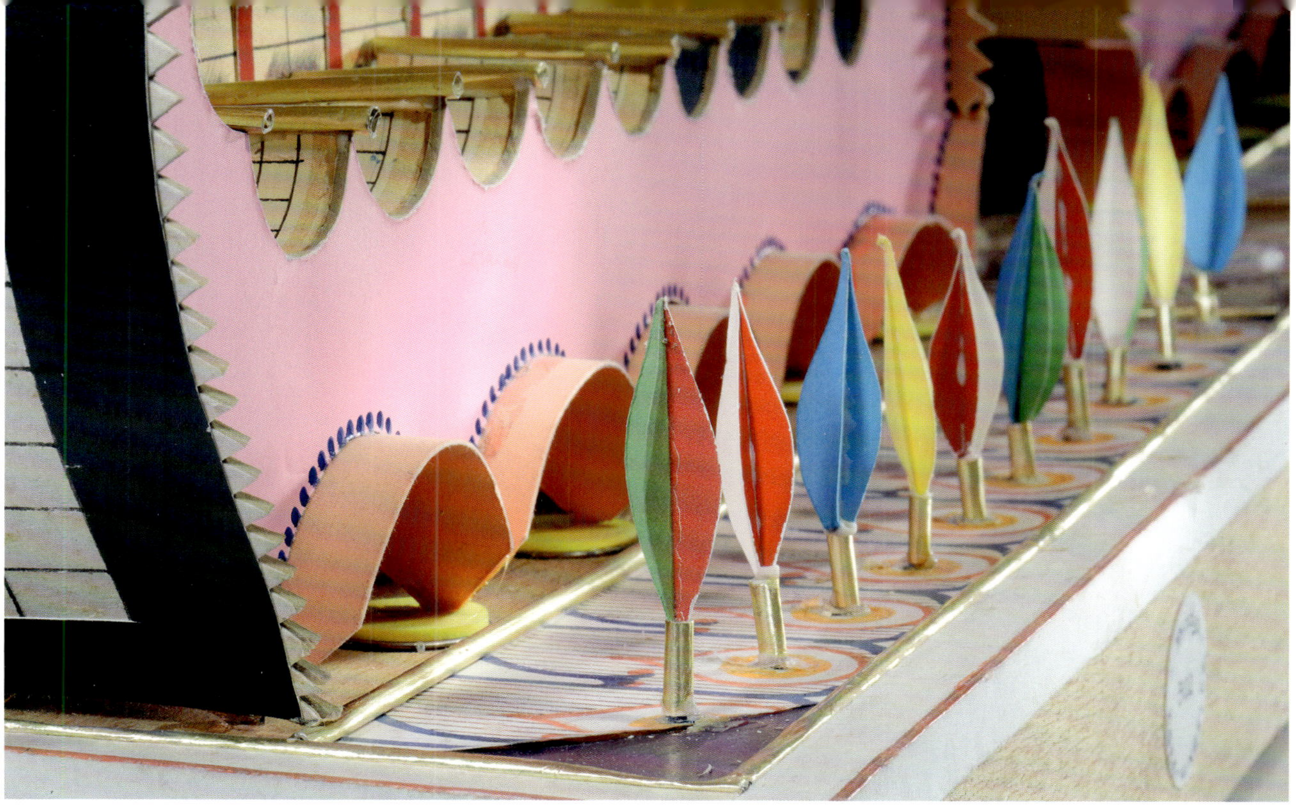

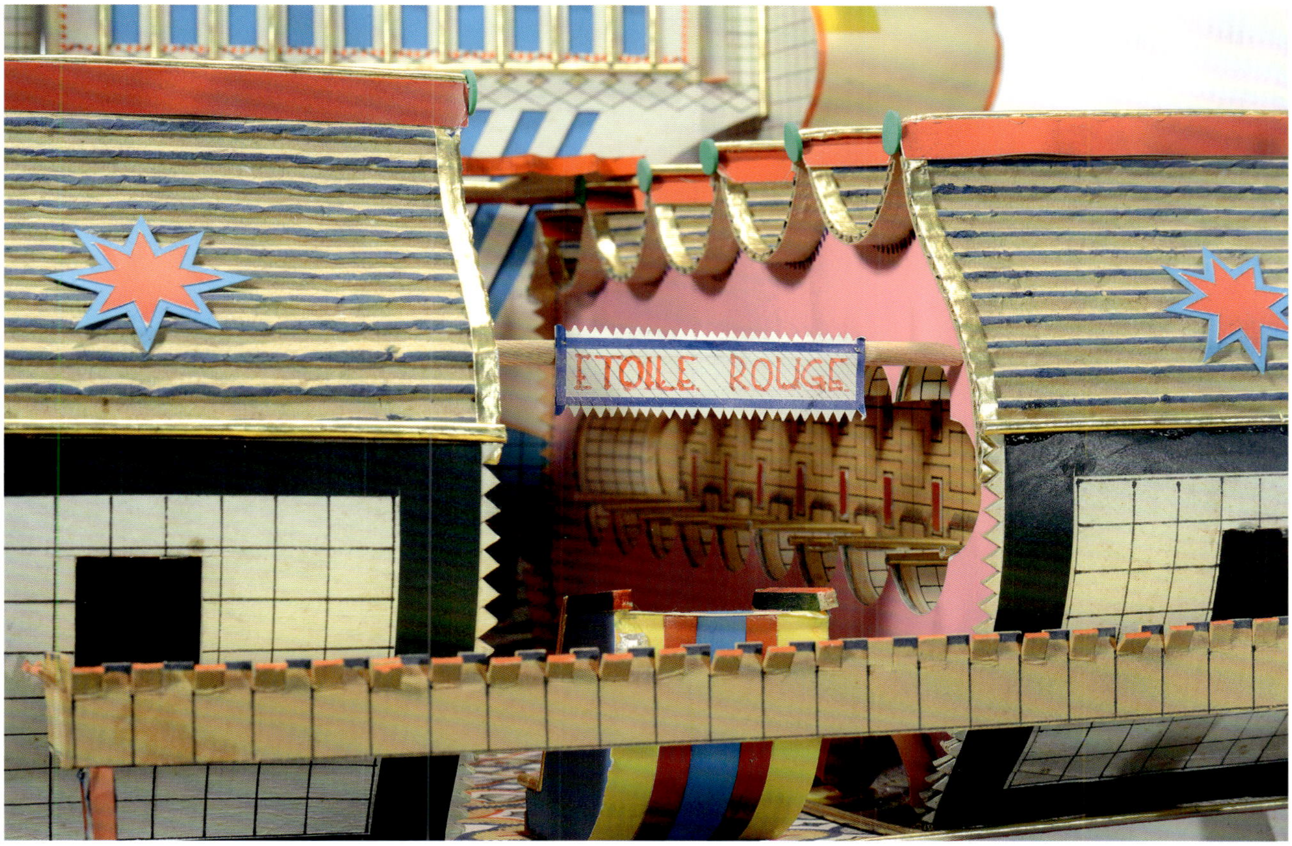
ETOILE ROUGE

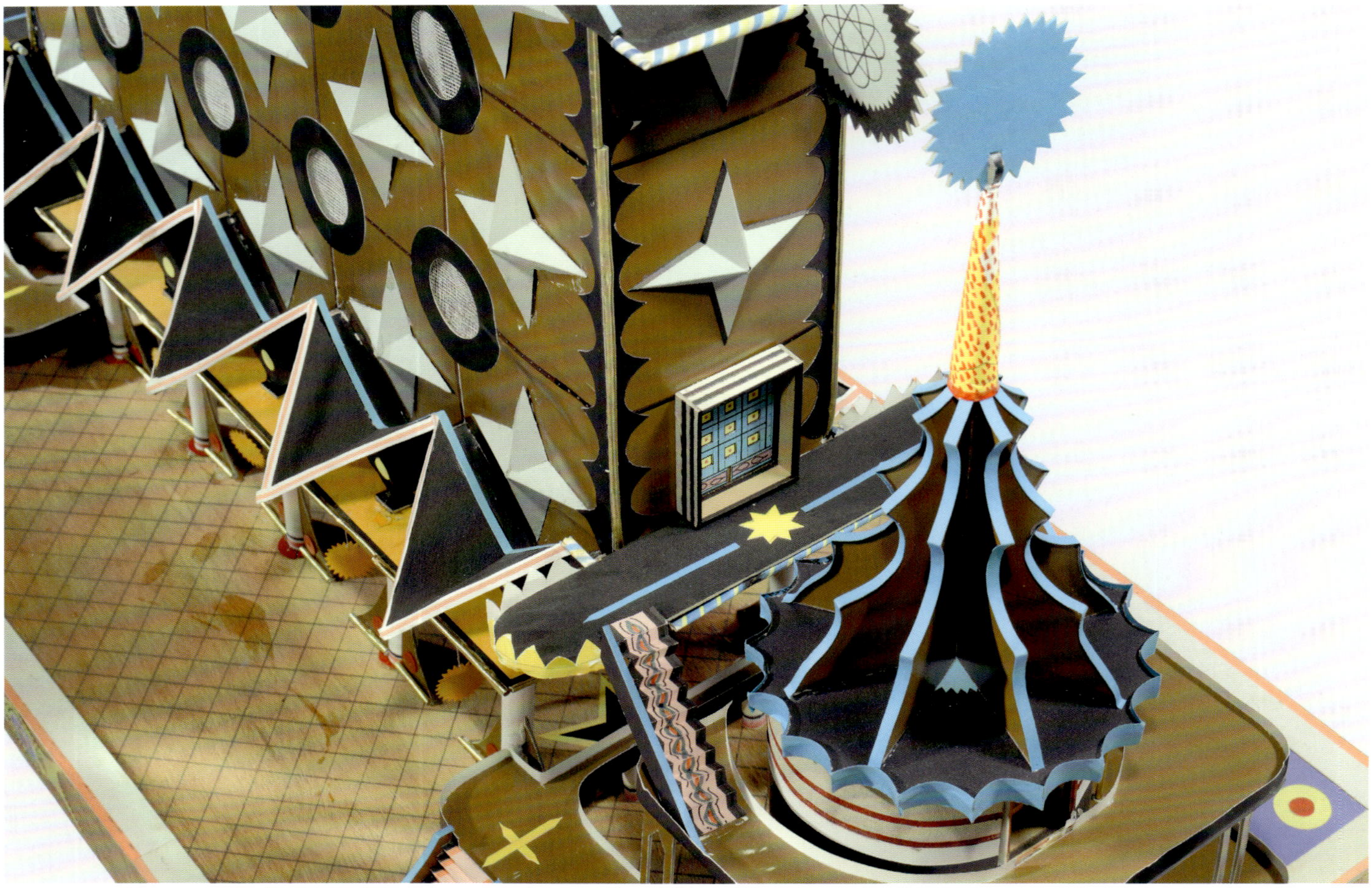

12

Air Force. 1991
21 ¼ x 32 $^{11}/_{16}$ x 16 ⅛" (54 x 83 x 41 cm)
CAAC—The Pigozzi Collection, Geneva

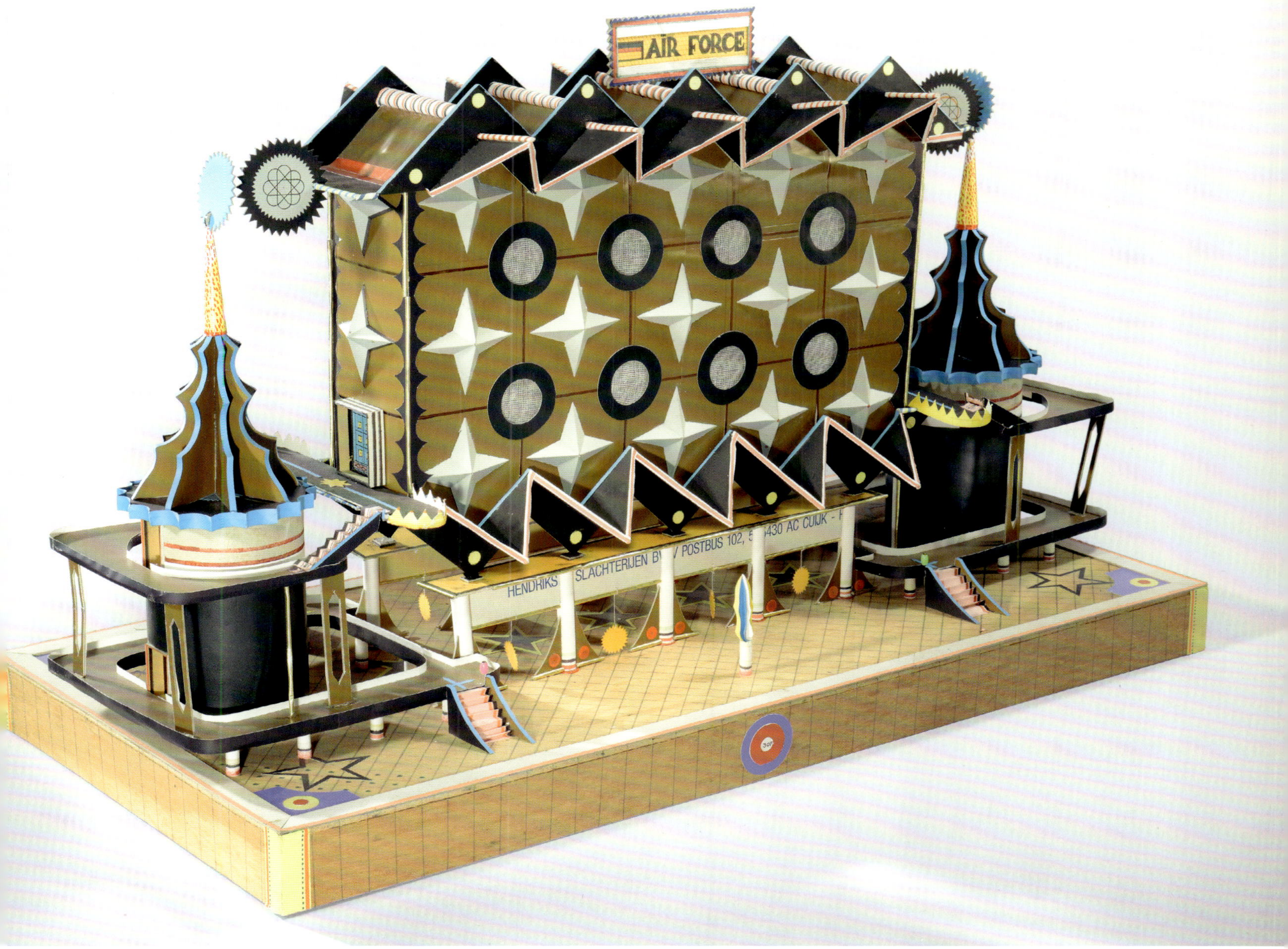
AIR FORCE
HENDRIKS SLACHTERIJEN BV POSTBUS 102, 5430 AC CUIJK

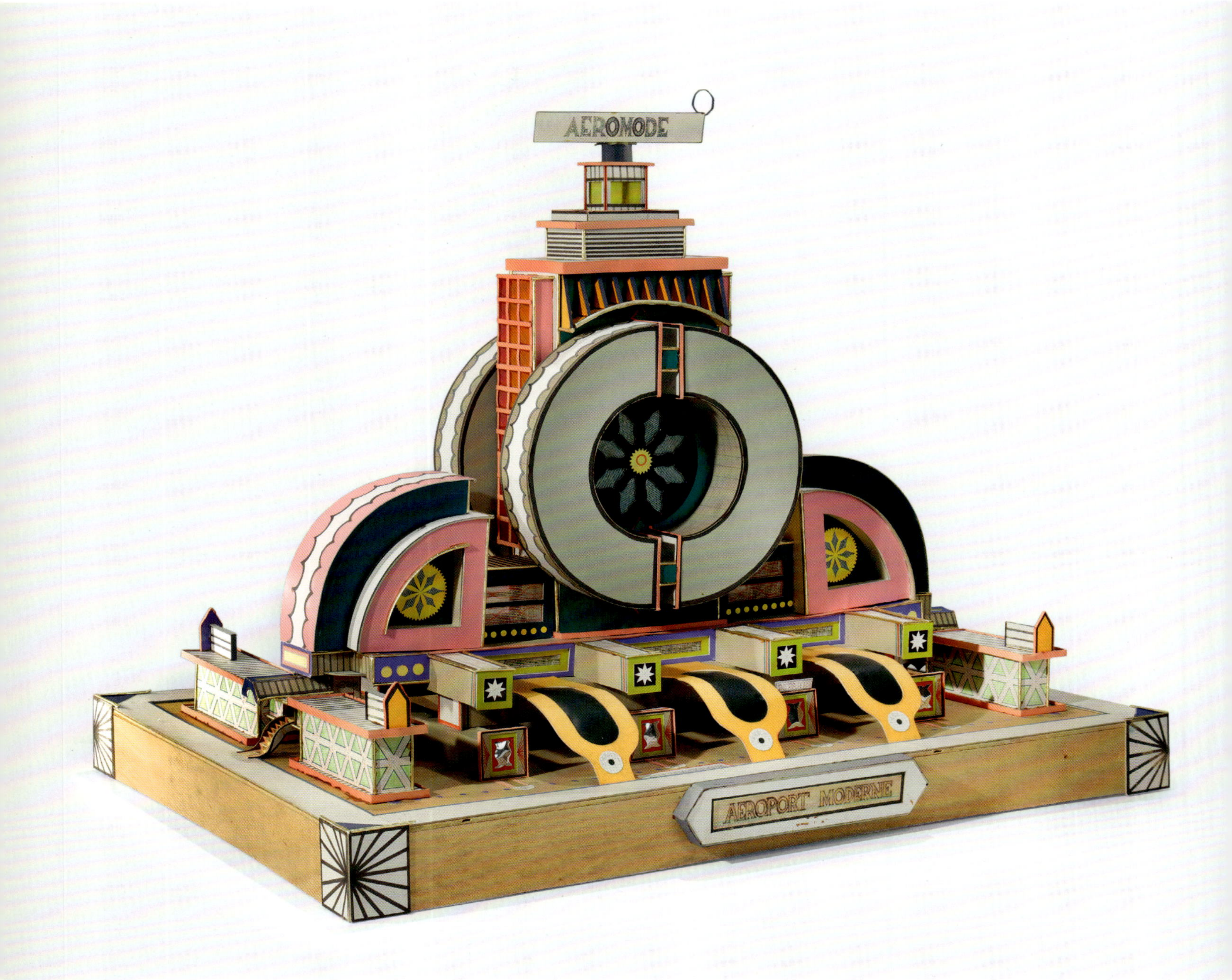

13

Aéromode (Aéroport Moderne). 1991
21 ¼ x 31 ½ x 21 ⅝" (54 x 80 x 55 cm)
CAAC—The Pigozzi Collection, Geneva

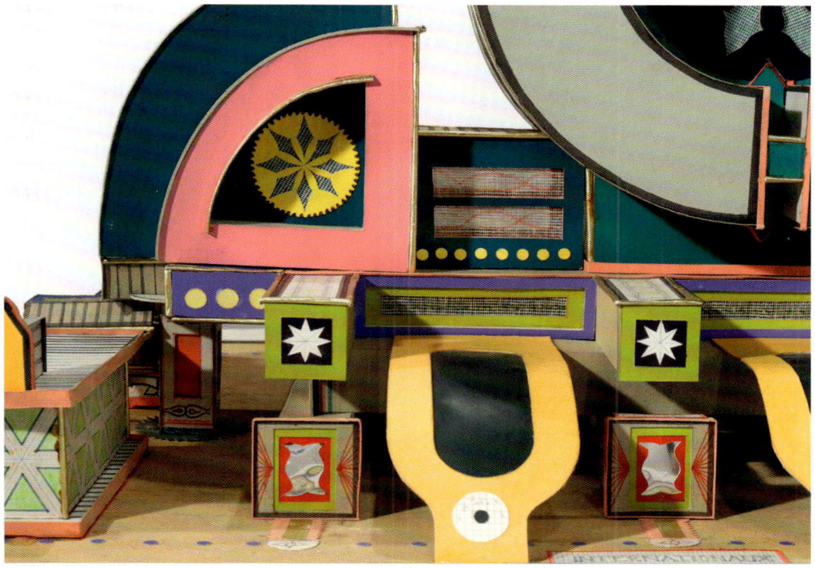

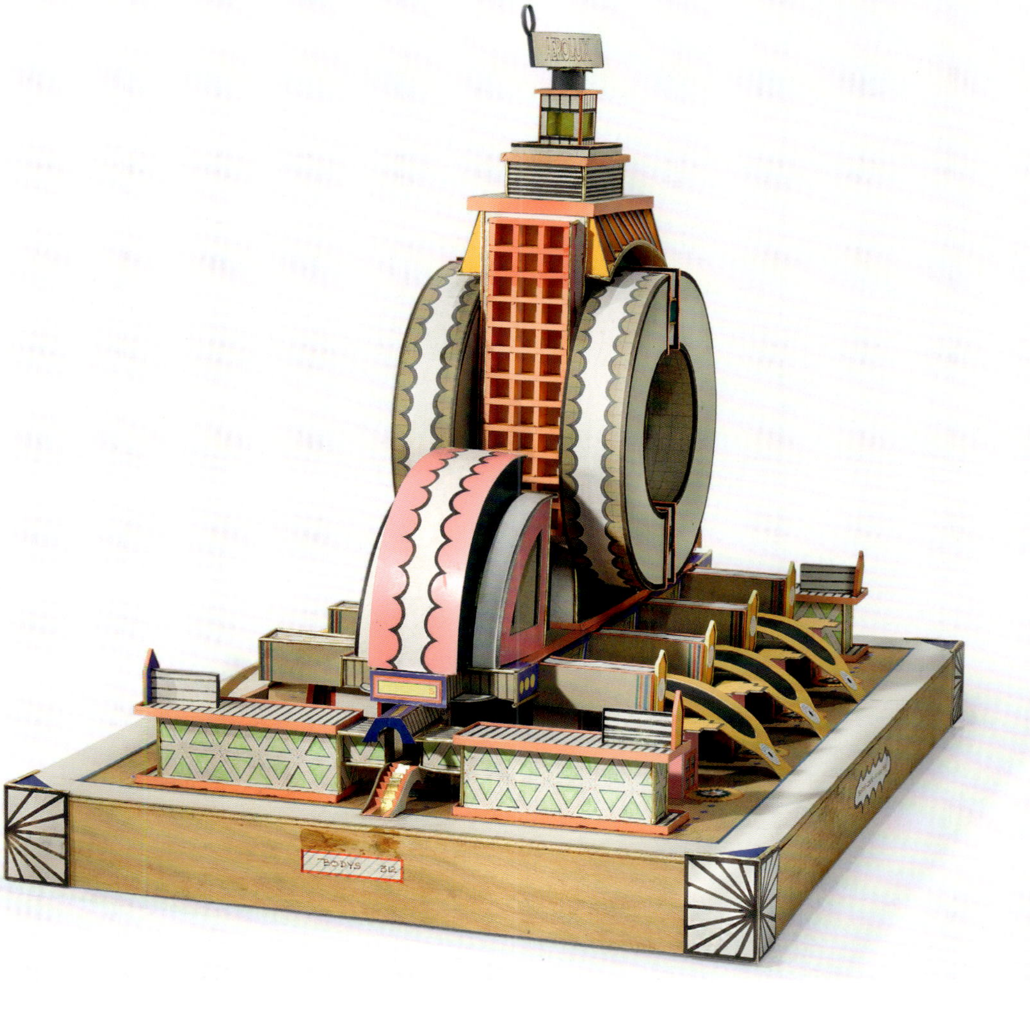
BODYS

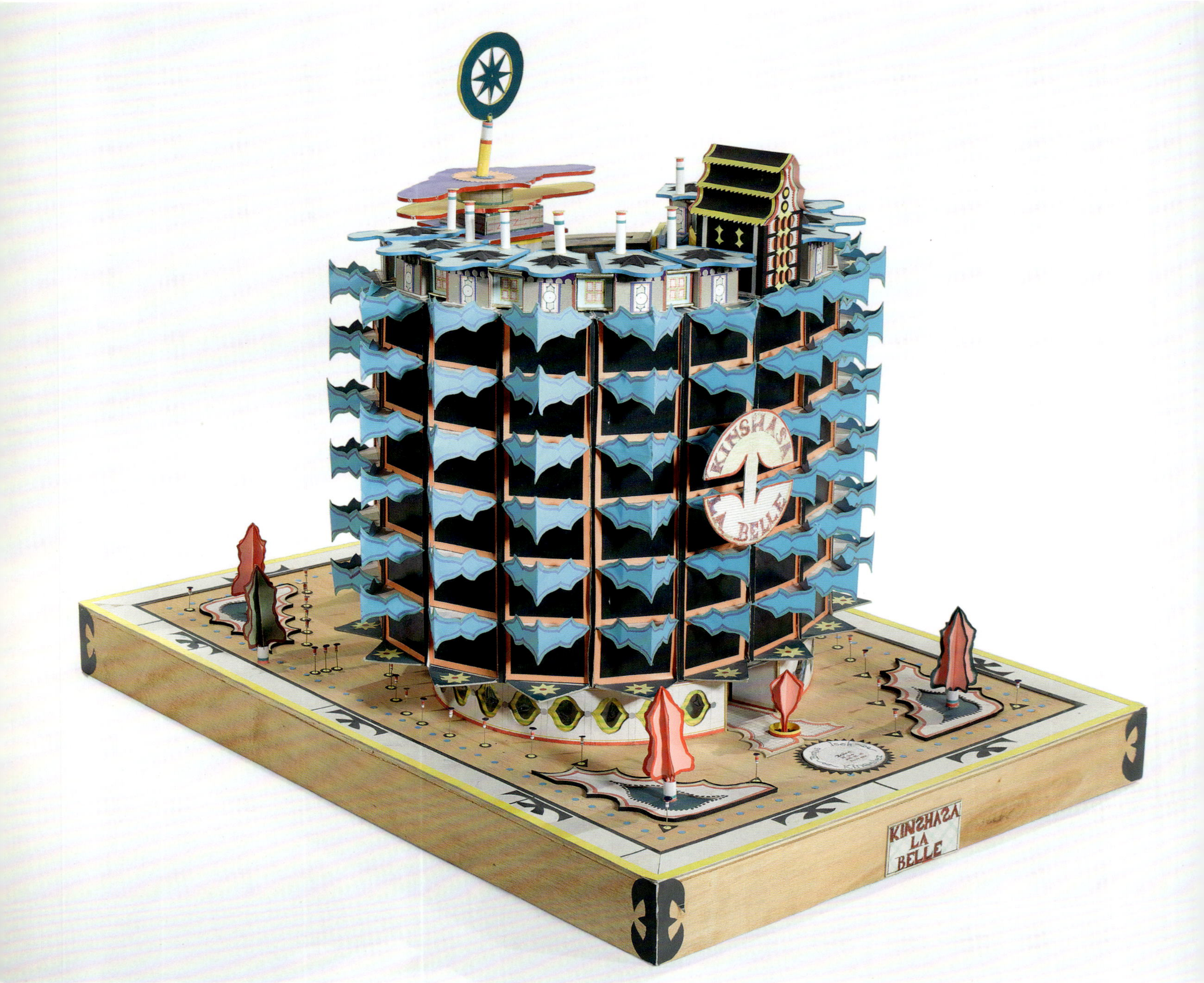

14

Kinshasa la Belle. 1991
24 $\frac{13}{16}$ x 21 $\frac{5}{8}$ x 31 $\frac{1}{2}$" (63 x 55 x 80 cm)
CAAC—The Pigozzi Collection, Geneva

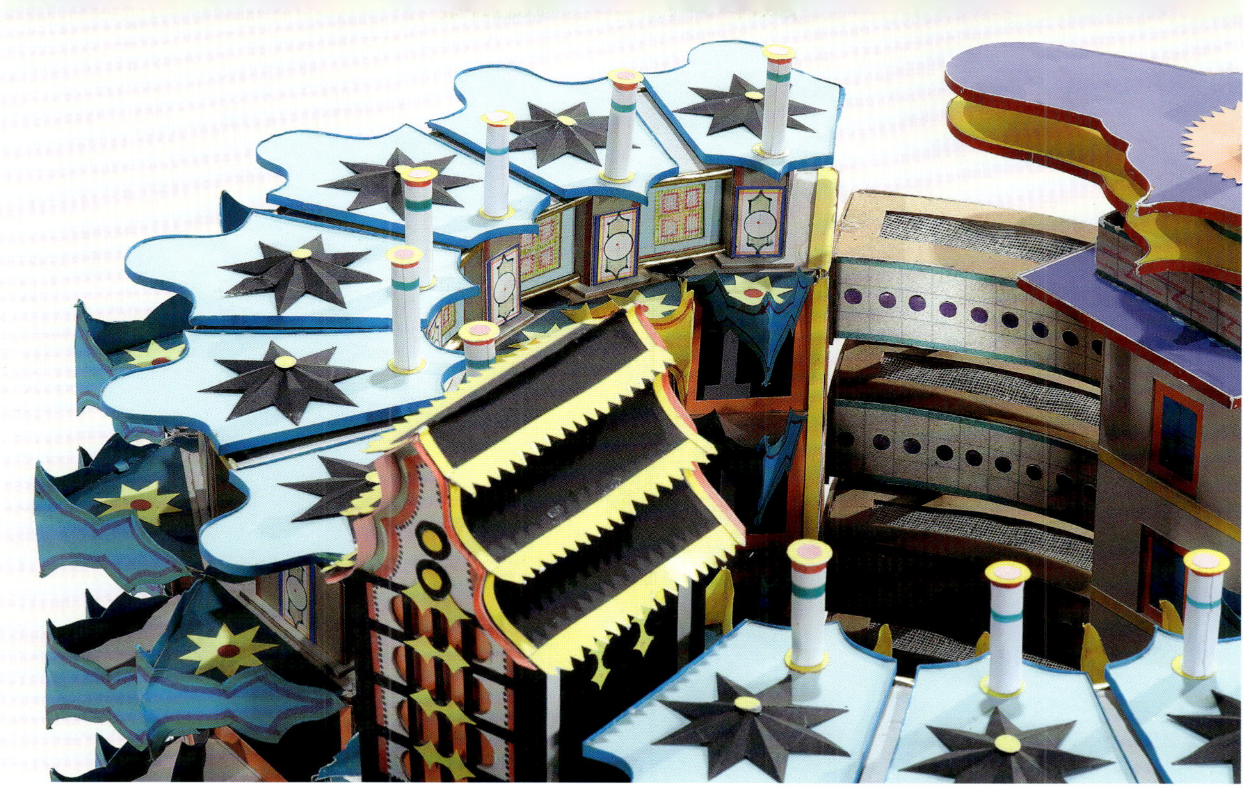

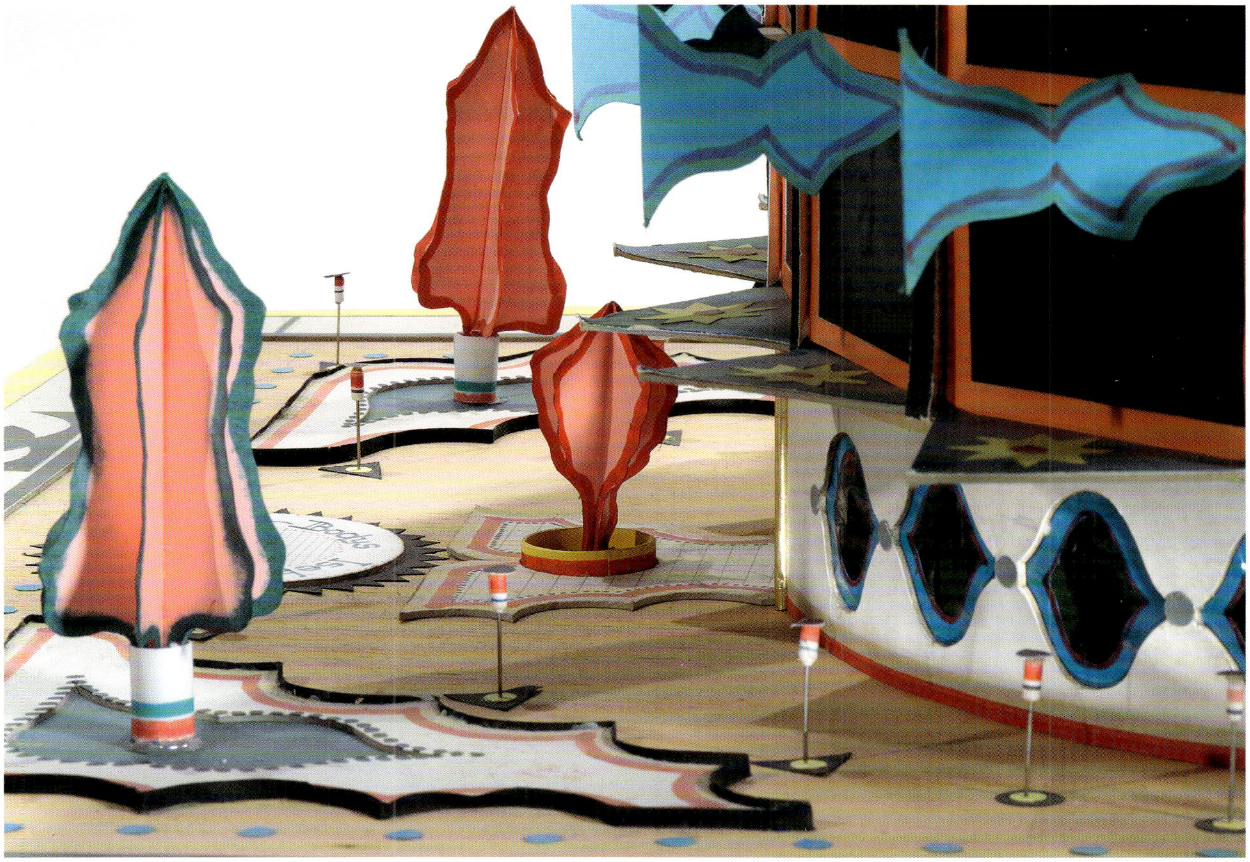

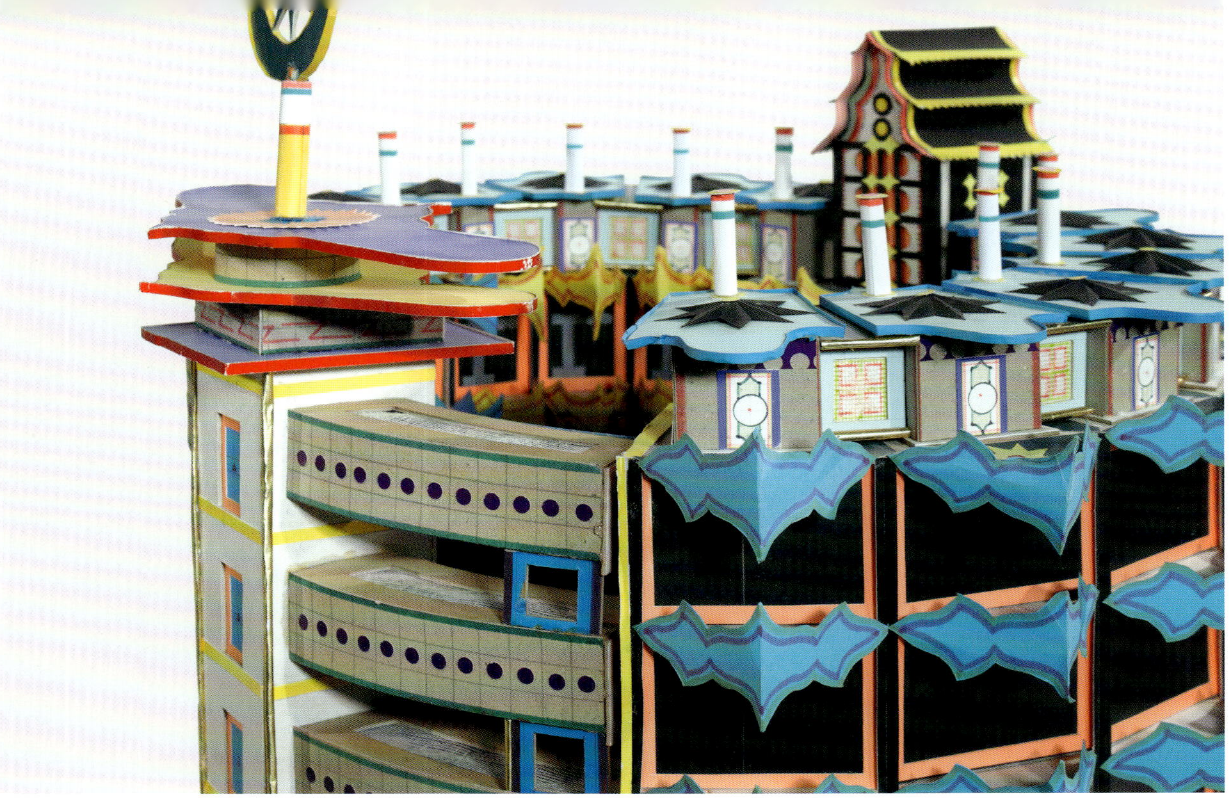

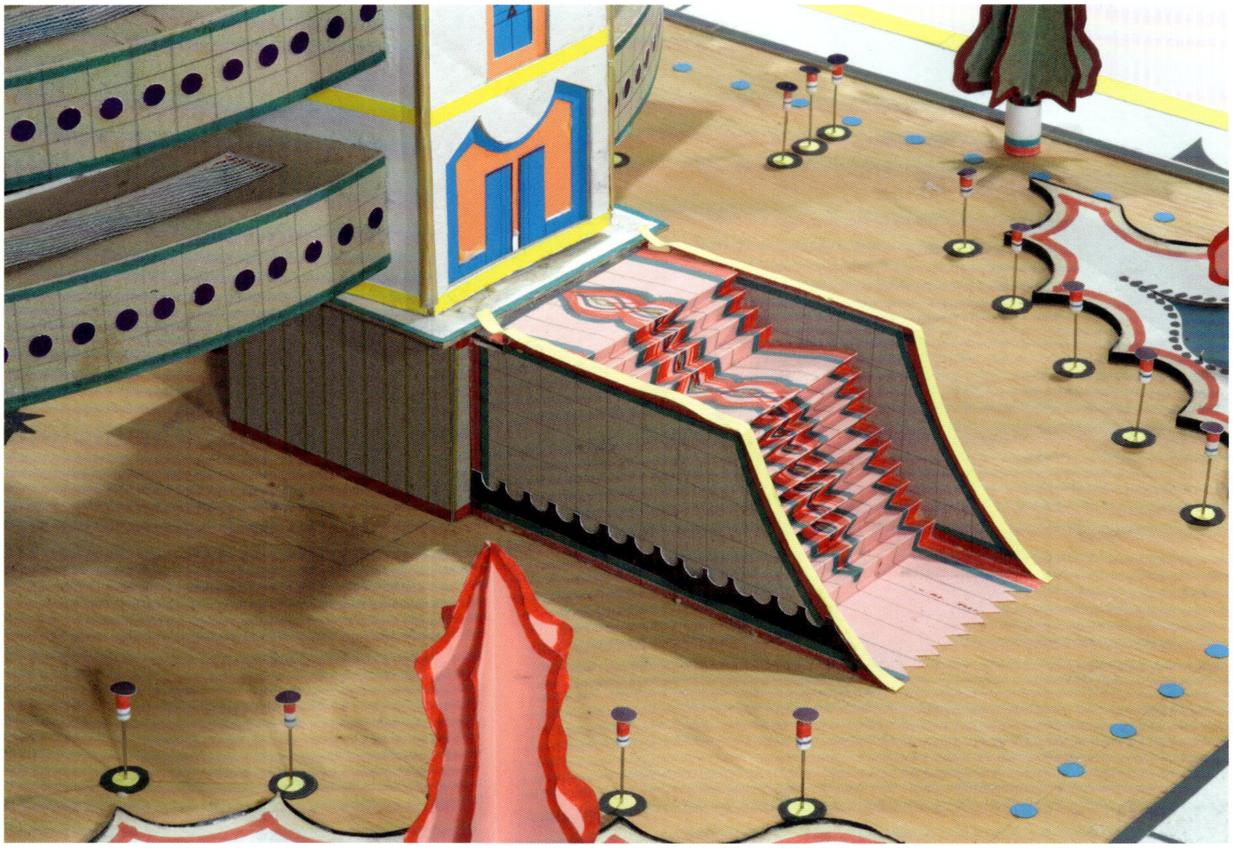

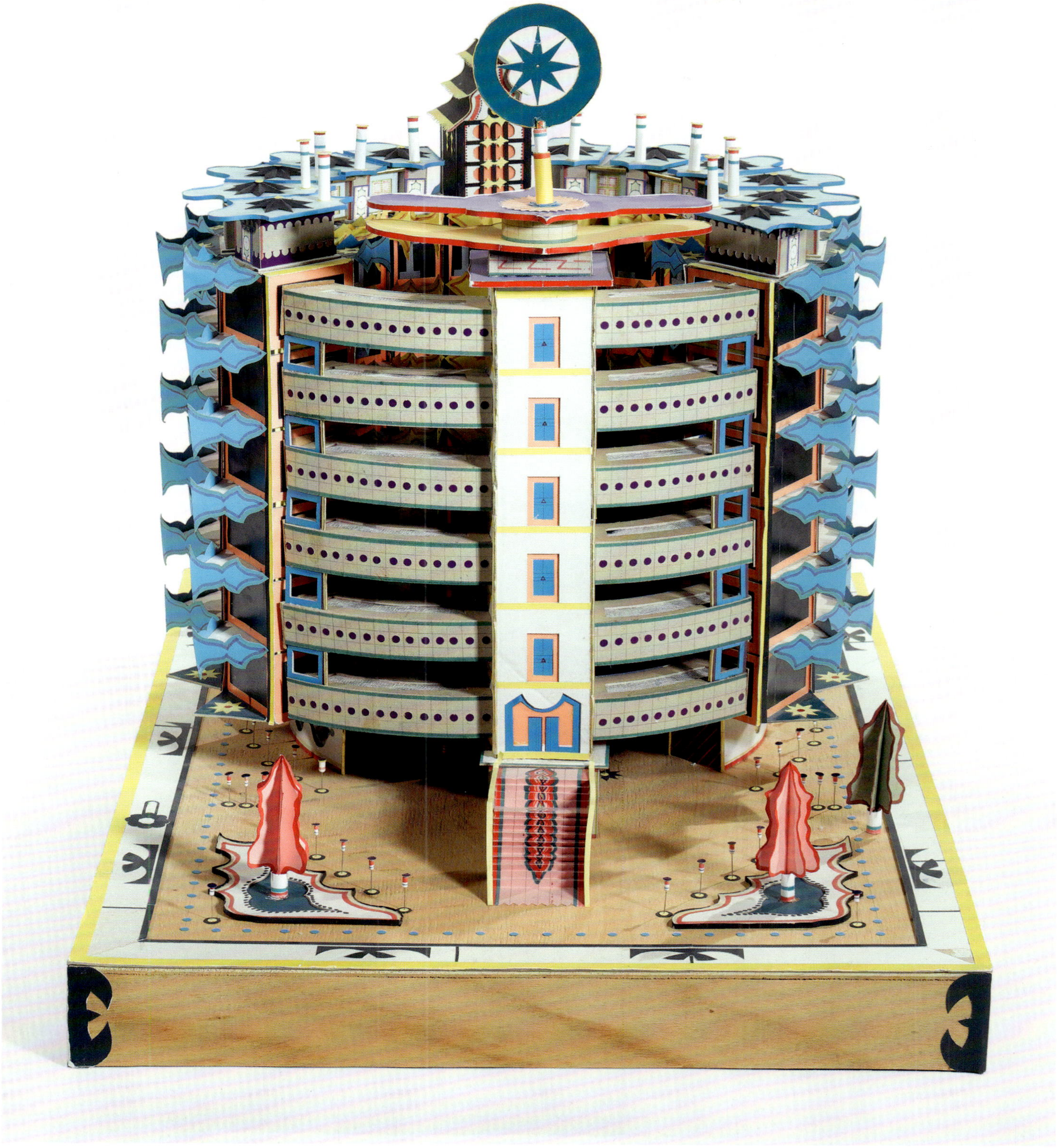

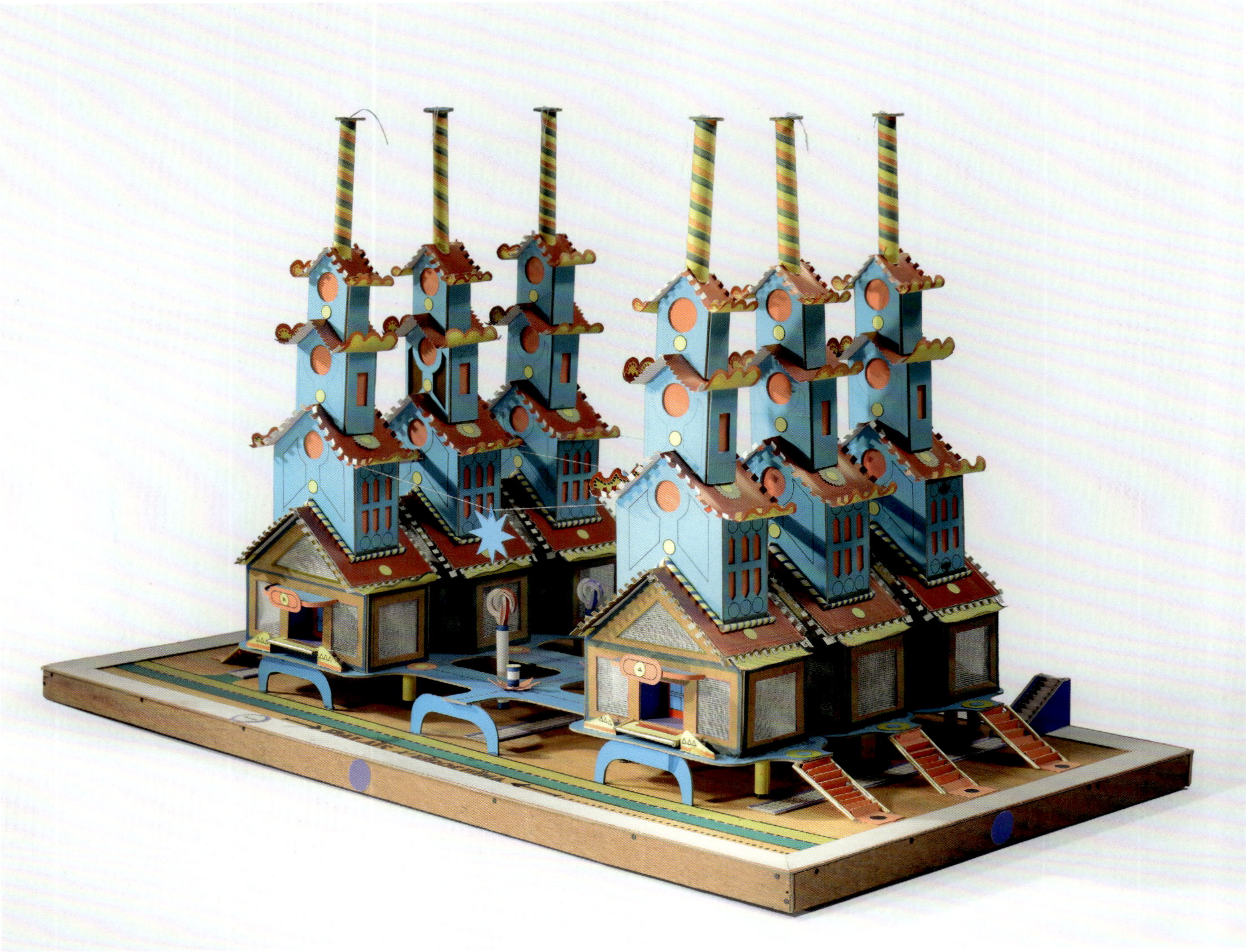

15

Palais d'Hirochima. 1991
18 ⅞ x 30 $^{11}/_{16}$ x 16 ⅛" (48 x 78 x 41 cm)
CAAC—The Pigozzi Collection, Geneva

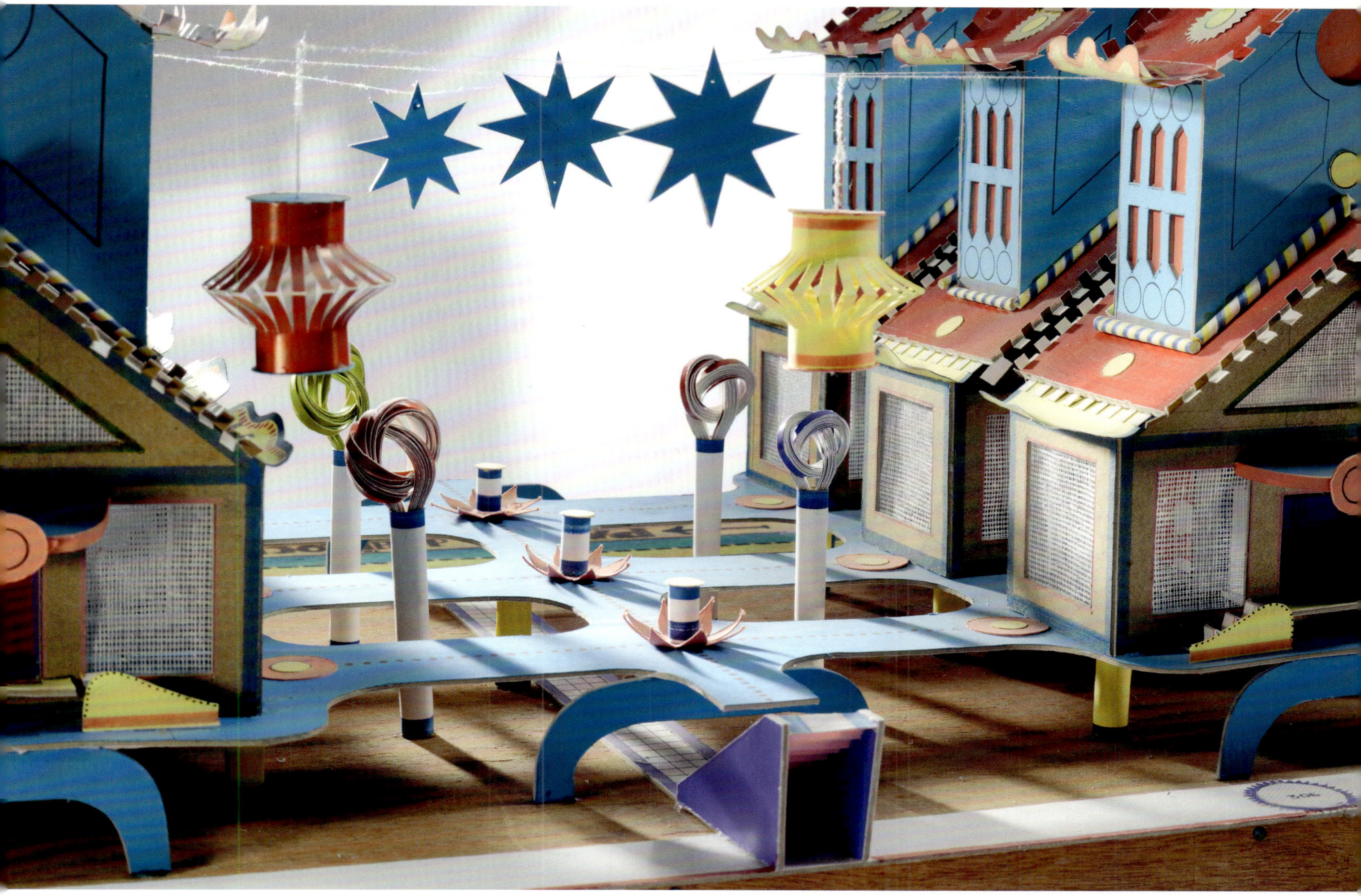

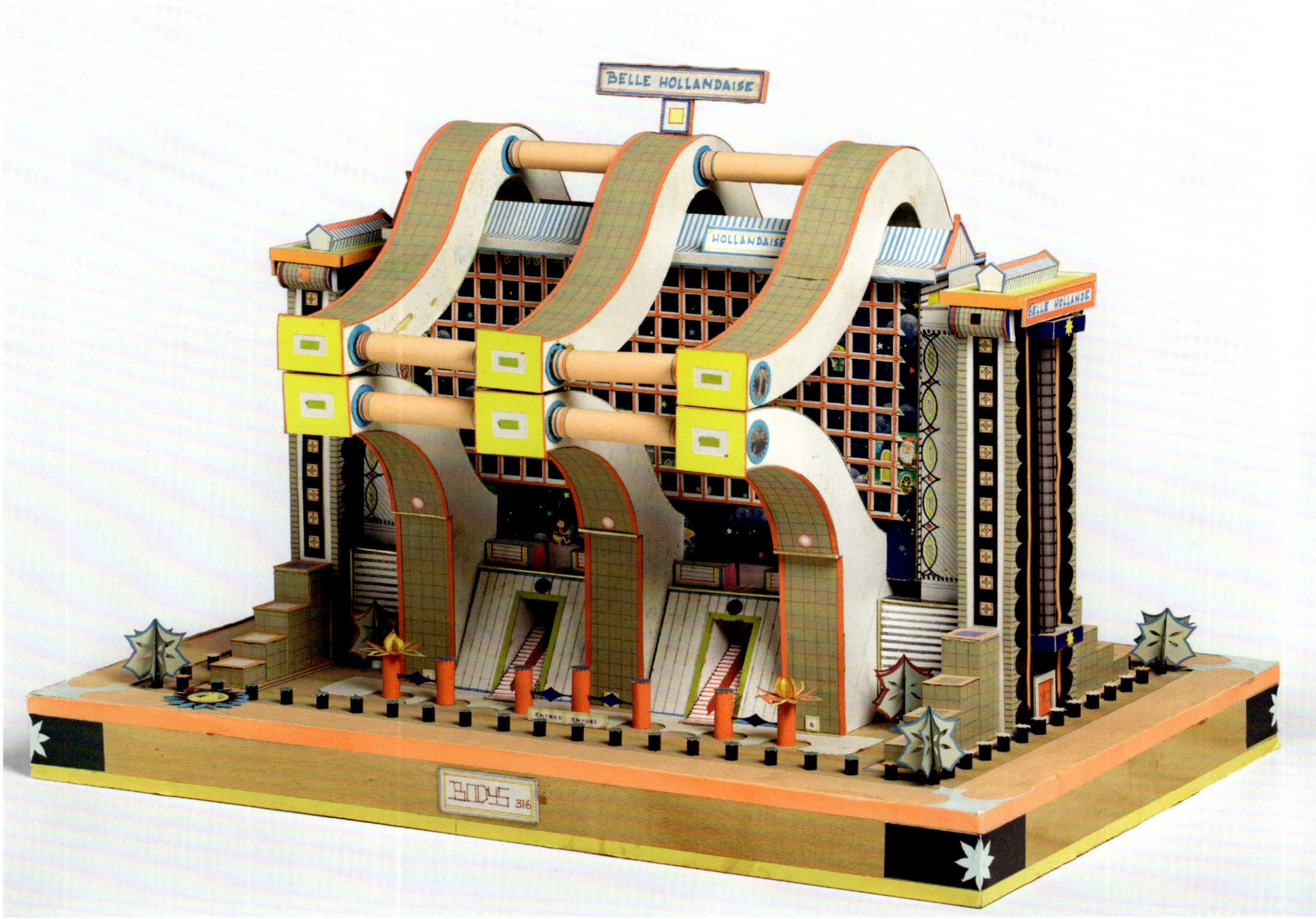

16

Belle Hollandaise. 1991
21 5⁄8 x 31 11⁄16 x 22 1⁄16" (55 x 80.5 x 56 cm)
Groninger Museum, Groningen, Netherlands

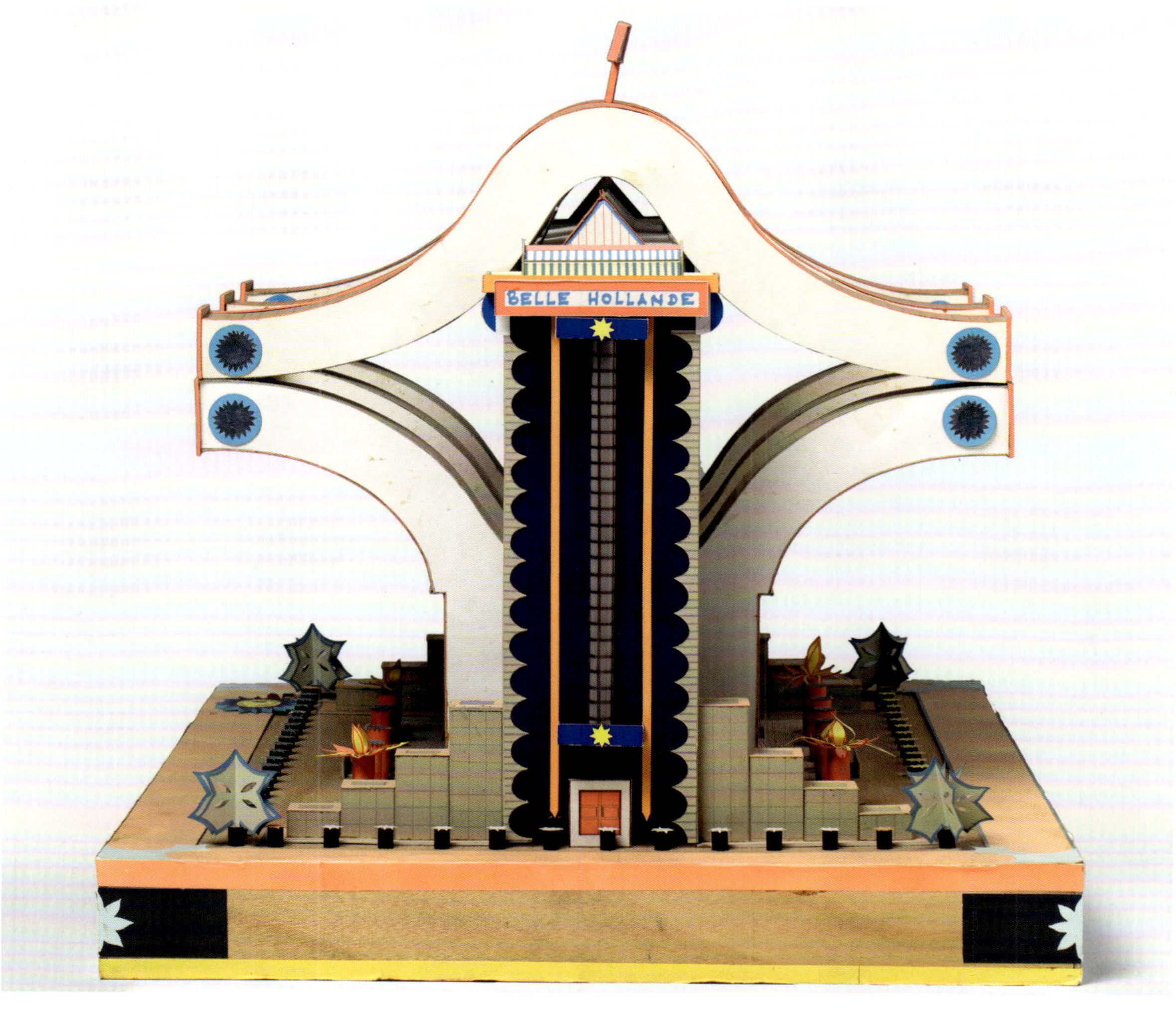
BELLE HOLLANDE

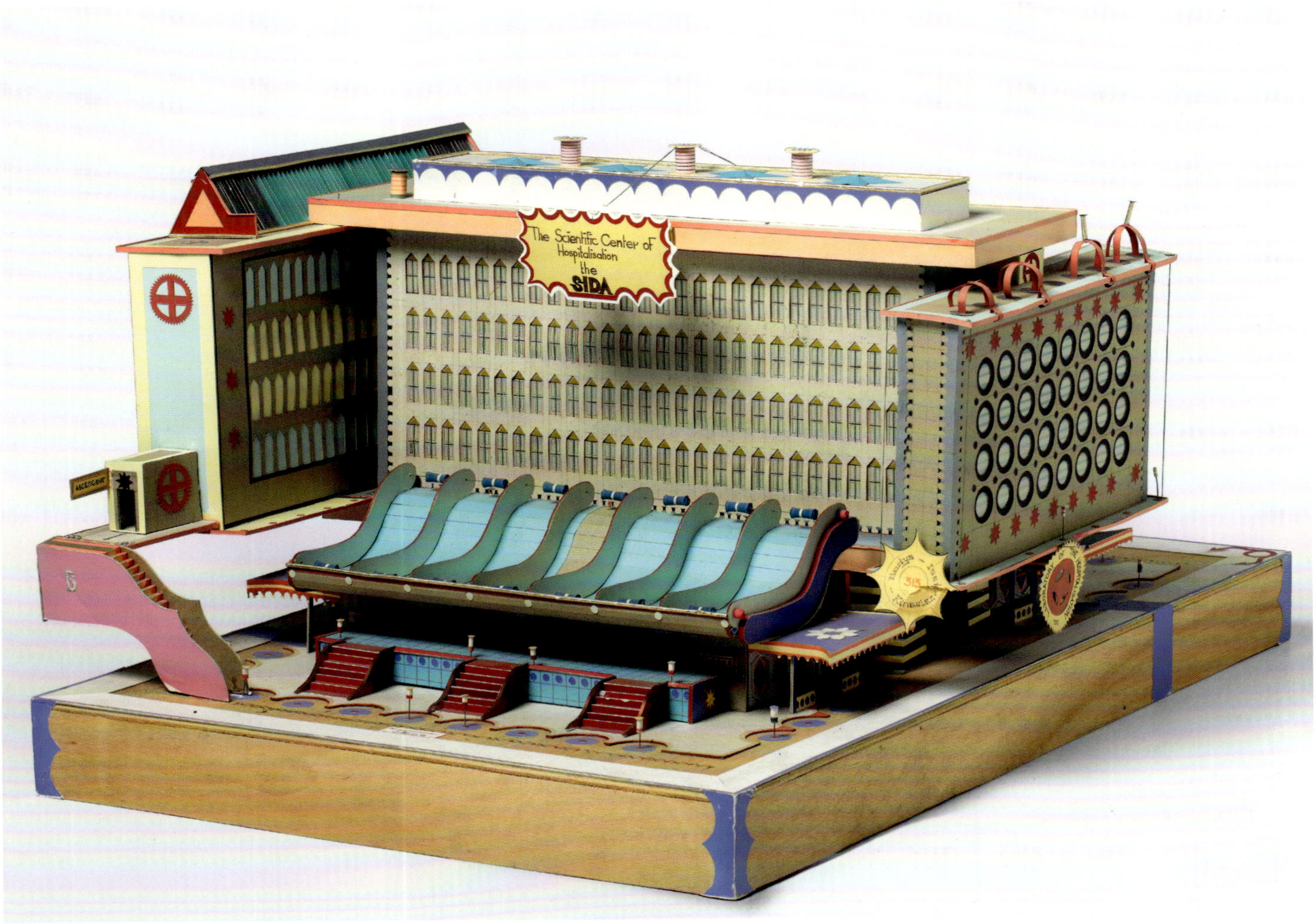

17

The Scientific Center of Hospitalisation the SIDA. 1991
16 $\frac{15}{16}$ x 25 $\frac{9}{16}$ x 31 $\frac{1}{2}$" (43 x 65 x 80 cm)
Groninger Museum, Groningen, Netherlands

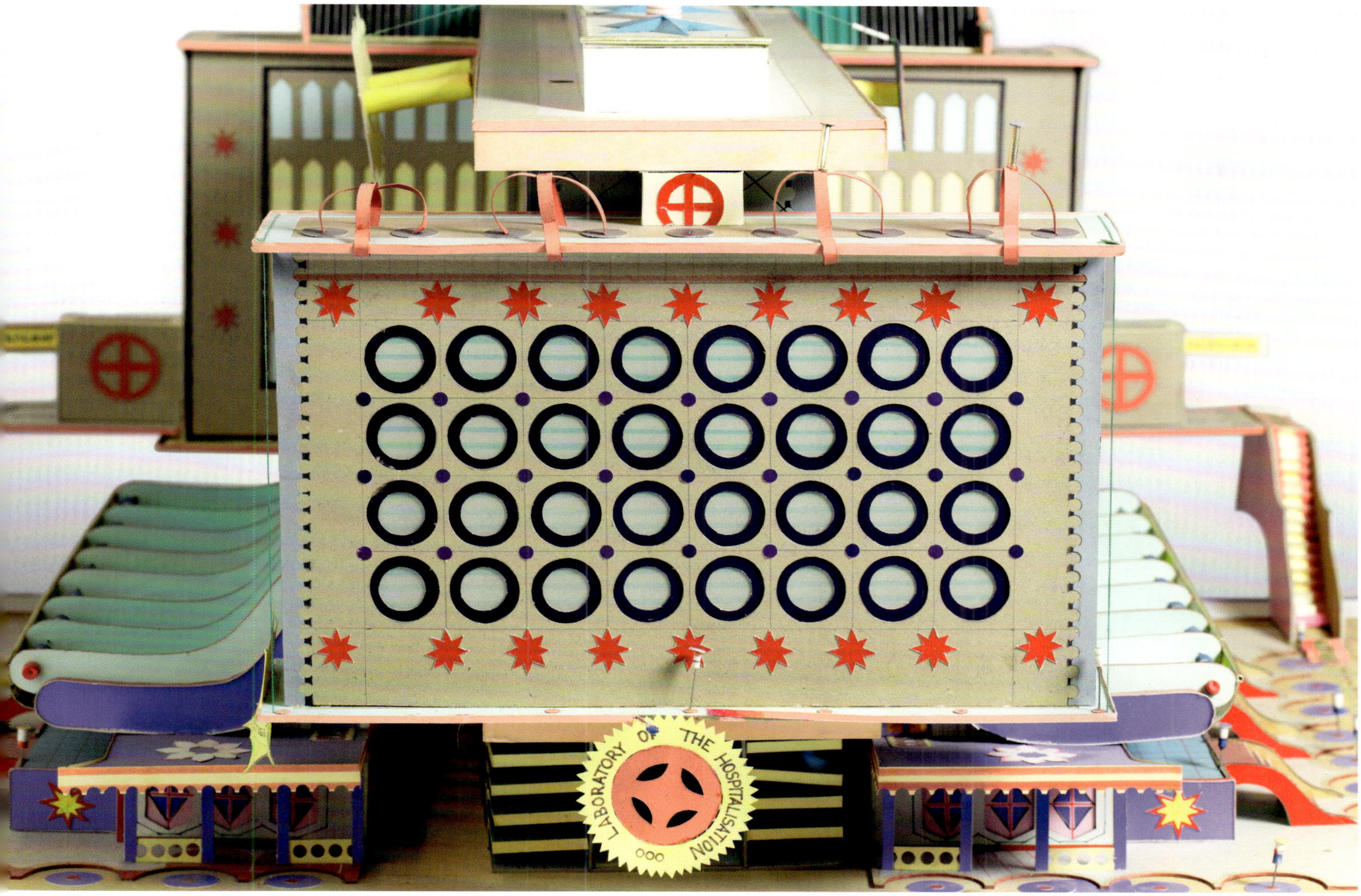
LABORATORY OF THE HOSPITALISATION

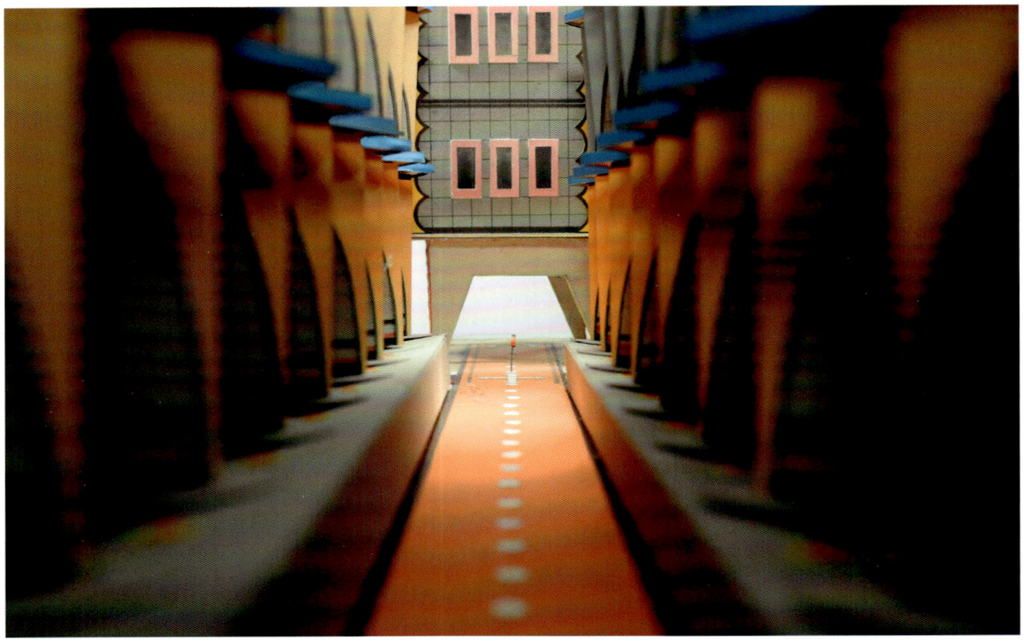

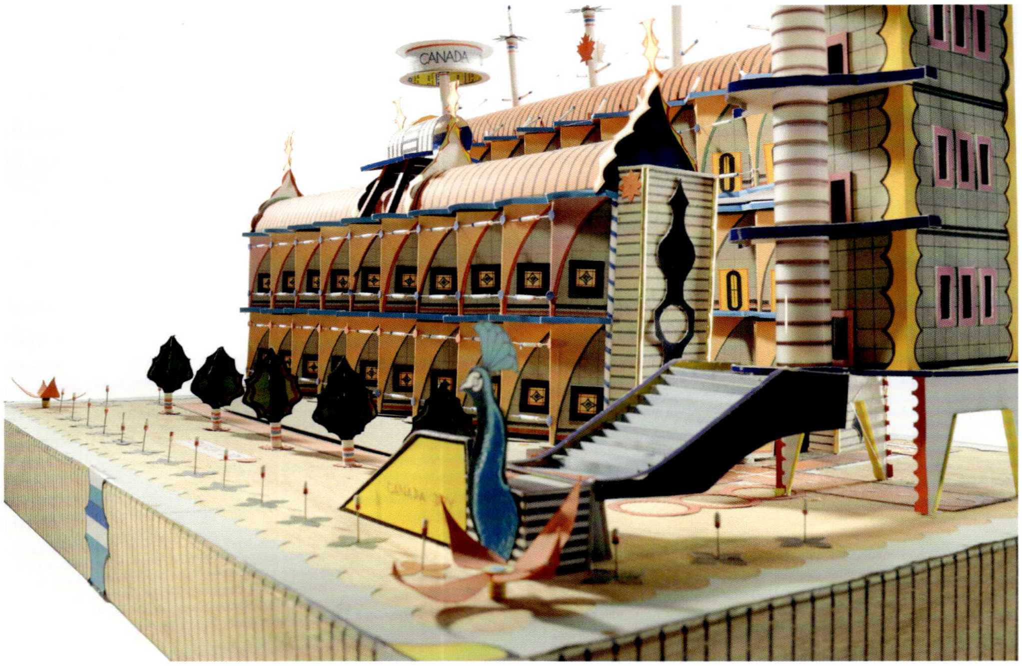

18

Canada Dry. 1991
20 ⅞ x 31 ½ x 21 ⅝" (53 x 80 x 55 cm)
CAAC—The Pigozzi Collection, Geneva

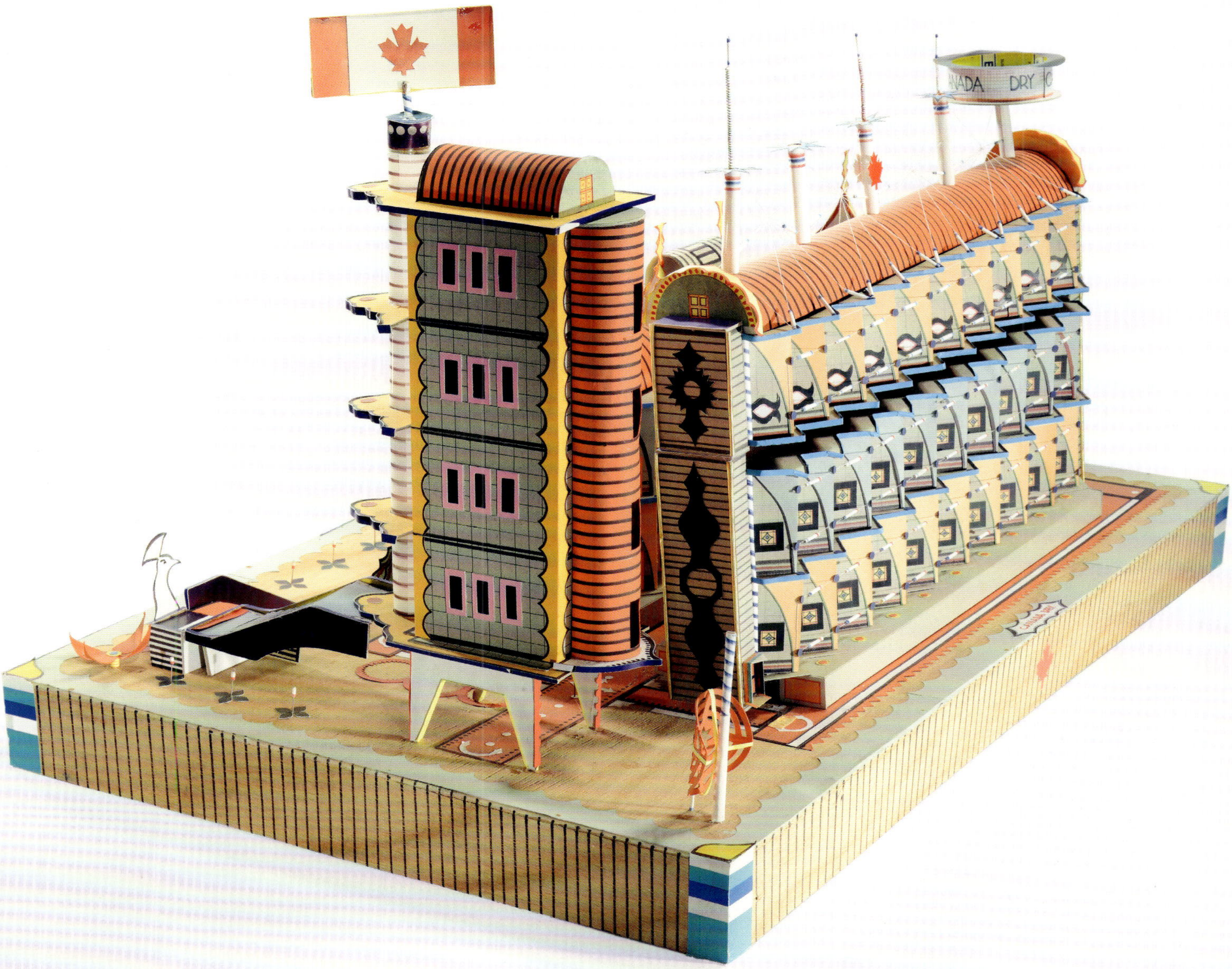
DRY

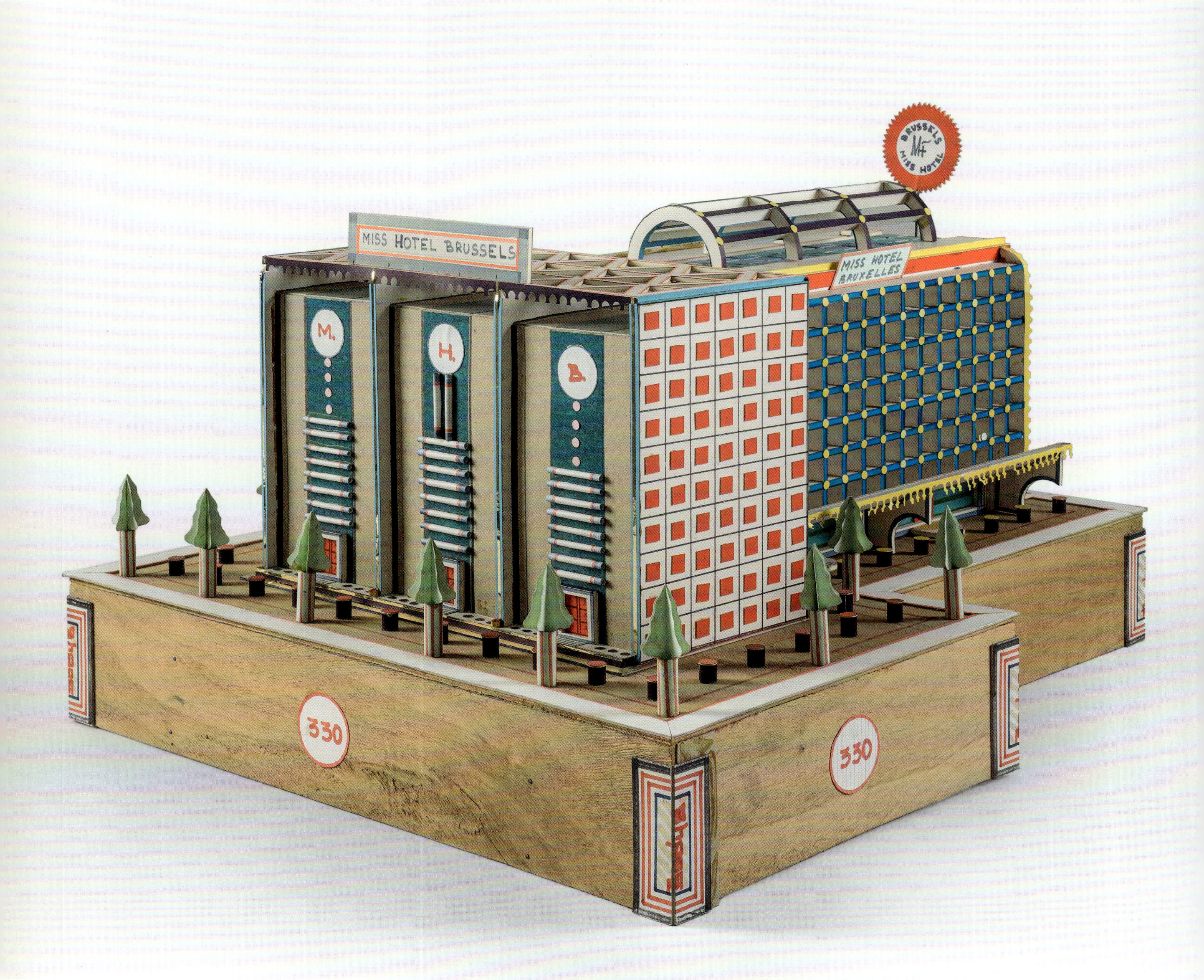

19

Miss Hotel Brussels. 1992
19 11/16 x 15 9/16 x 24" (50 x 39.5 x 61 cm)
Lucien Bilinelli Collection, Brussels/Milan

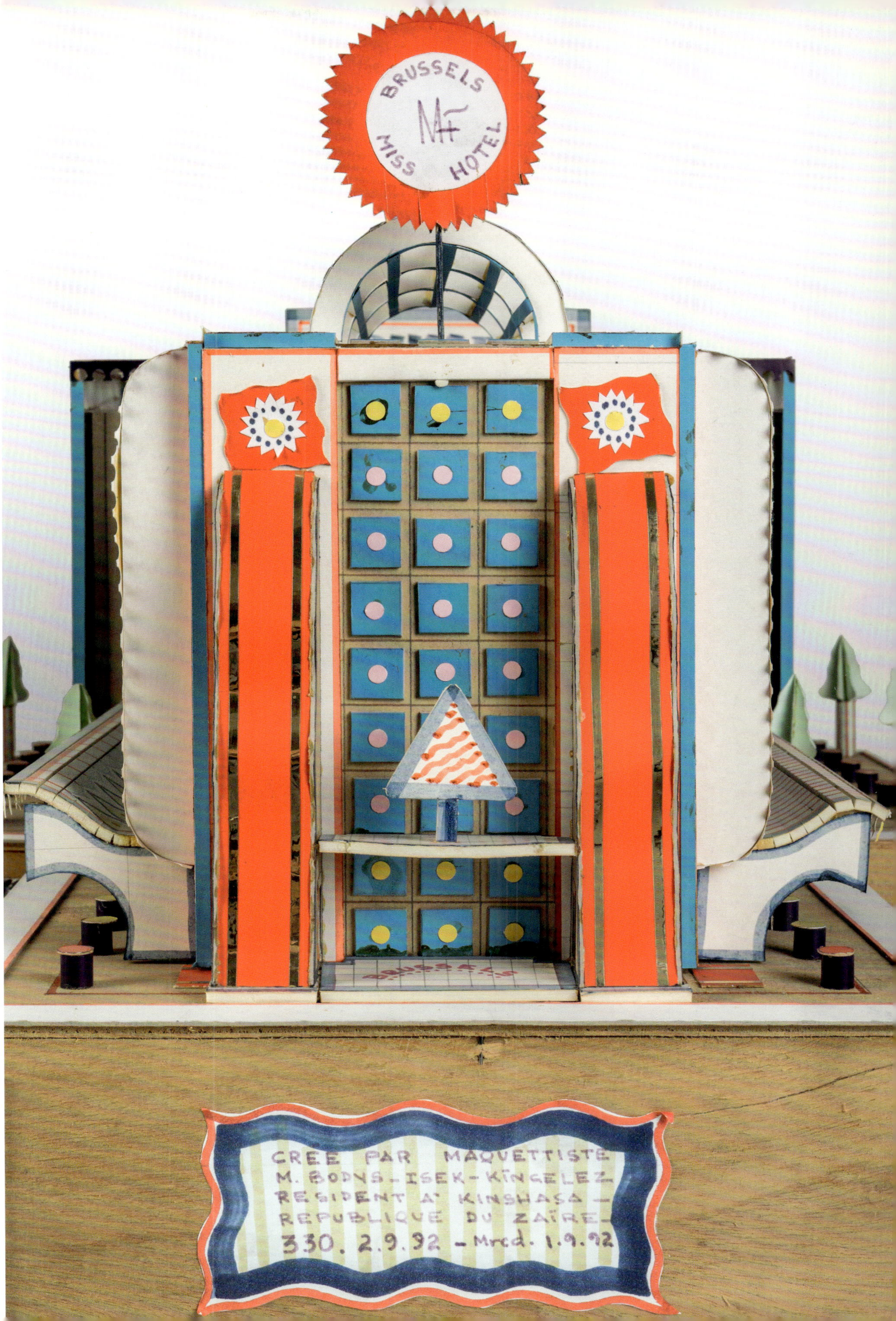
BRUSSELS
MF
MISS HOTEL
CREE PAR MAQUETTISTE
M. BODYS_ISEK-KĨNGELEZ
RESIDENT A' KINSHASA -
REPUBLIQUE DU ZAÏRE_
330. 2.9.92 - Mrcd. 1.9.92

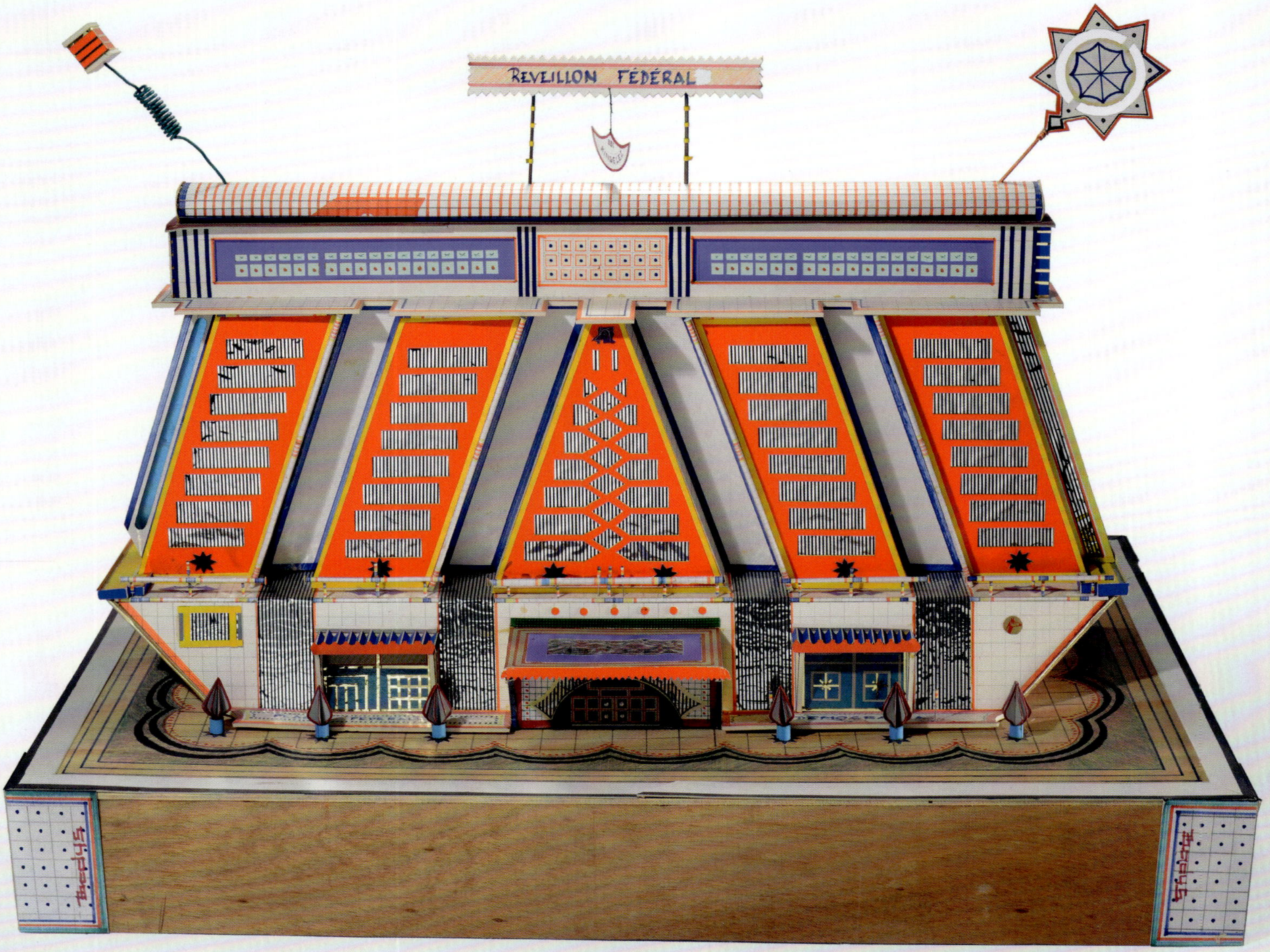

20

Reveillon Fédéral. 1992
23 ⅝ x 31 ½ x 20 ⅞" (60 x 80 x 53 cm)
CAAC—The Pigozzi Collection, Geneva

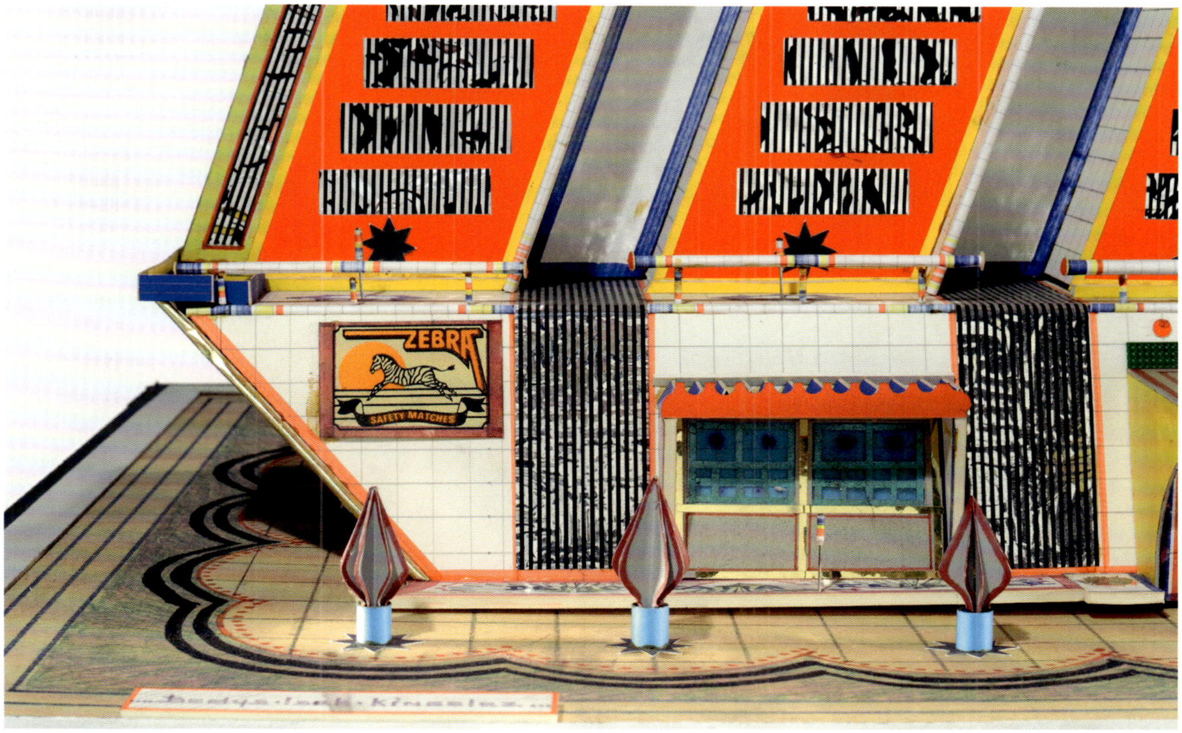
ZEBRA
SAFETY MATCHES

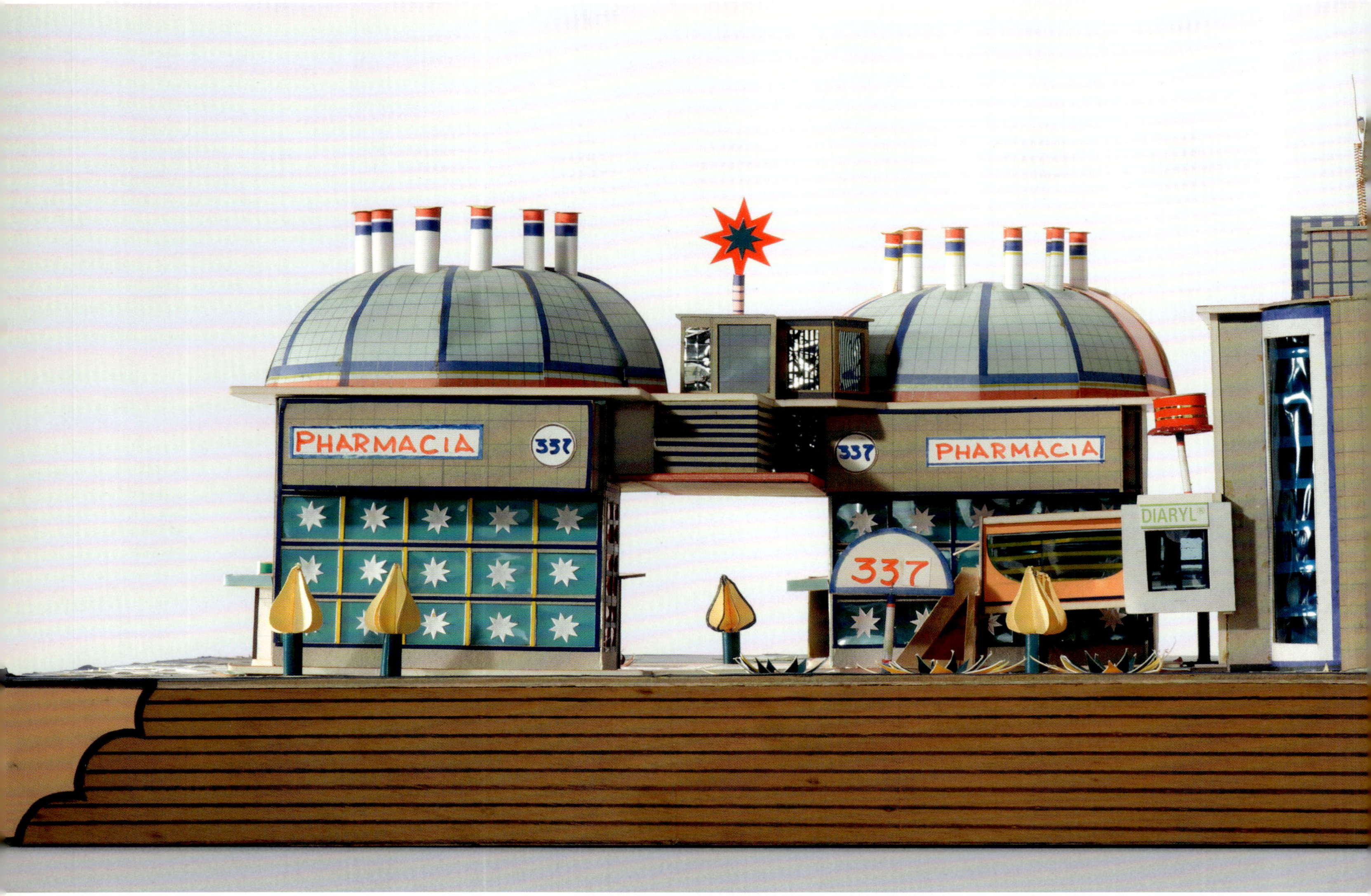

21

Industria da Pharmacia. 1992
14 15/16 x 31 1/8 x 21 5/8" (38 x 79 x 55 cm)
CAAC—The Pigozzi Collection, Geneva

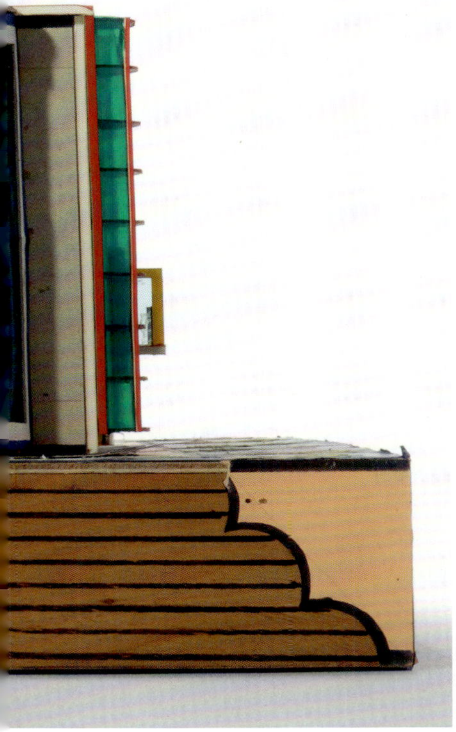

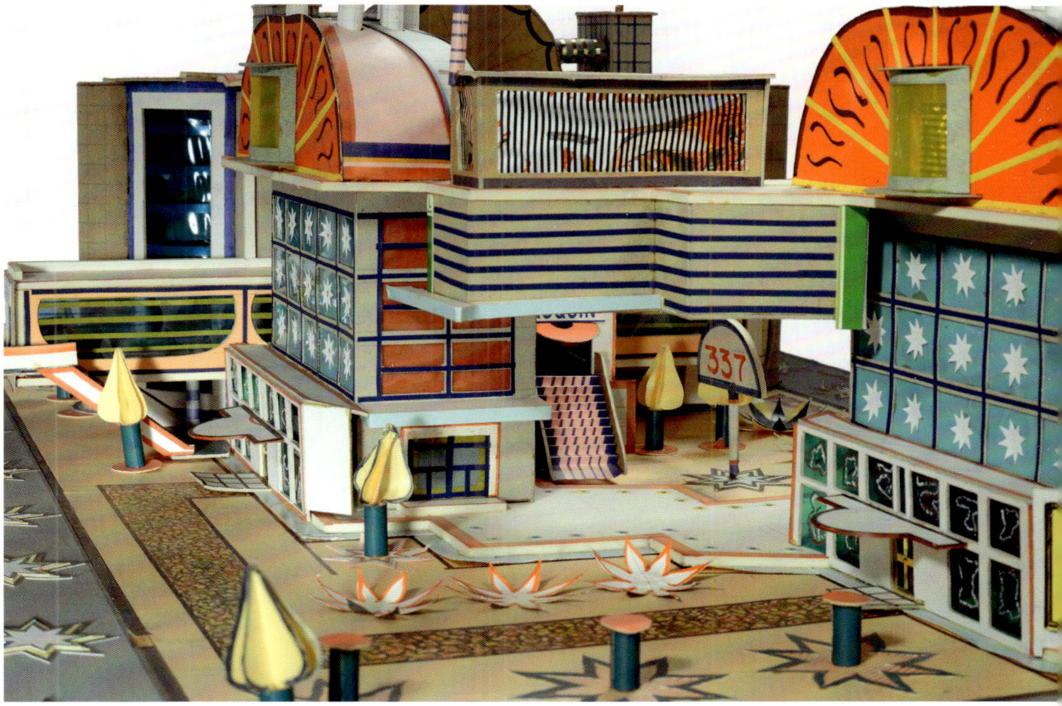
337

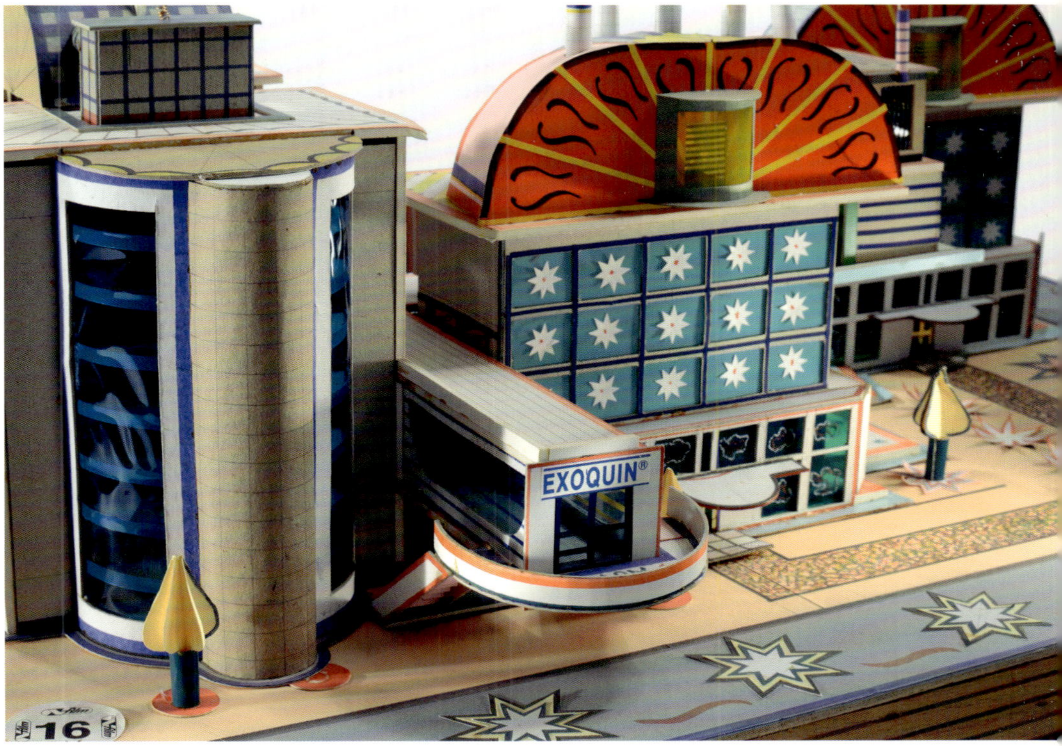
EXOQUIN®
16

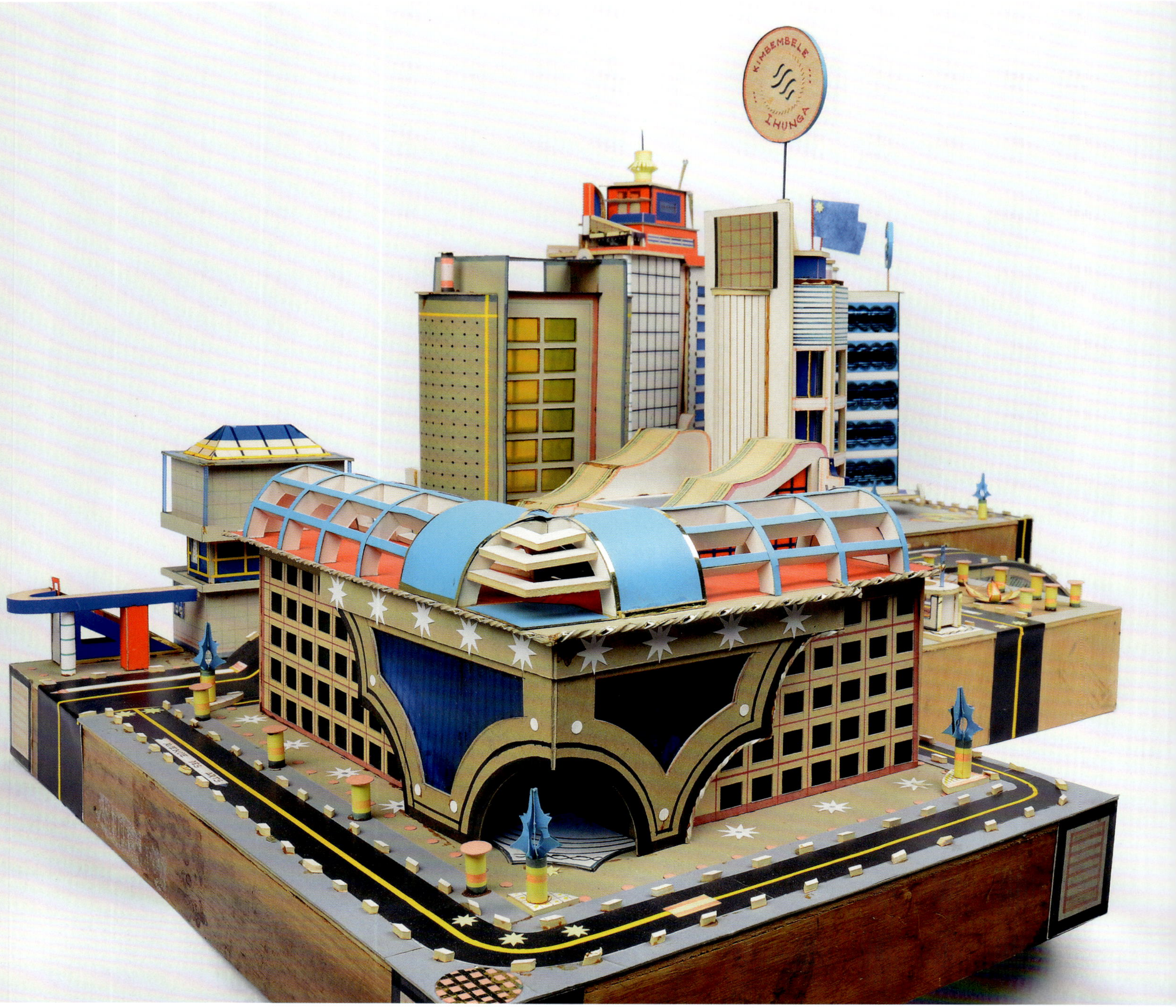

22

Kimbembele Ihunga (Kimbembele Ville). 1992
20 1⁄16 x 42 ½ x 34 1⁄16" (51 x 108 x 86.5 cm)
Courtesy The Museum of Everything

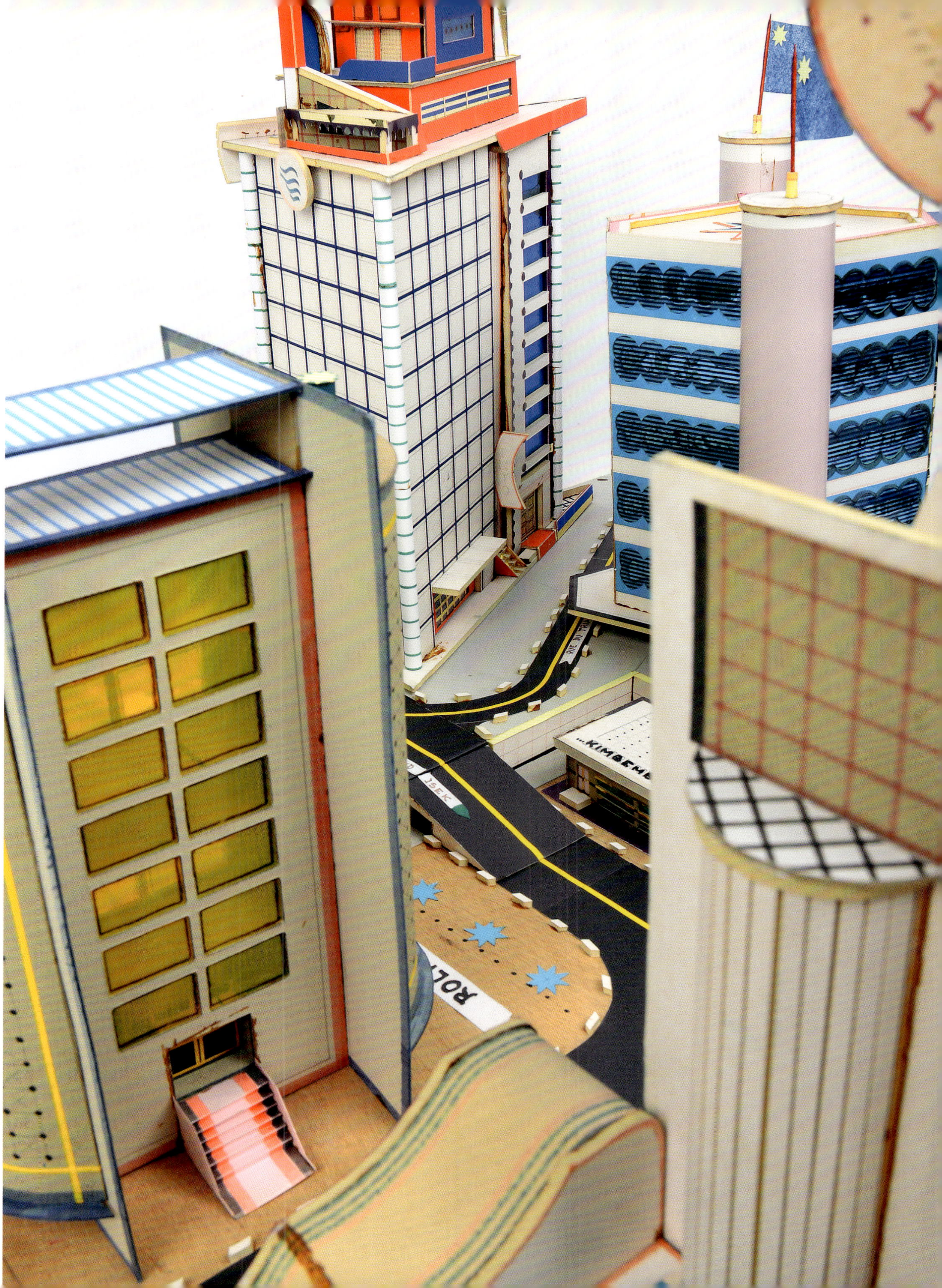

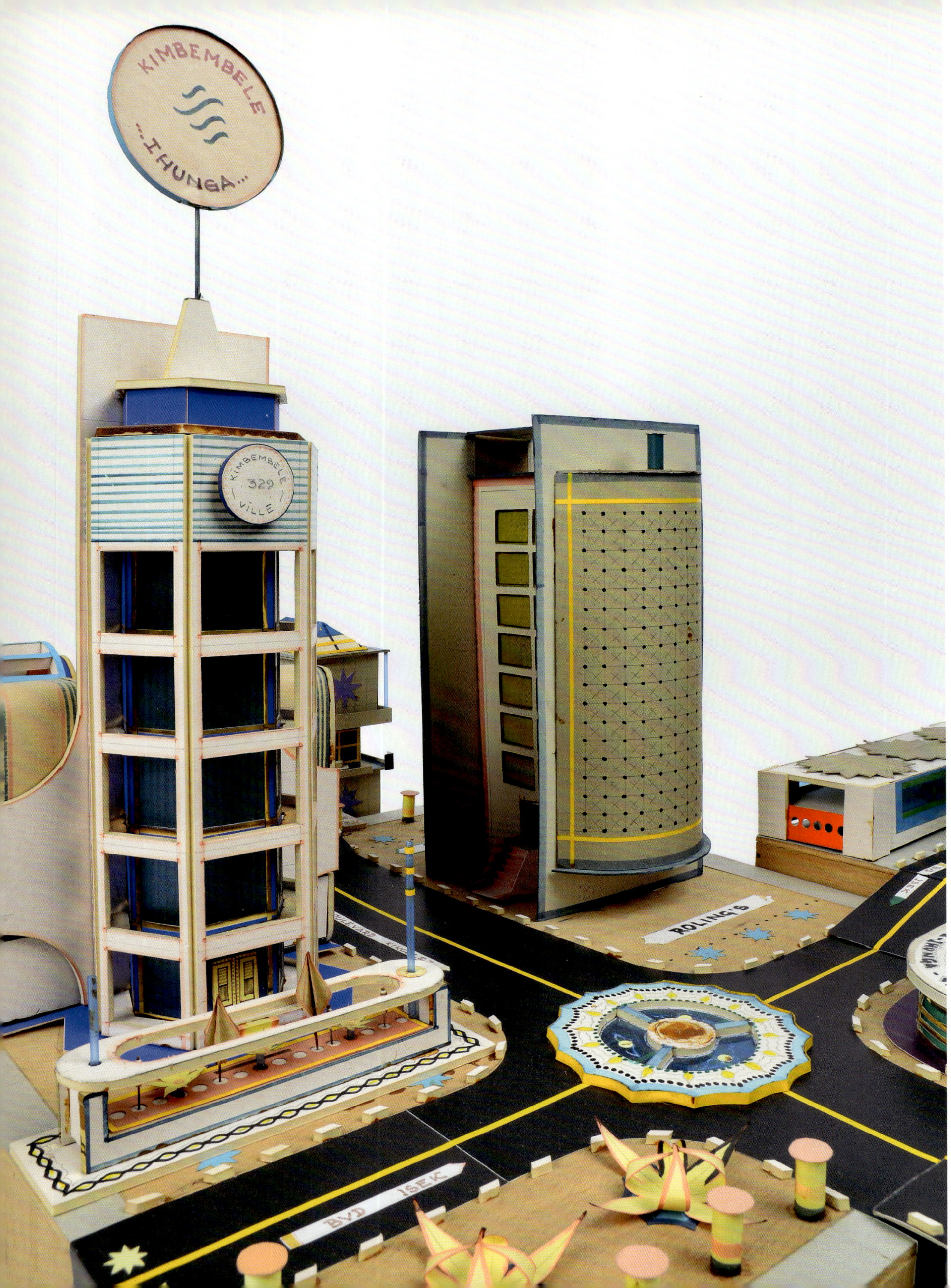
KIMBEMBELE
...I HUNGA...
KIMBEMBELE
329
VILLE
ROLING'S
BVD ISEK

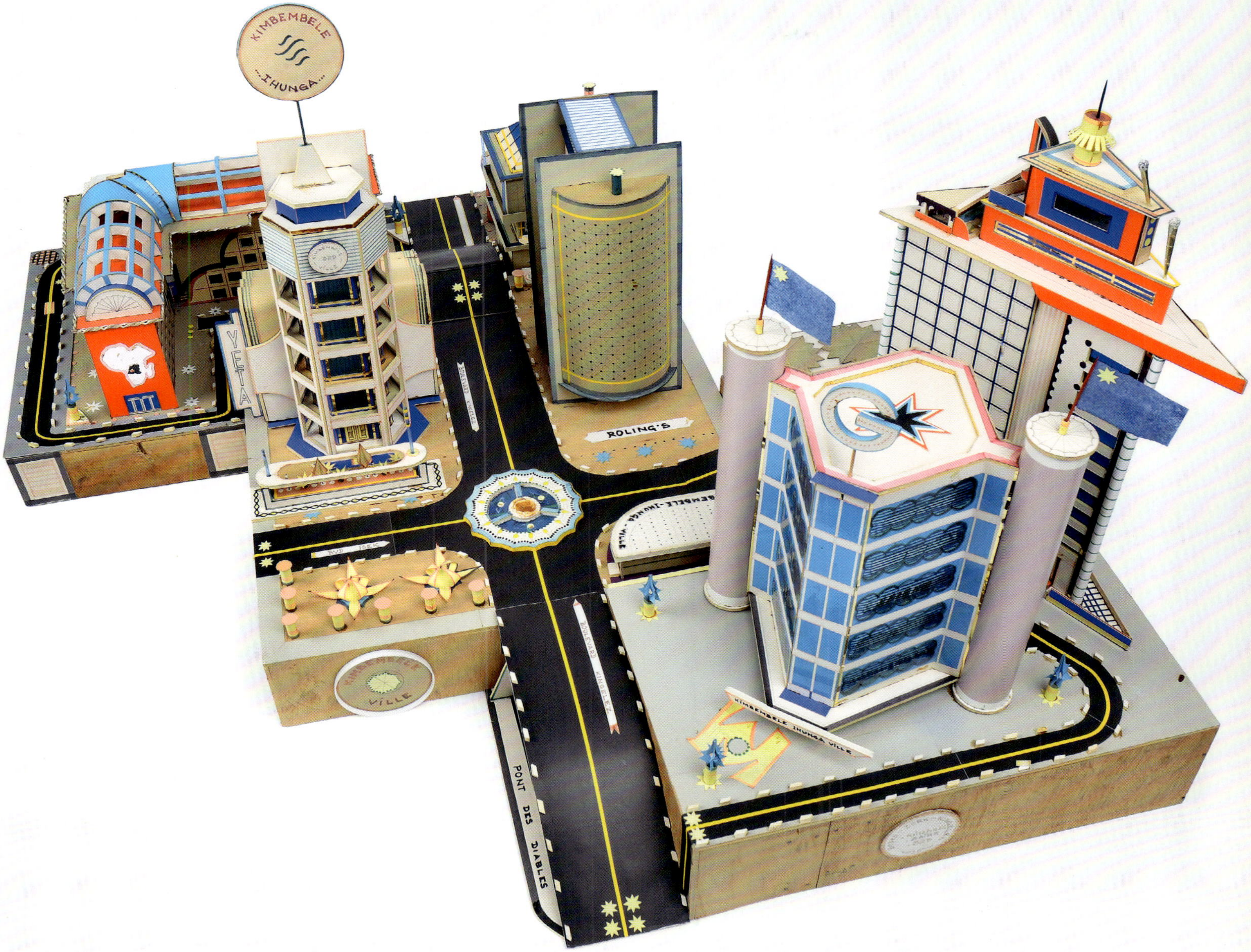
KIMBEMBELE
IHUNGA
YETA
ROLING'S
KIMBEMBELE
VILLE
KIMBEMBELE IHUNGA VILLE
PONT DES DIABLES

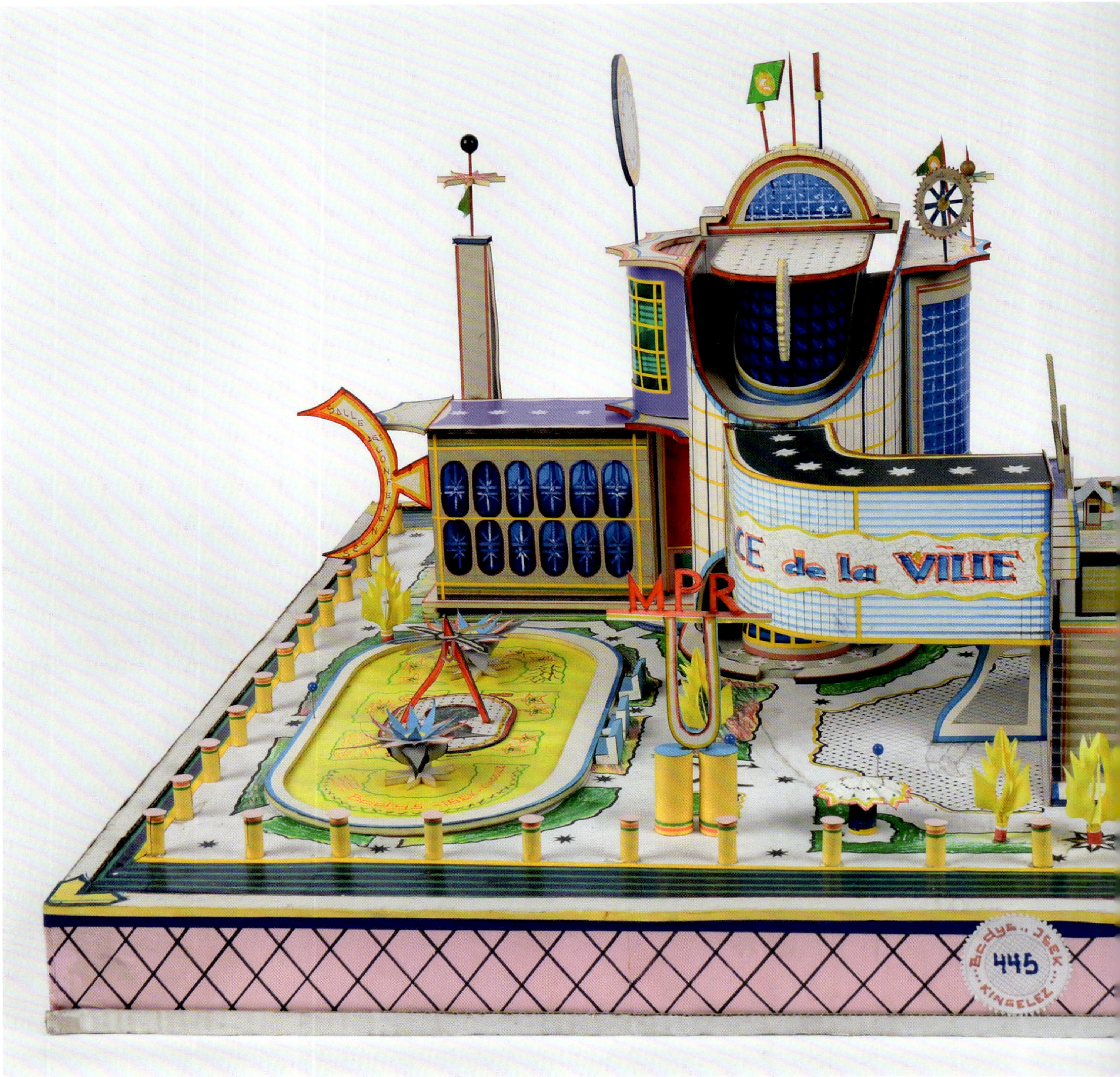

23

Place de la Ville. 1993
15 3/4 x 33 7/16 x 29 1/2" (40 x 85 x 75 cm)
Courtesy The Museum of Everything

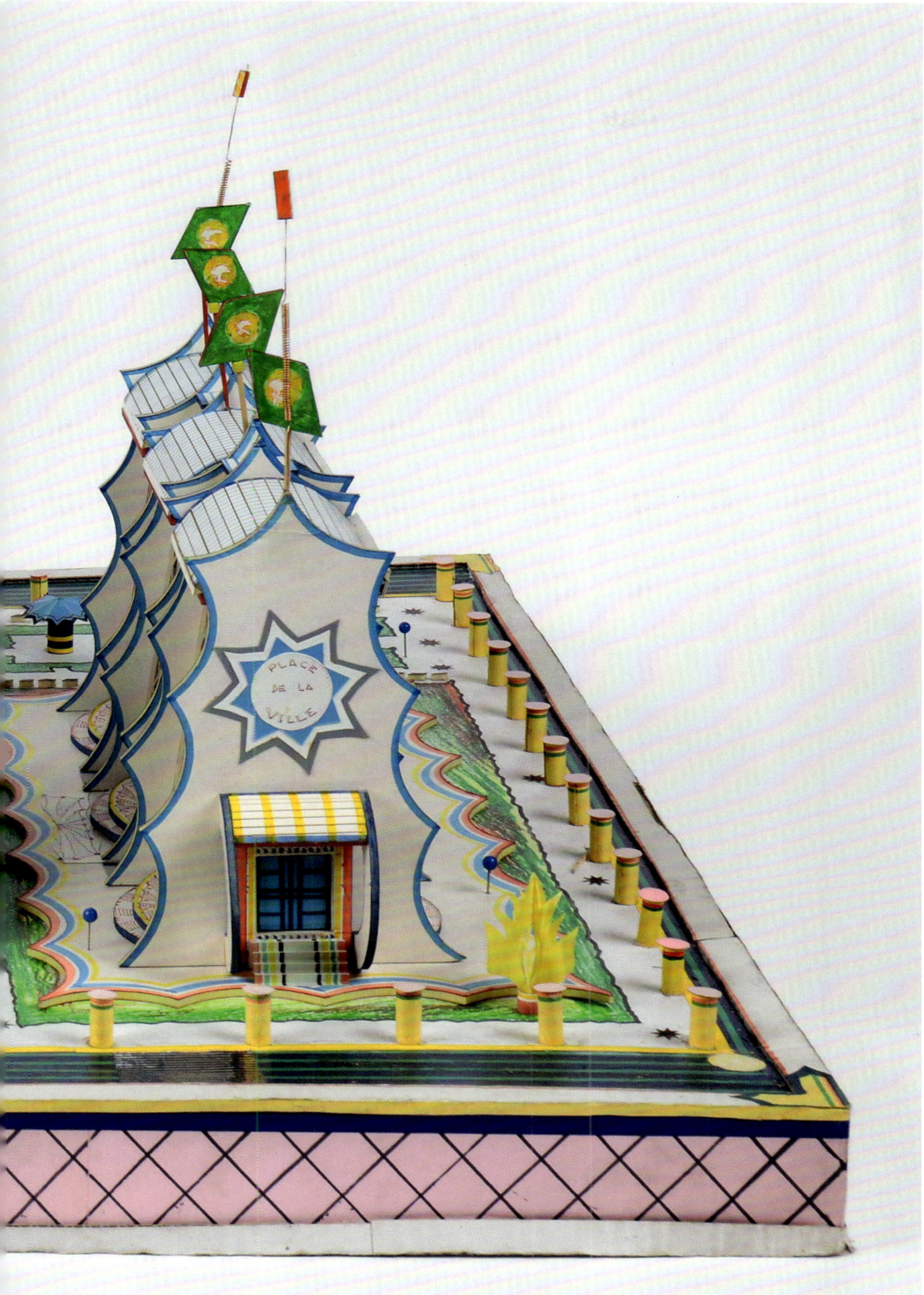
PLACE
DE LA
VILLE

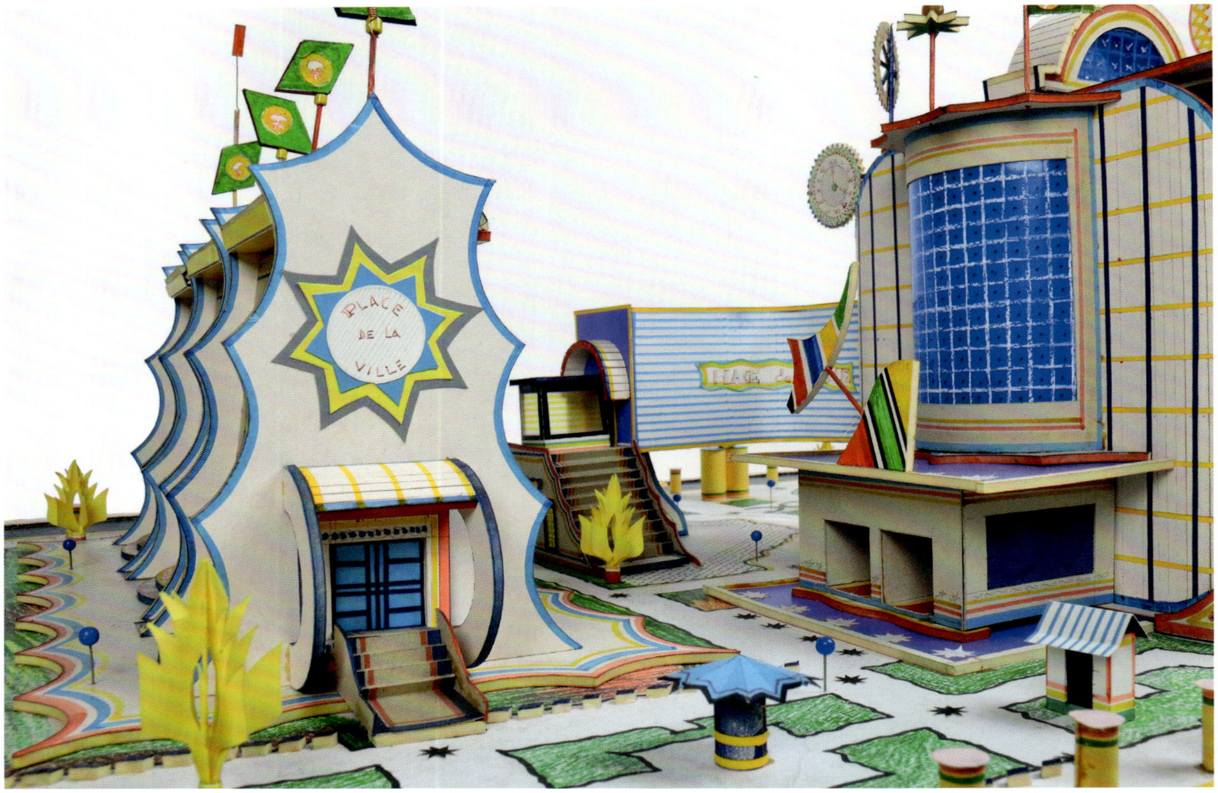
PLACE
DE LA
VILLE

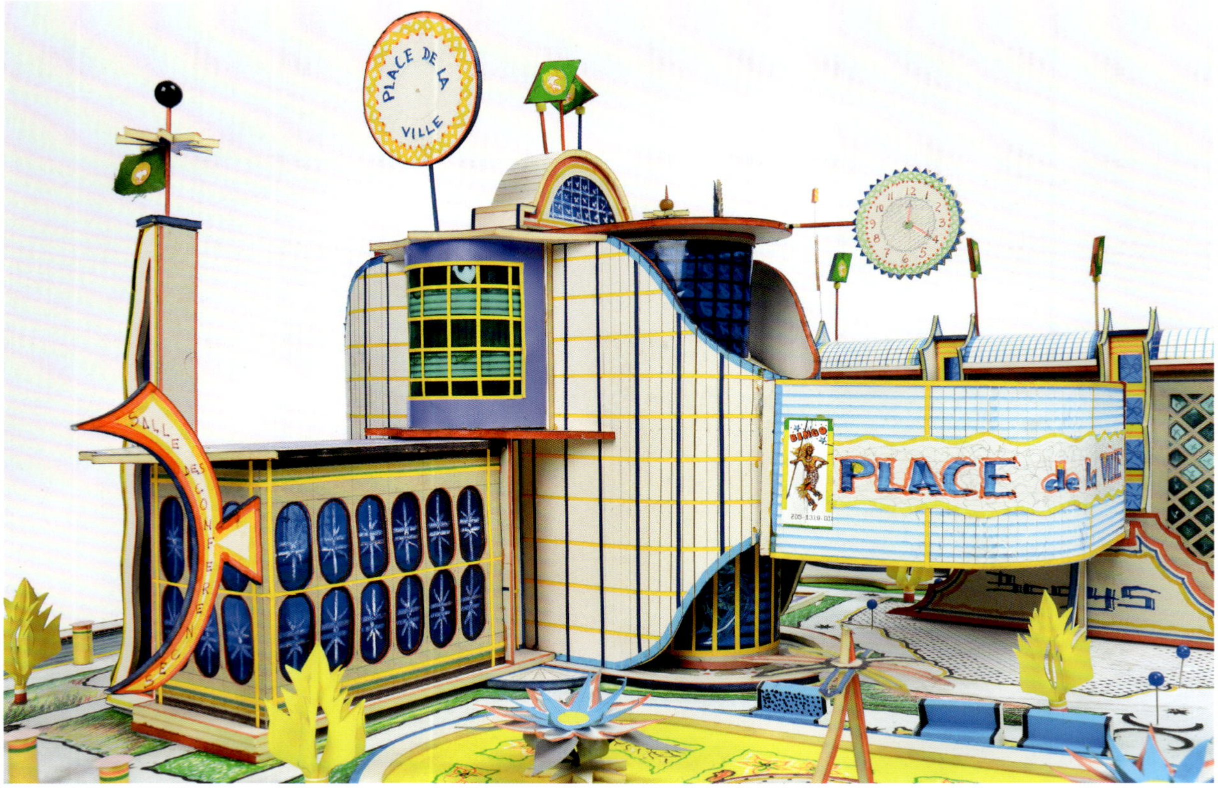
PLACE DE LA
VILLE
PLACE de la VILLE

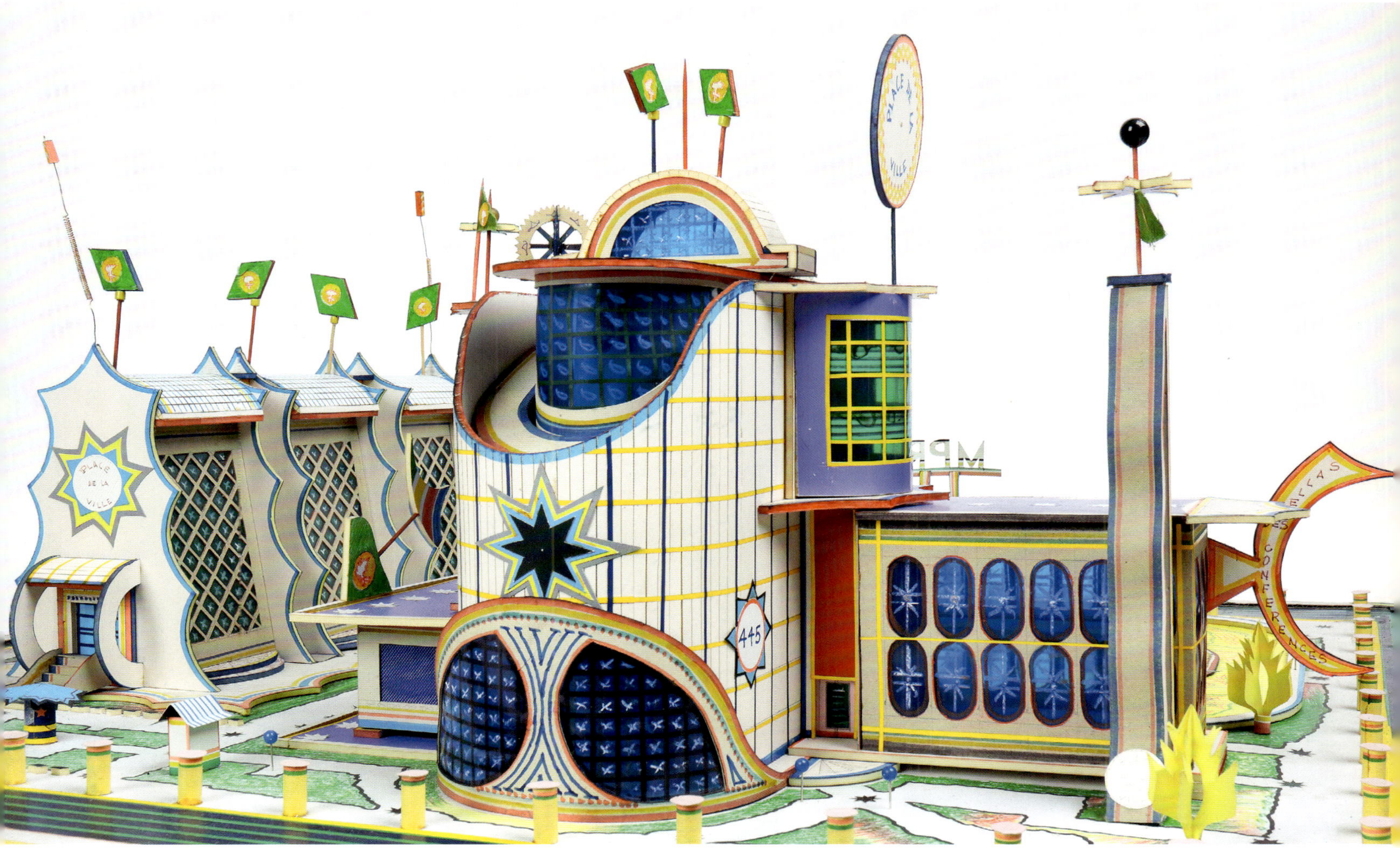
PLACE DE LA VILLE
445

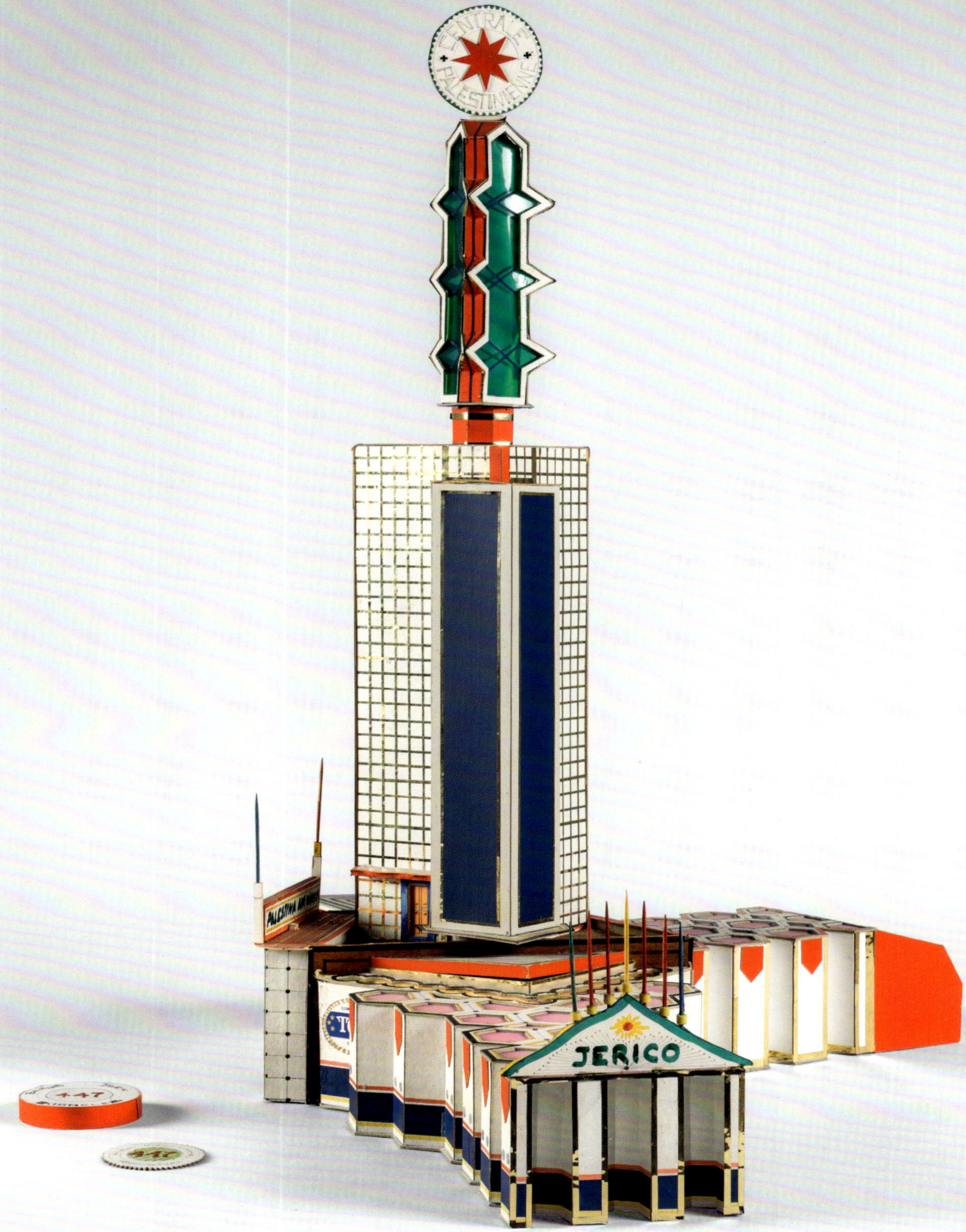

24

Centrale Palestinienne. 1993
$31\frac{7}{8}$ x $28\frac{3}{8}$ x $26\frac{3}{8}$" (81 x 72 x 67 cm), irreg.
COLLECTION PROSPER—The Prosper Collection.
Courtesy Aeroplastics Contemporary, Brussels

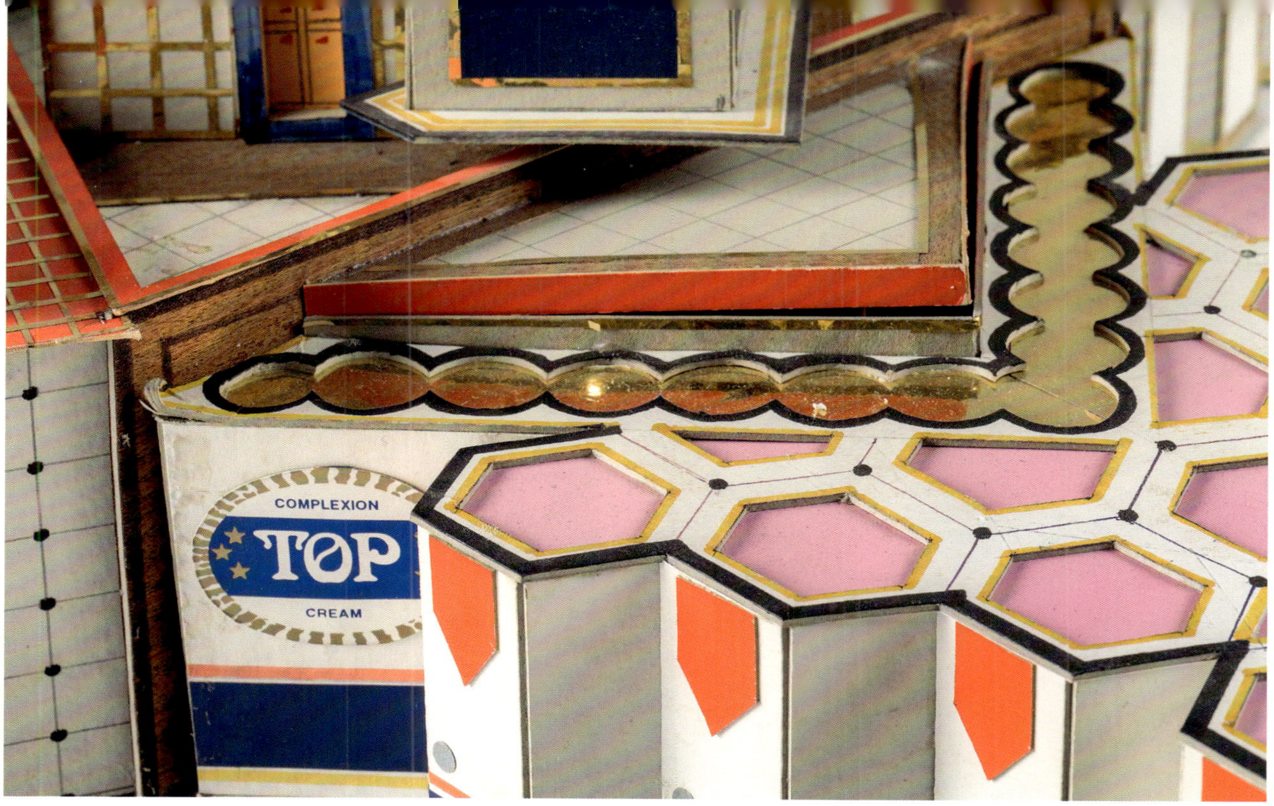
COMPLEXION
TOP
CREAM

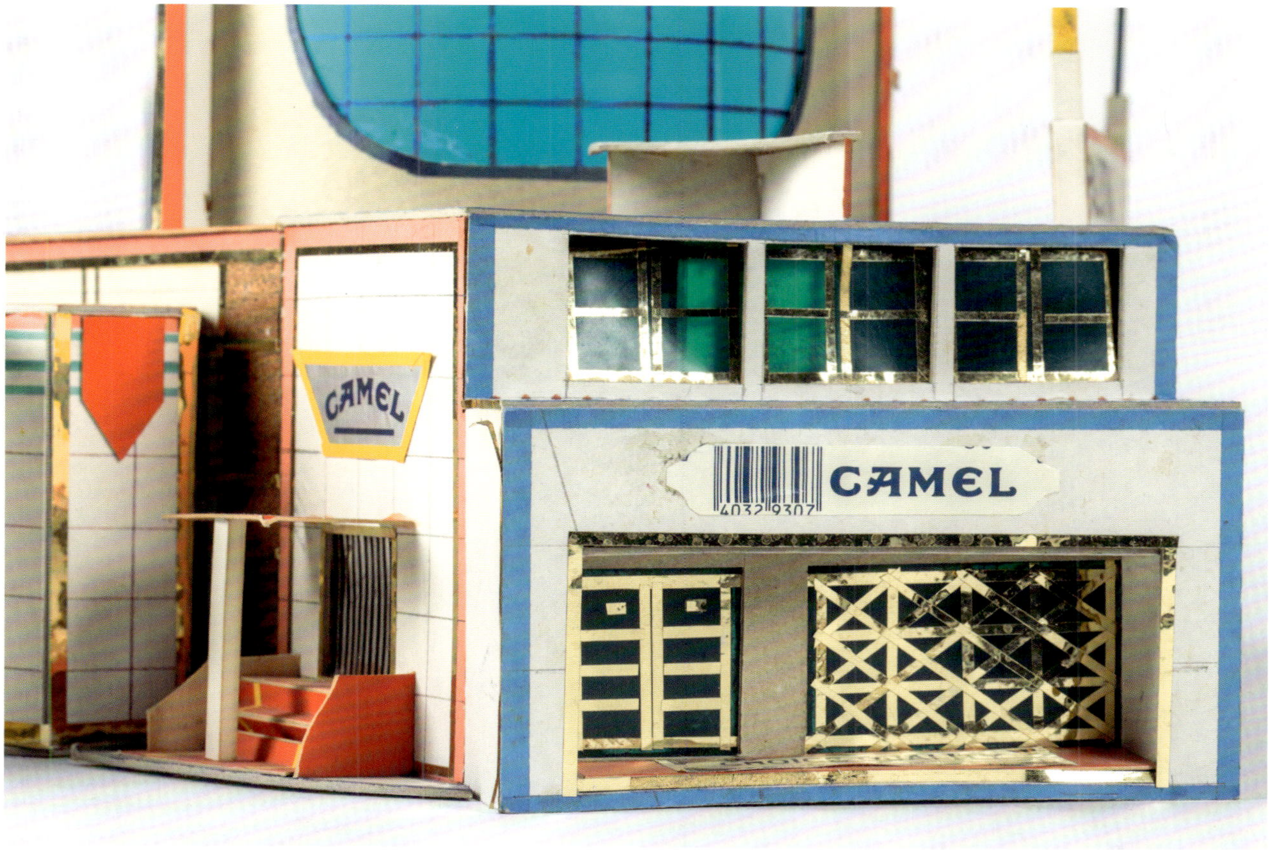
CAMEL
CAMEL
4032 9307

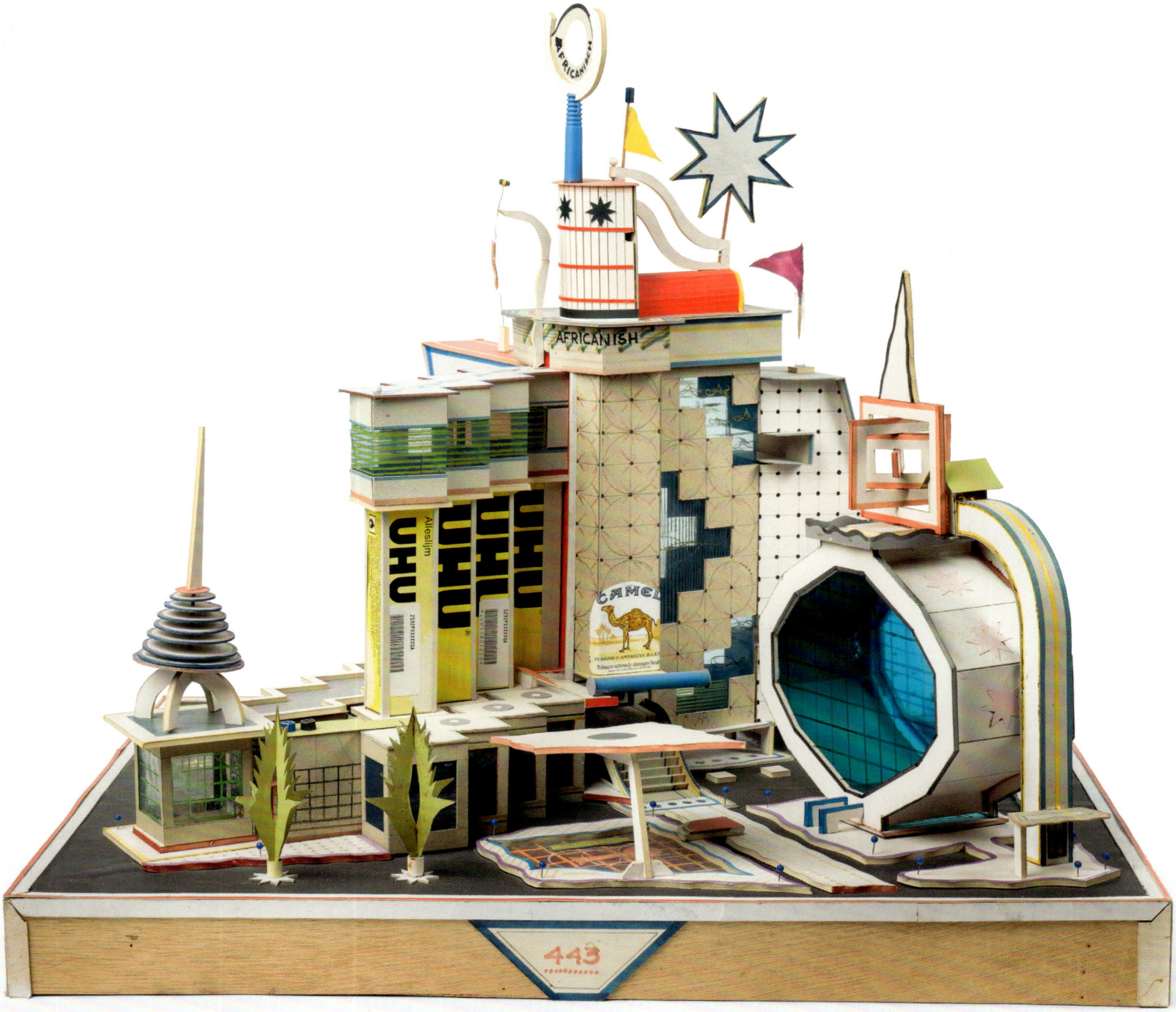

25

Africanisch. 1994
19 11/16 x 22 7/16 x 24" (50 x 57 x 61 cm)
Private collection, Paris

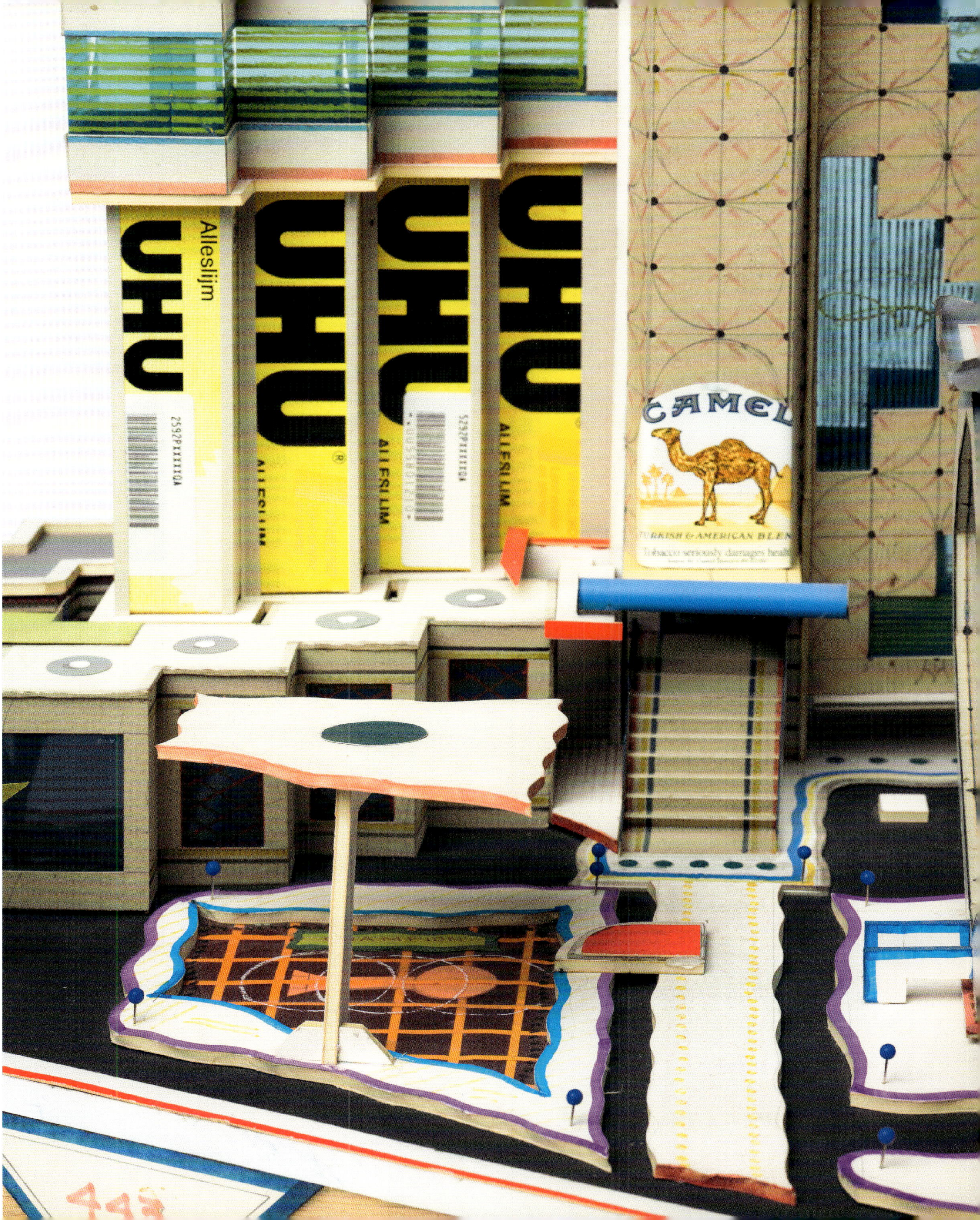
UHU
Alleslijm
UHU
ALLESLIJM
UHU
ALLESLIJM
UHU
ALLESLIJM
CAMEL
TURKISH & AMERICAN BLEN
Tobacco seriously damages healt

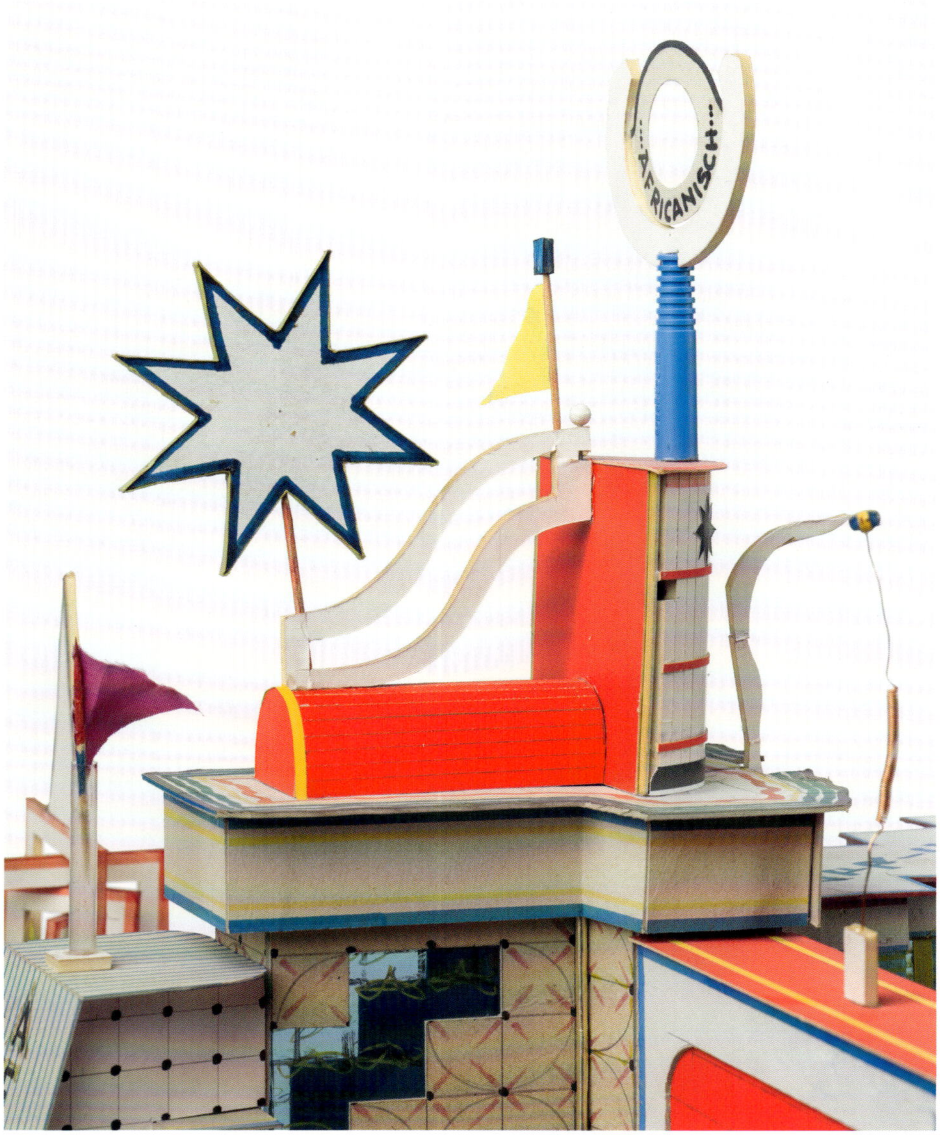
AFRICANISCH

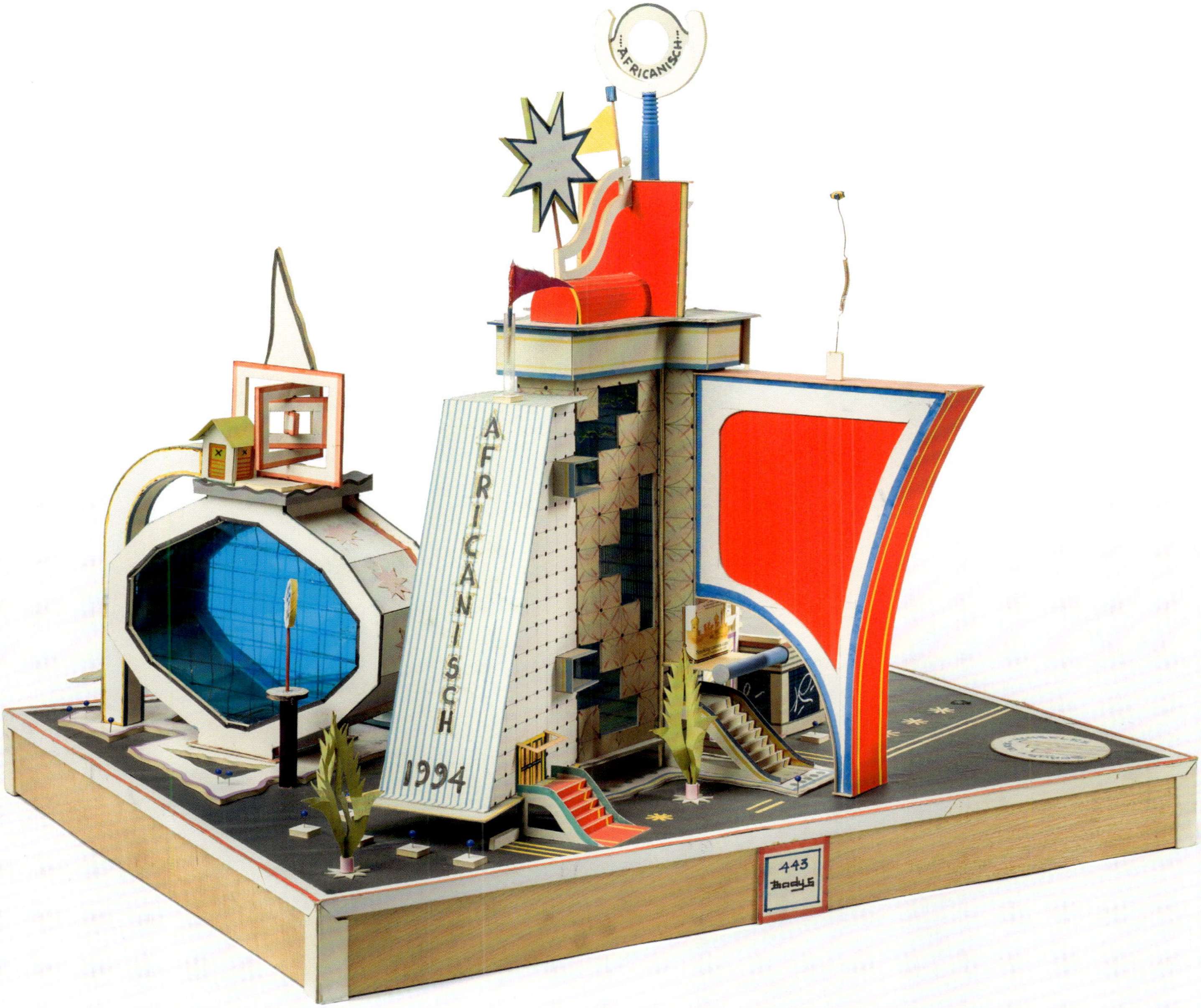
AFRICANISCH
AFRICANISCH
1994
443

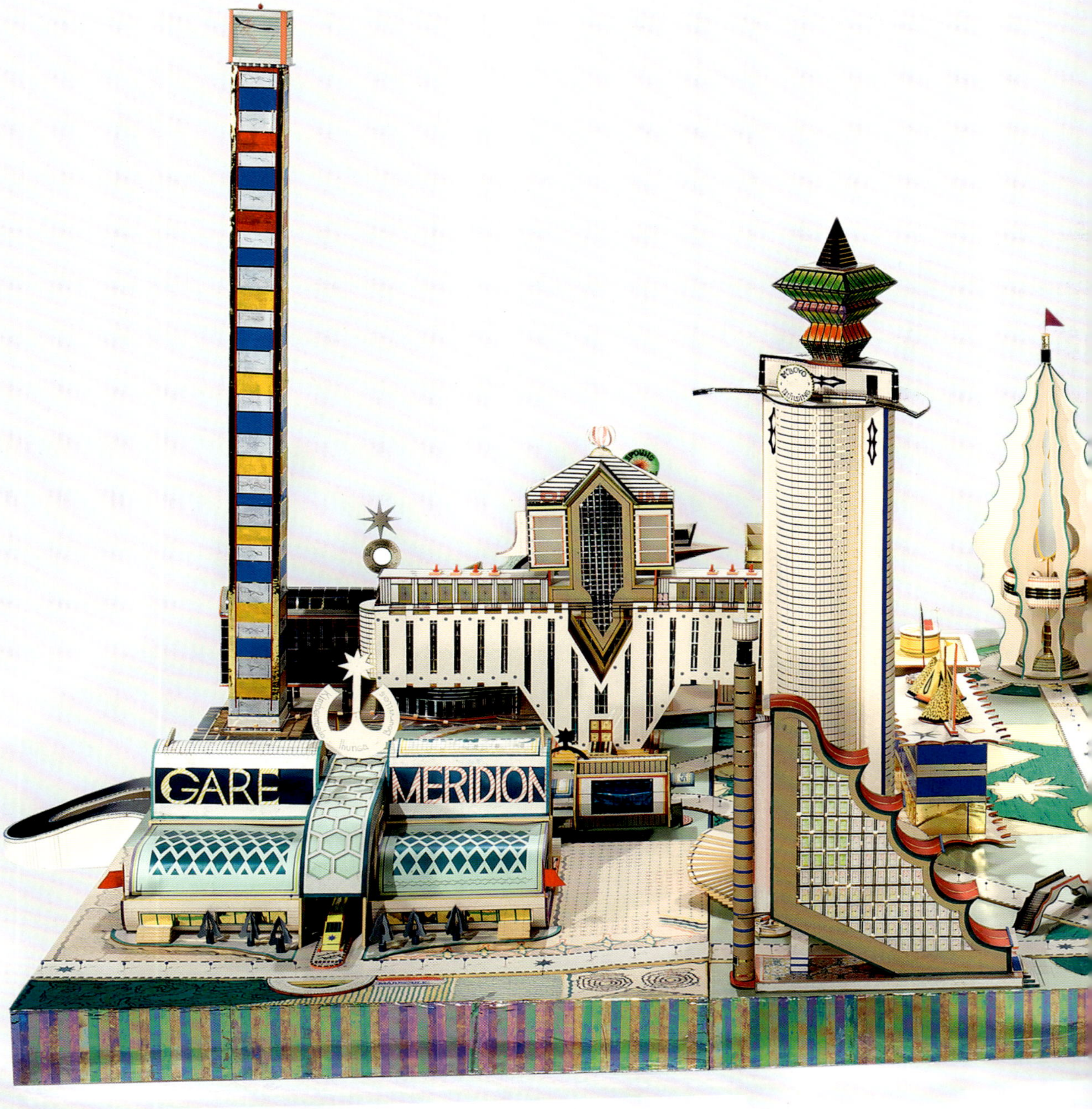

26

Kimbembele Ihunga. 1994
51 3/16" x 72 13/16" x 10' 5" (130 x 185 x 320 cm)
CAAC—The Pigozzi Collection, Geneva

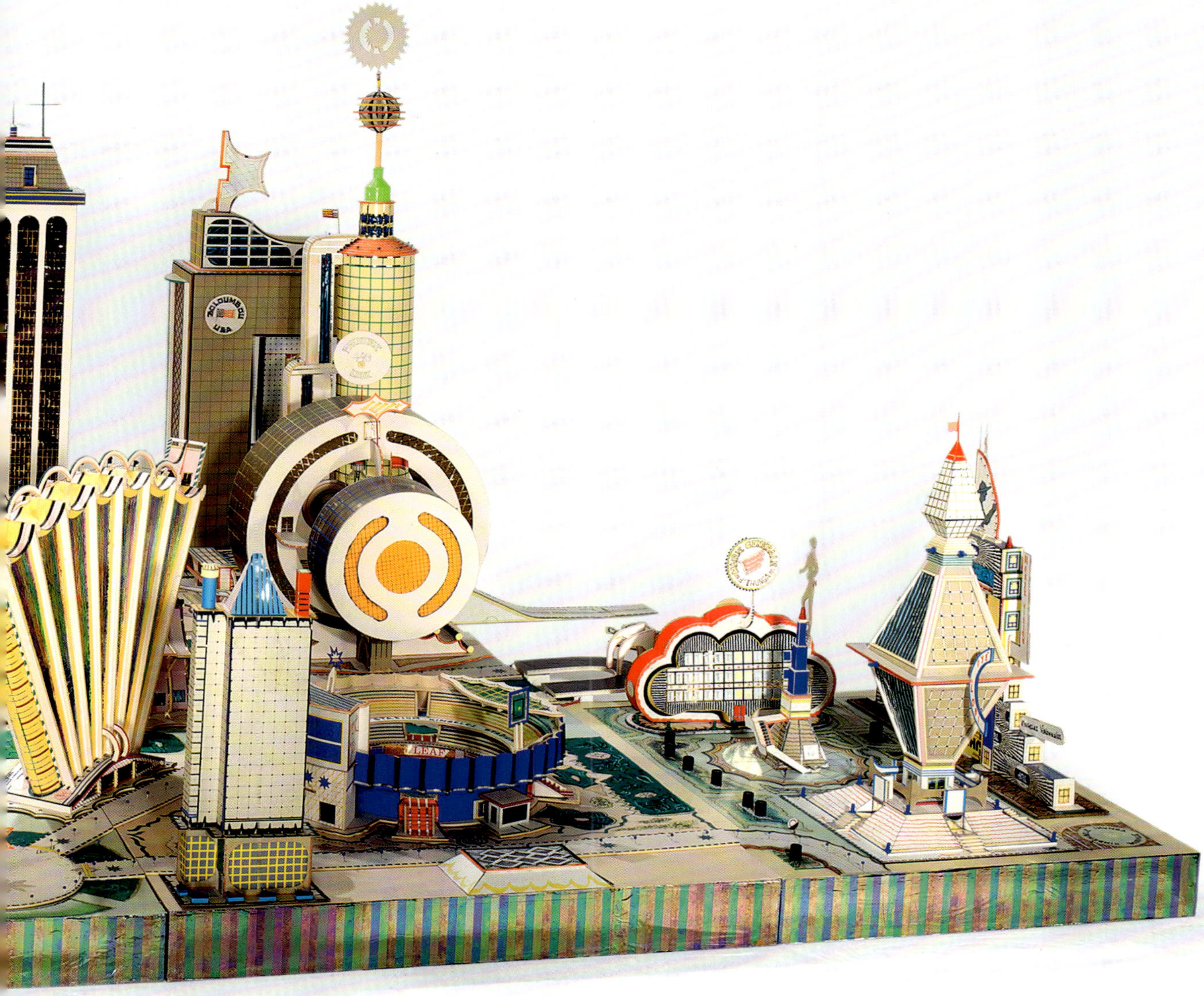

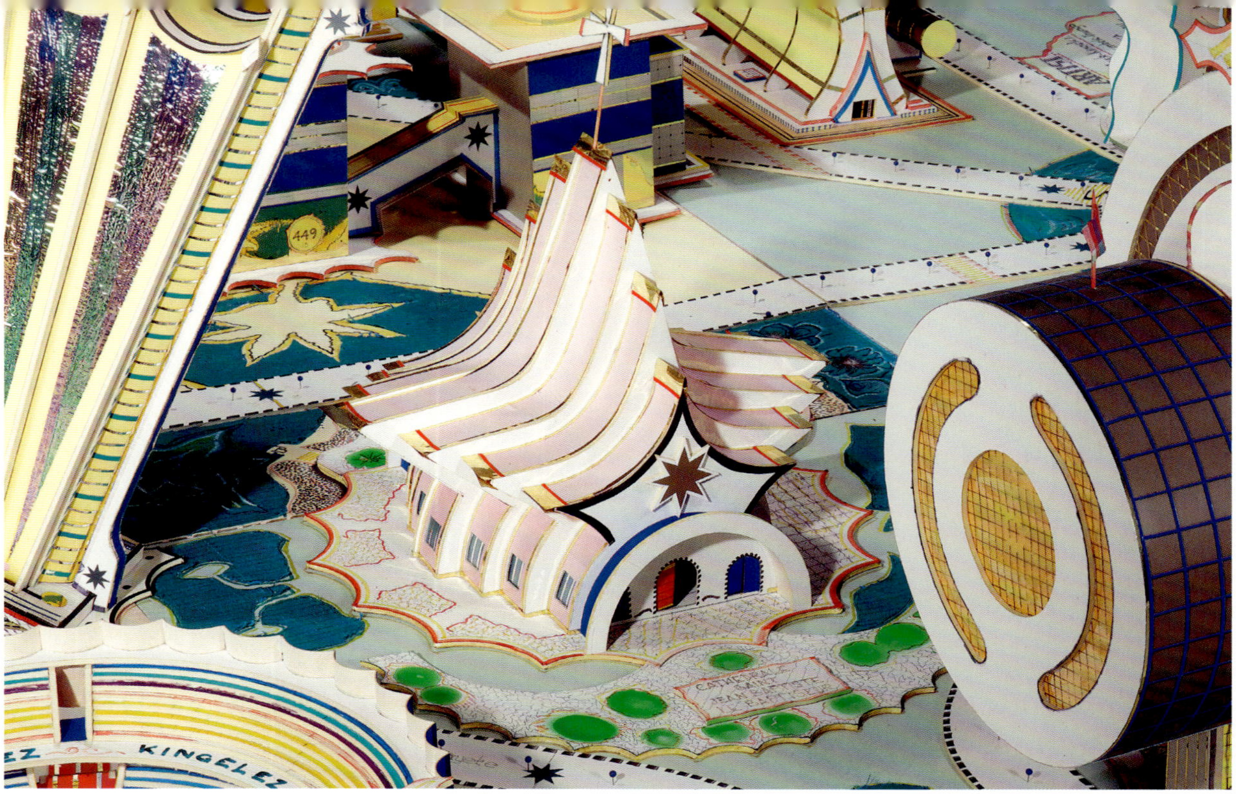
449
KINGELEZ

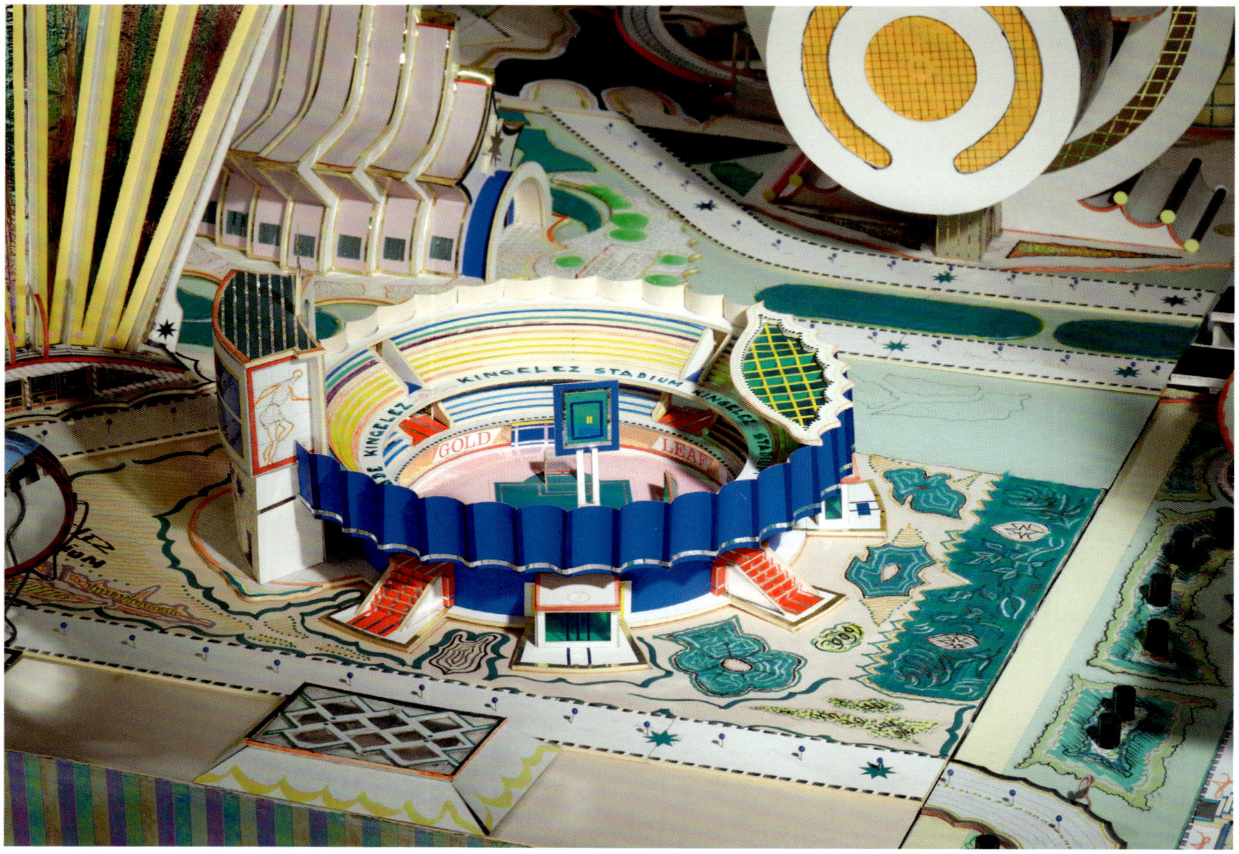
KINGELEZ STADIUM
GOLD
LEAF

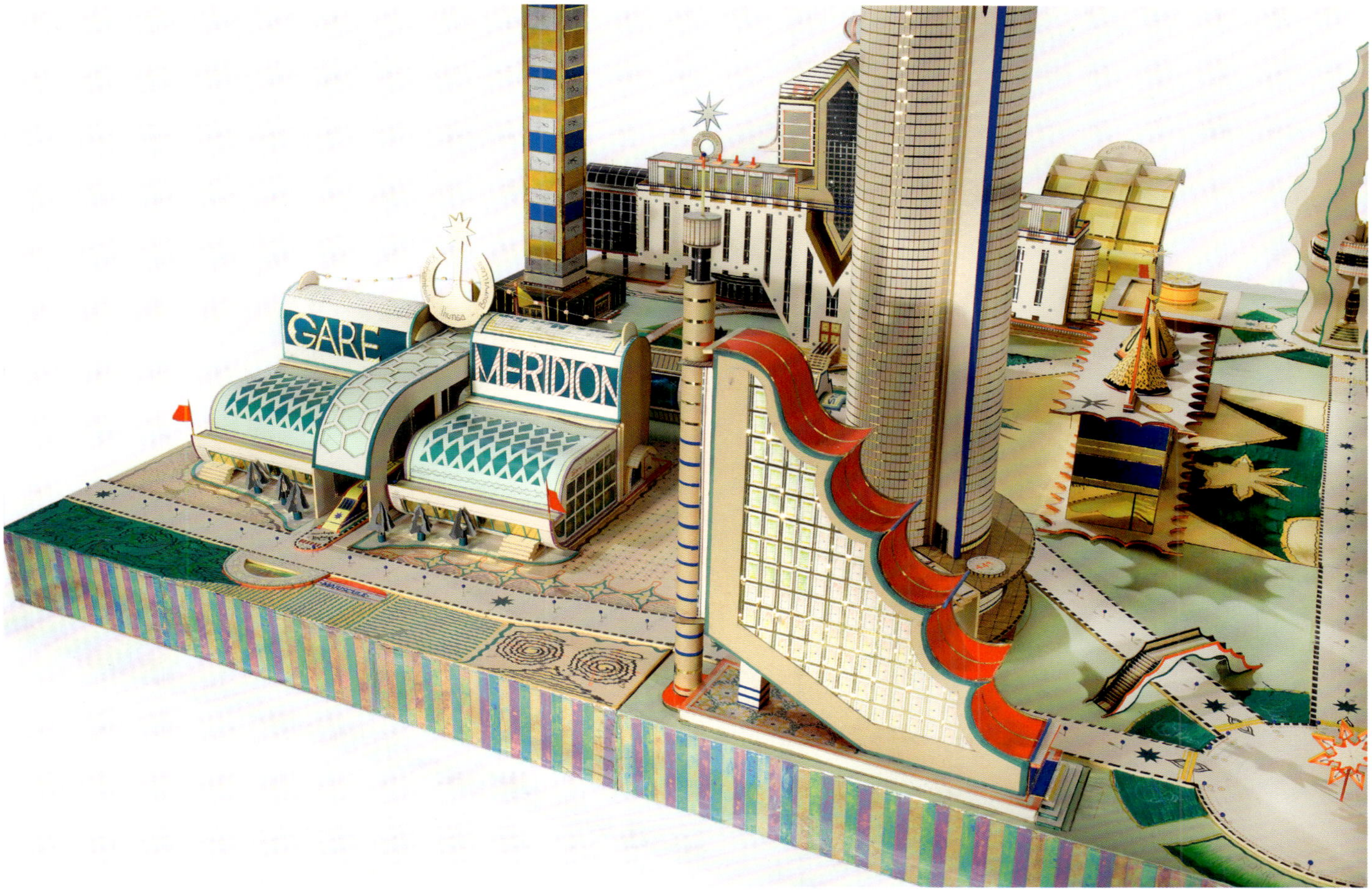
GARE
MERIDION

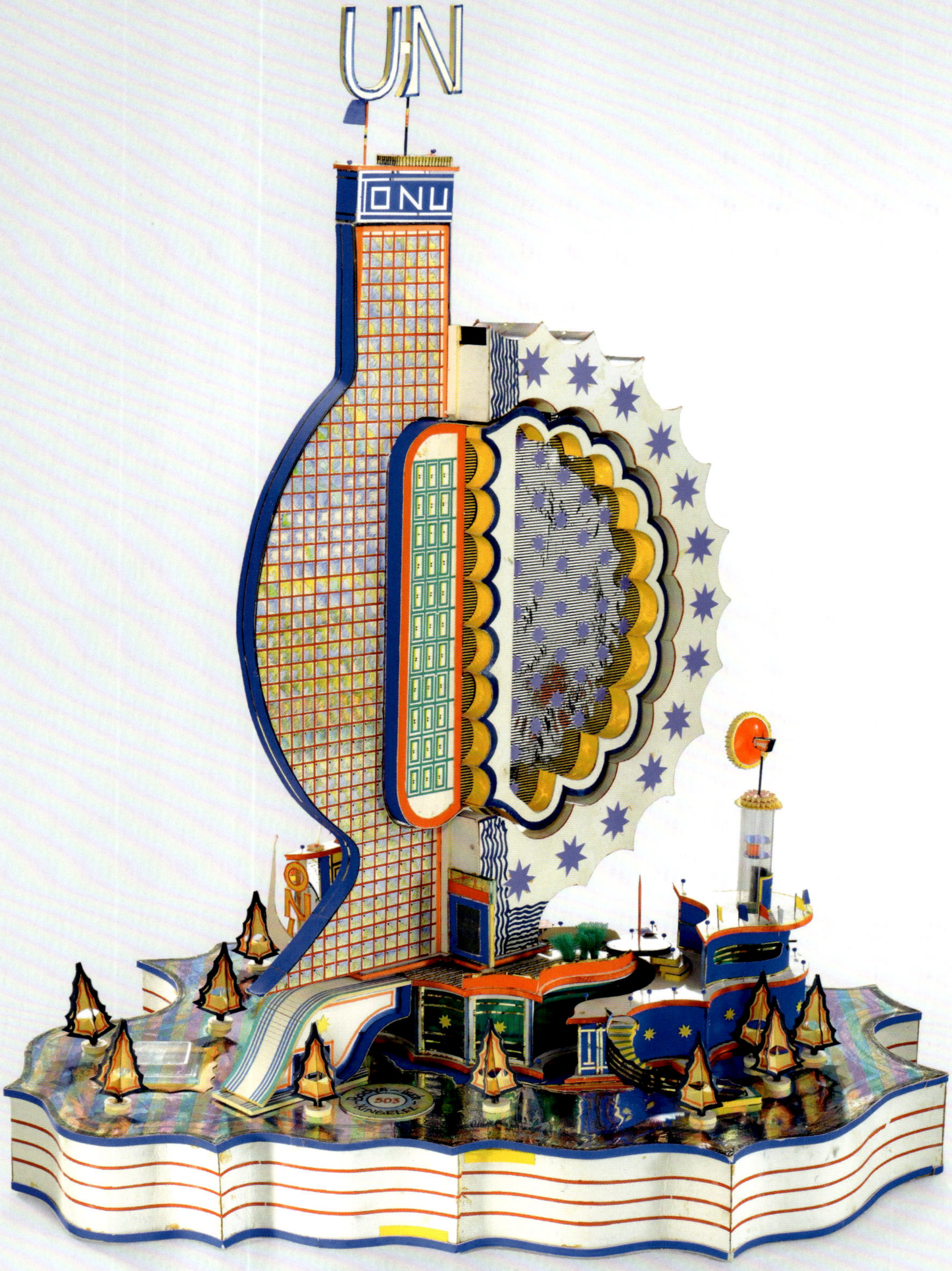

27

U.N. 1995

35 13⁄16 x 29 1⁄8 x 20 7⁄8" (91 x 74 x 53 cm), irreg.

CAAC—The Pigozzi Collection, Geneva

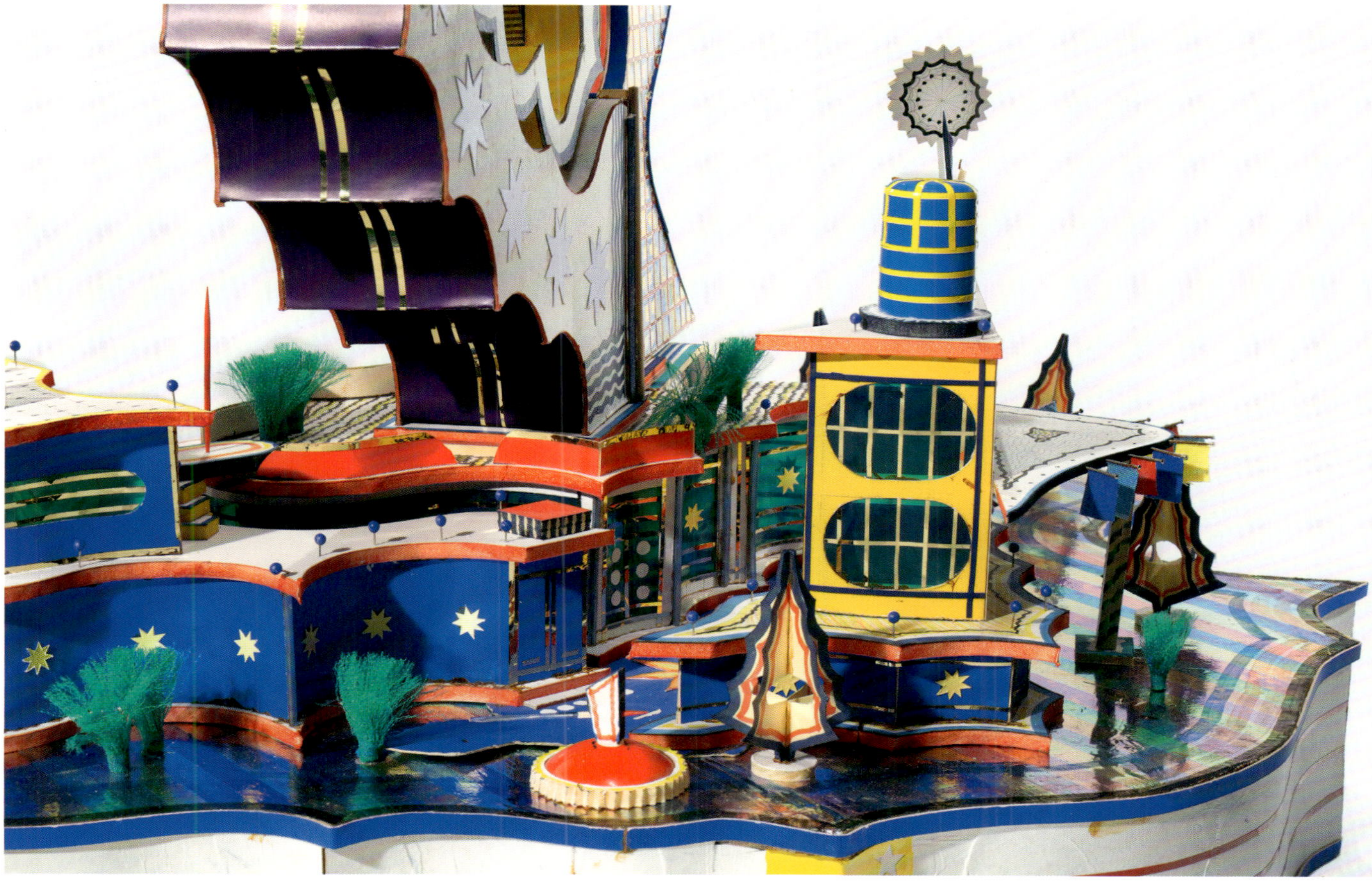

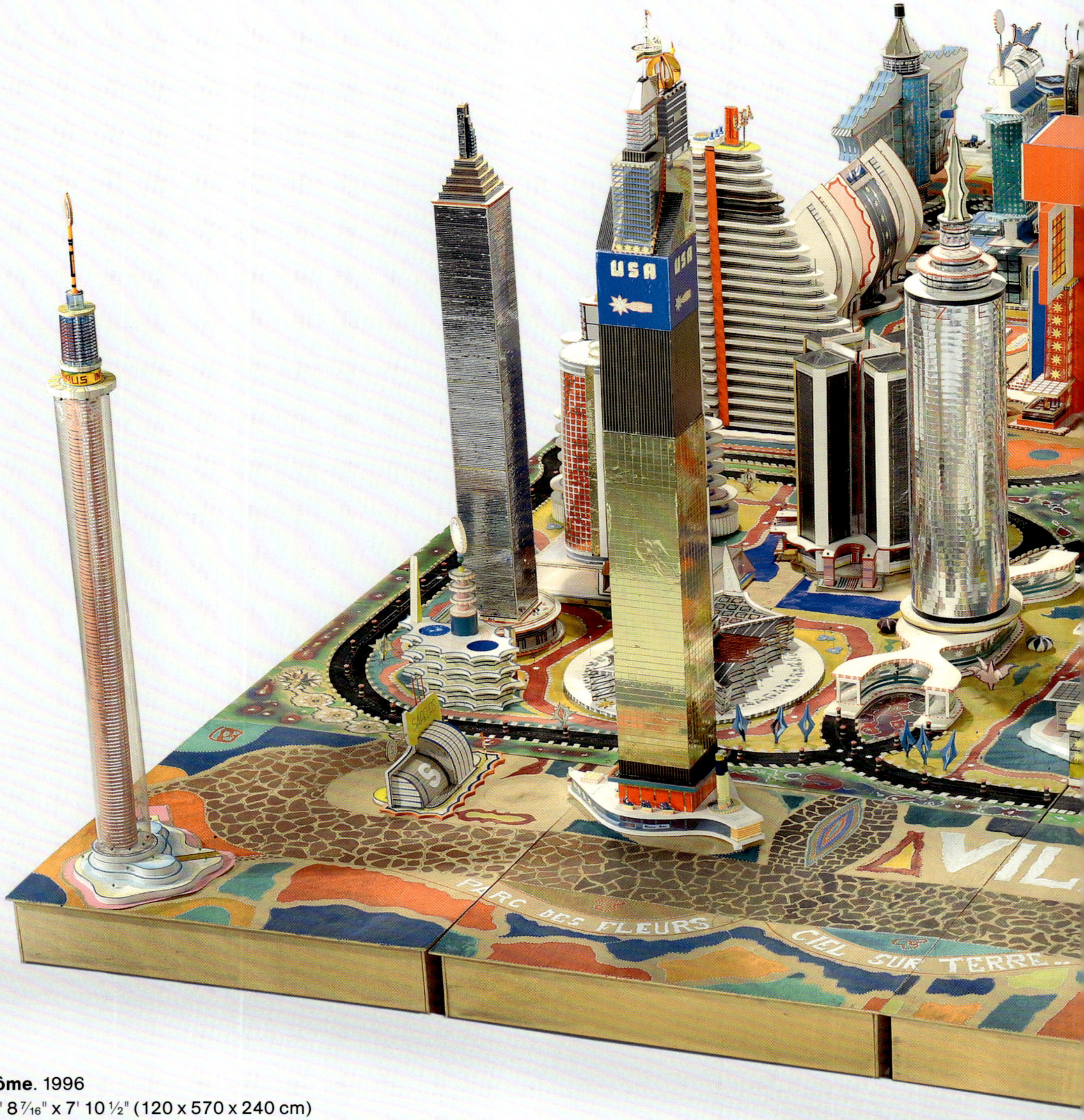

28

Ville Fantôme. 1996
47 ¼" x 18' 8 7⁄16" x 7' 10 ½" (120 x 570 x 240 cm)
CAAC—The Pigozzi Collection, Geneva

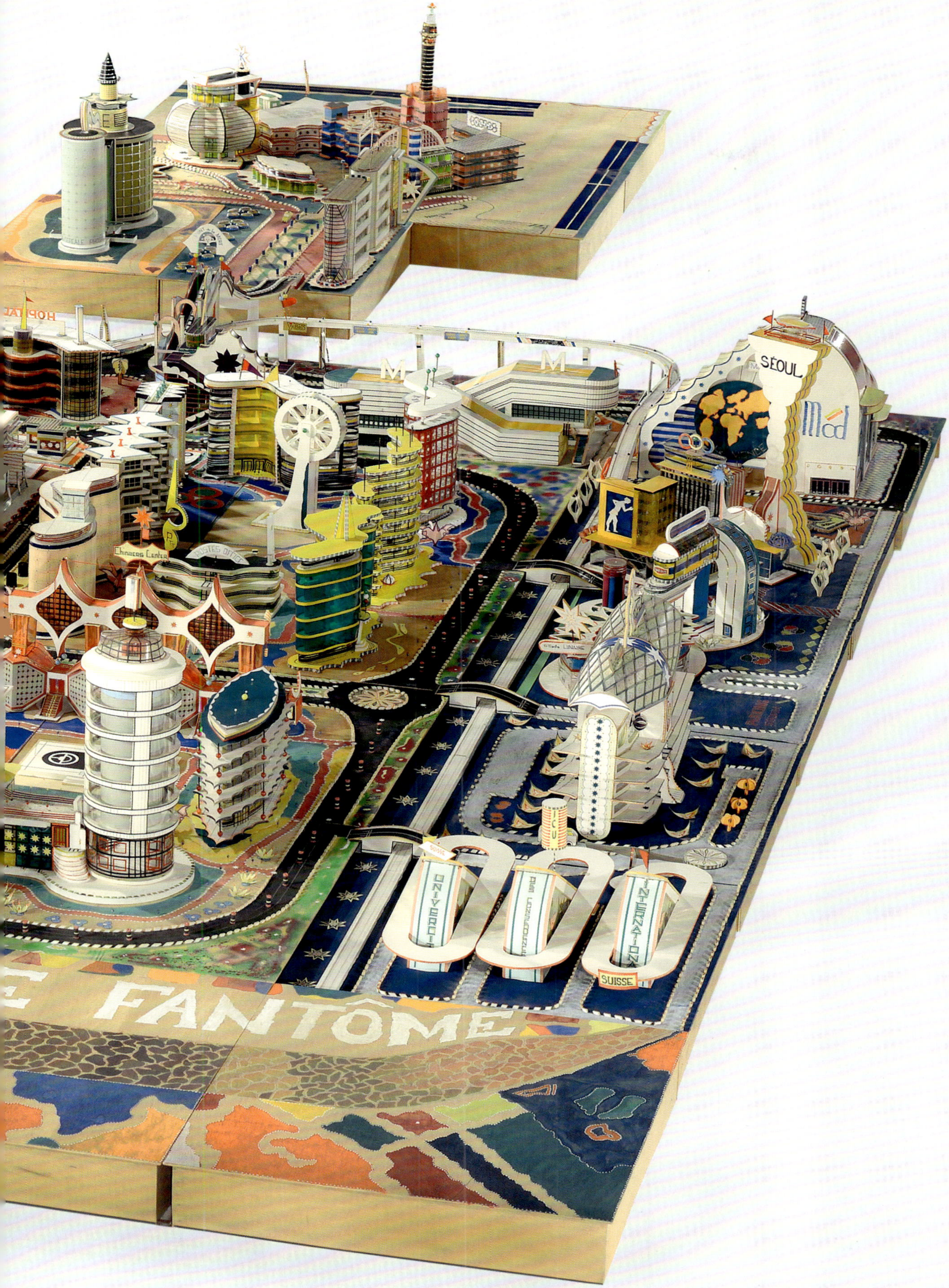
SÉOUL
FANTÔME
SUISSE

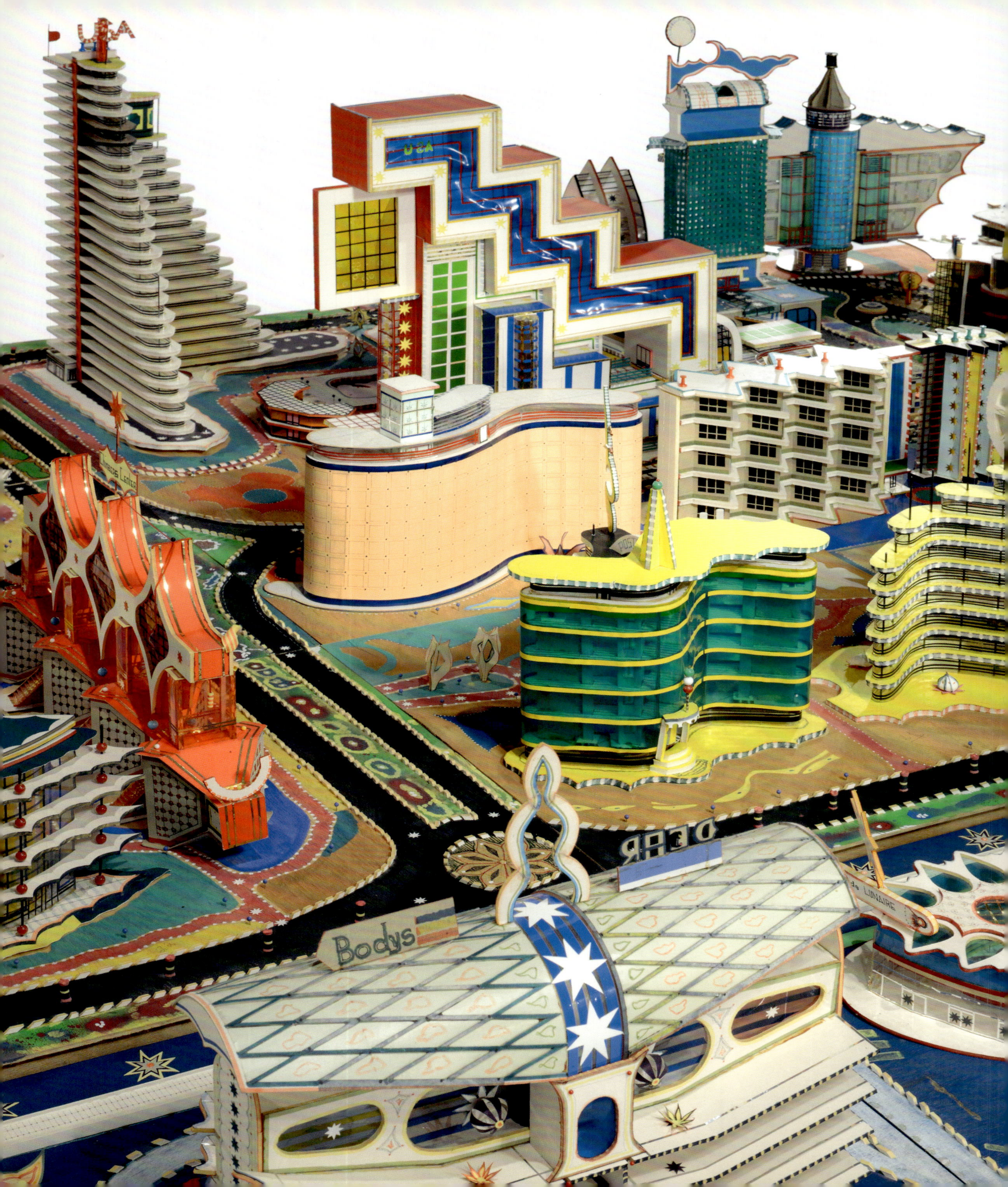
Bodys

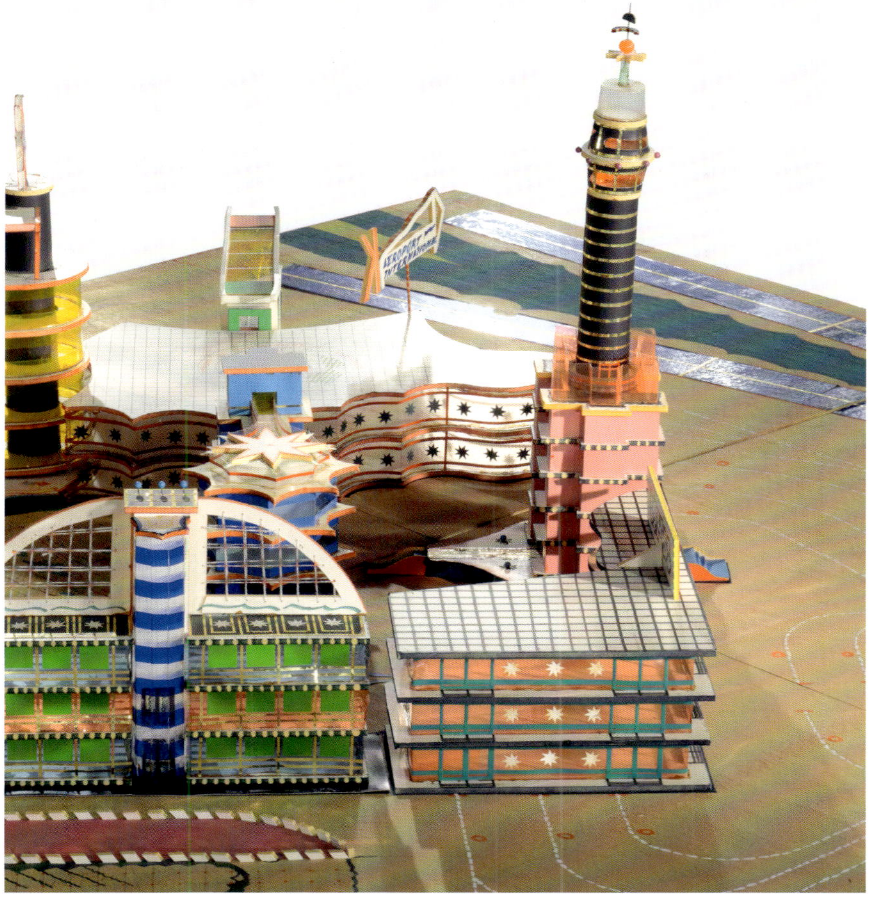

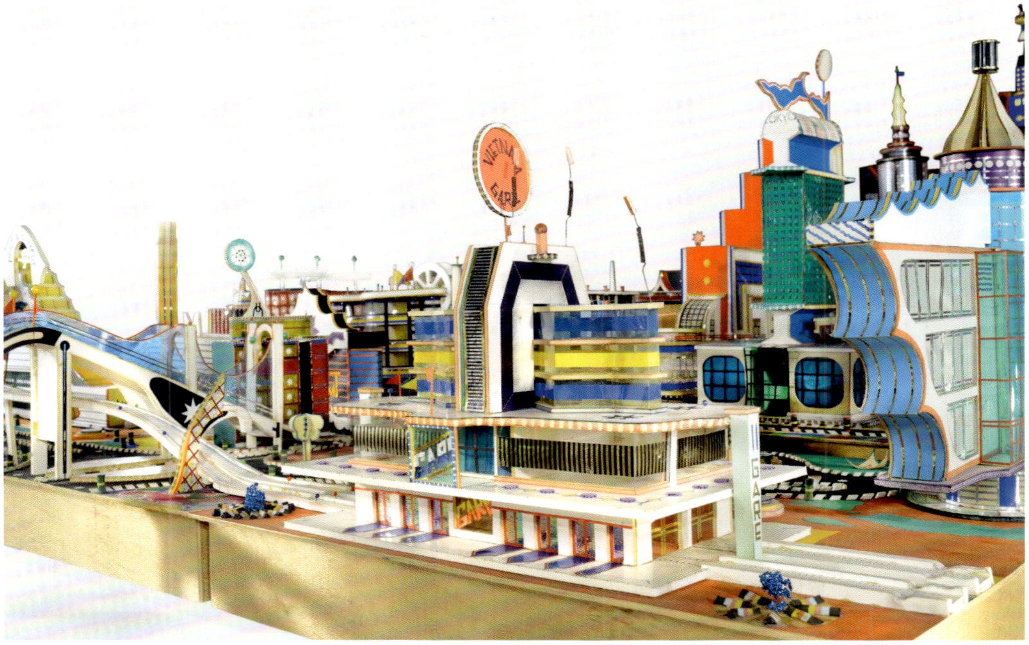
GARE

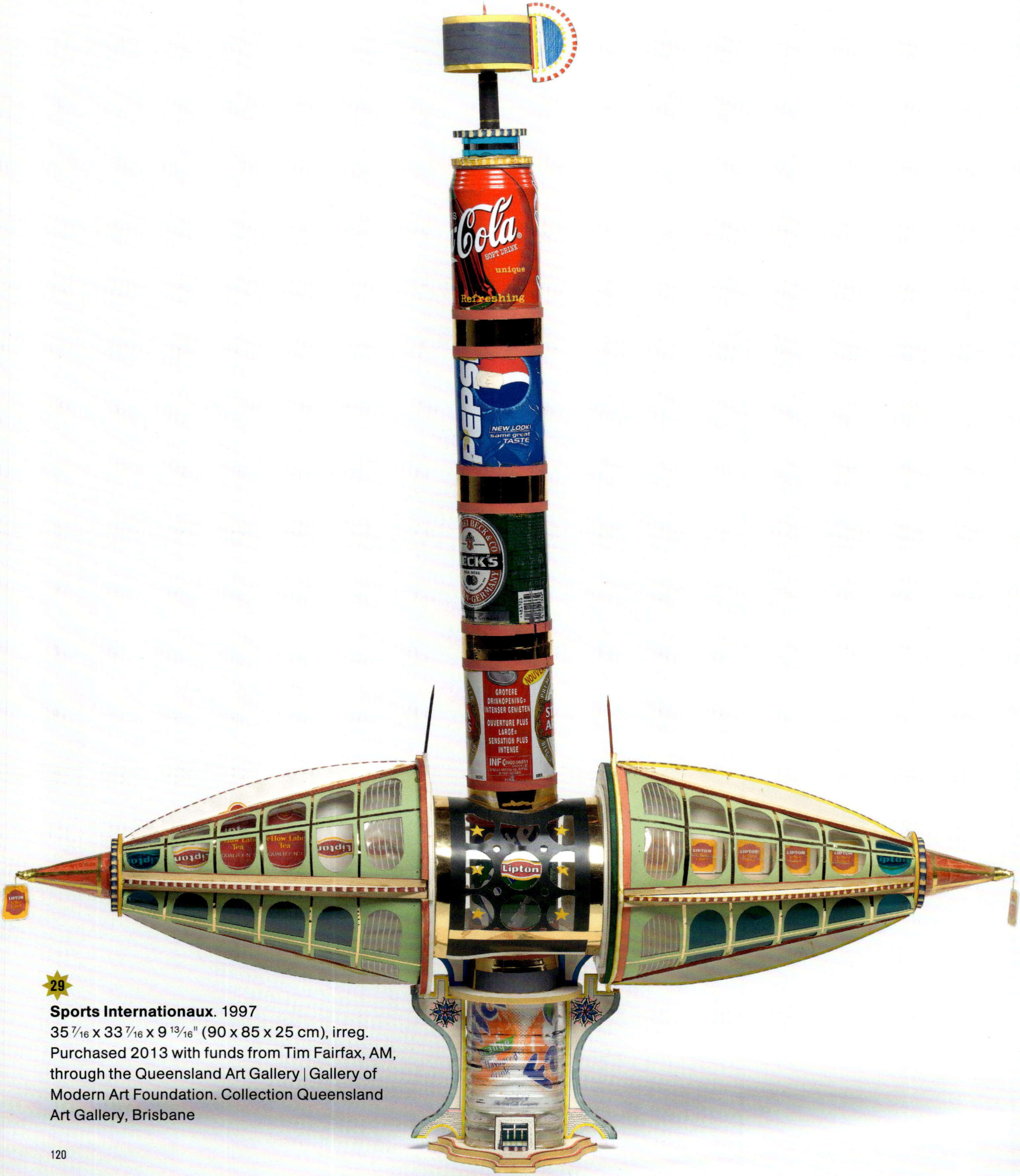

29

Sports Internationaux. 1997
35 7⁄16 x 33 7⁄16 x 9 13⁄16" (90 x 85 x 25 cm), irreg.
Purchased 2013 with funds from Tim Fairfax, AM, through the Queensland Art Gallery | Gallery of Modern Art Foundation. Collection Queensland Art Gallery, Brisbane

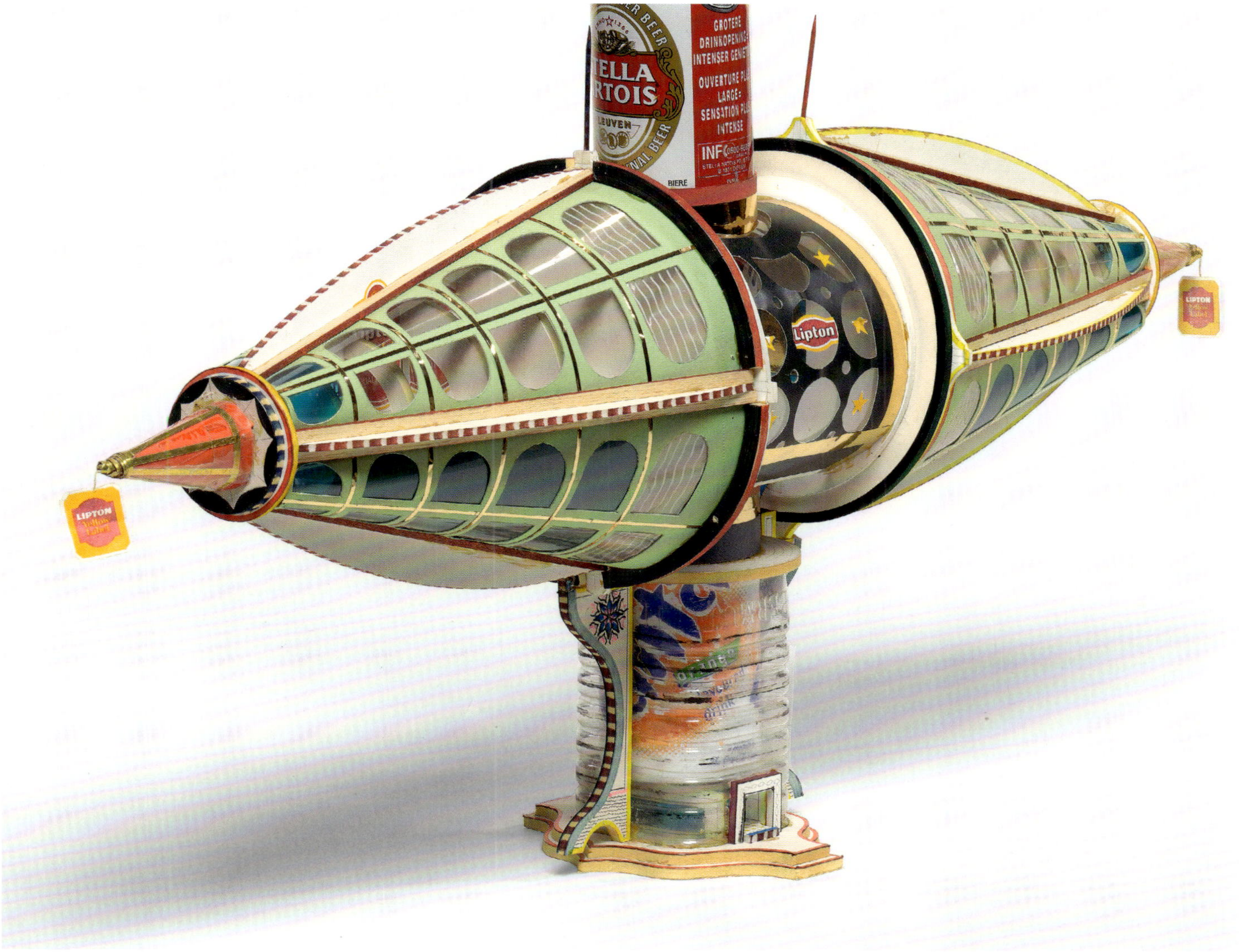
LEUVEN
GROTERE
INTENSE
BIERE
Lipton
LIPTON

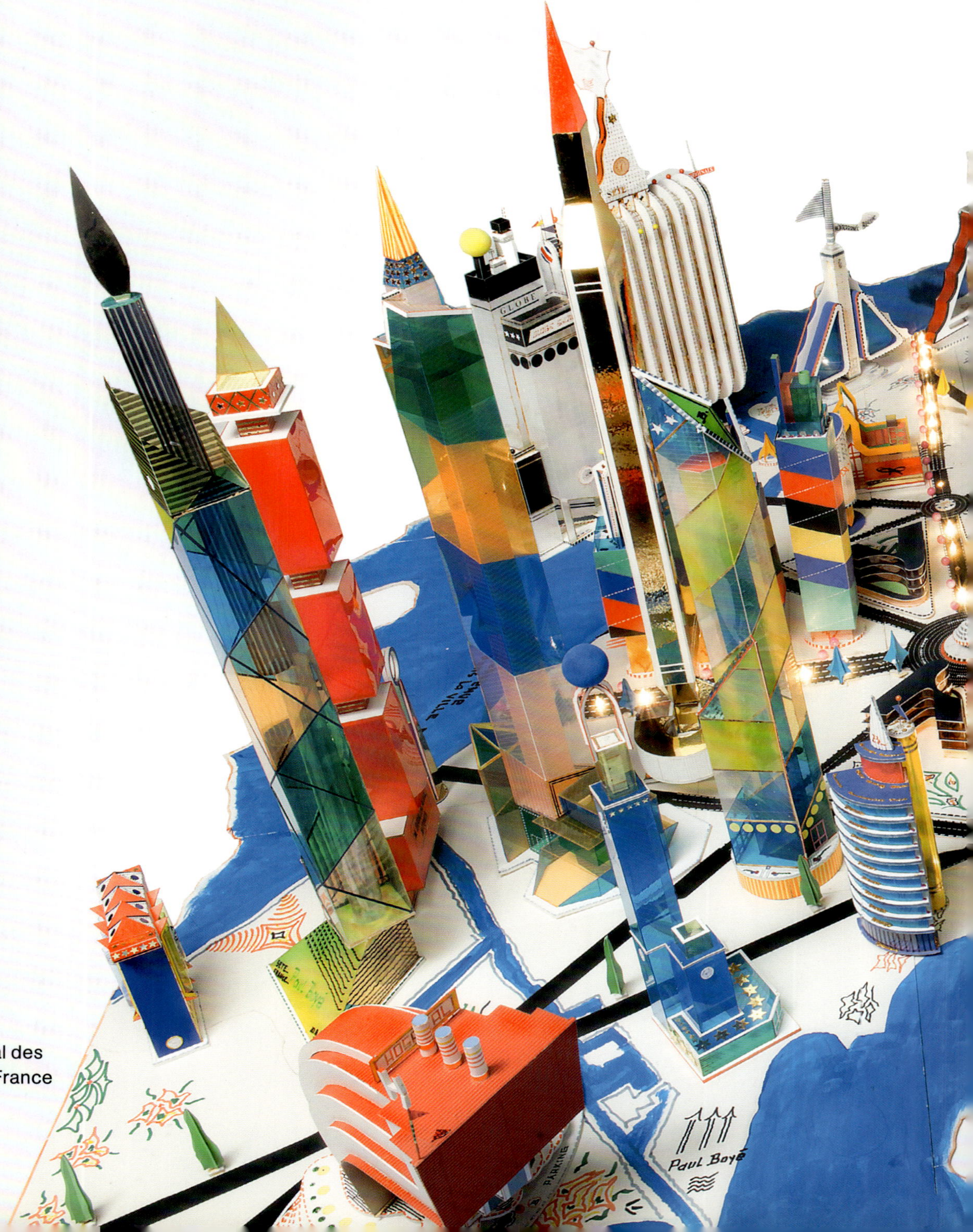

30

Ville de Sète 3009. 2000
31 1/2" x 9' 10 1/8" x 6' 10 11/16"
(80 x 300 x 210 cm)
Collection Musée International des Arts Modestes (MIAM), Sète, France

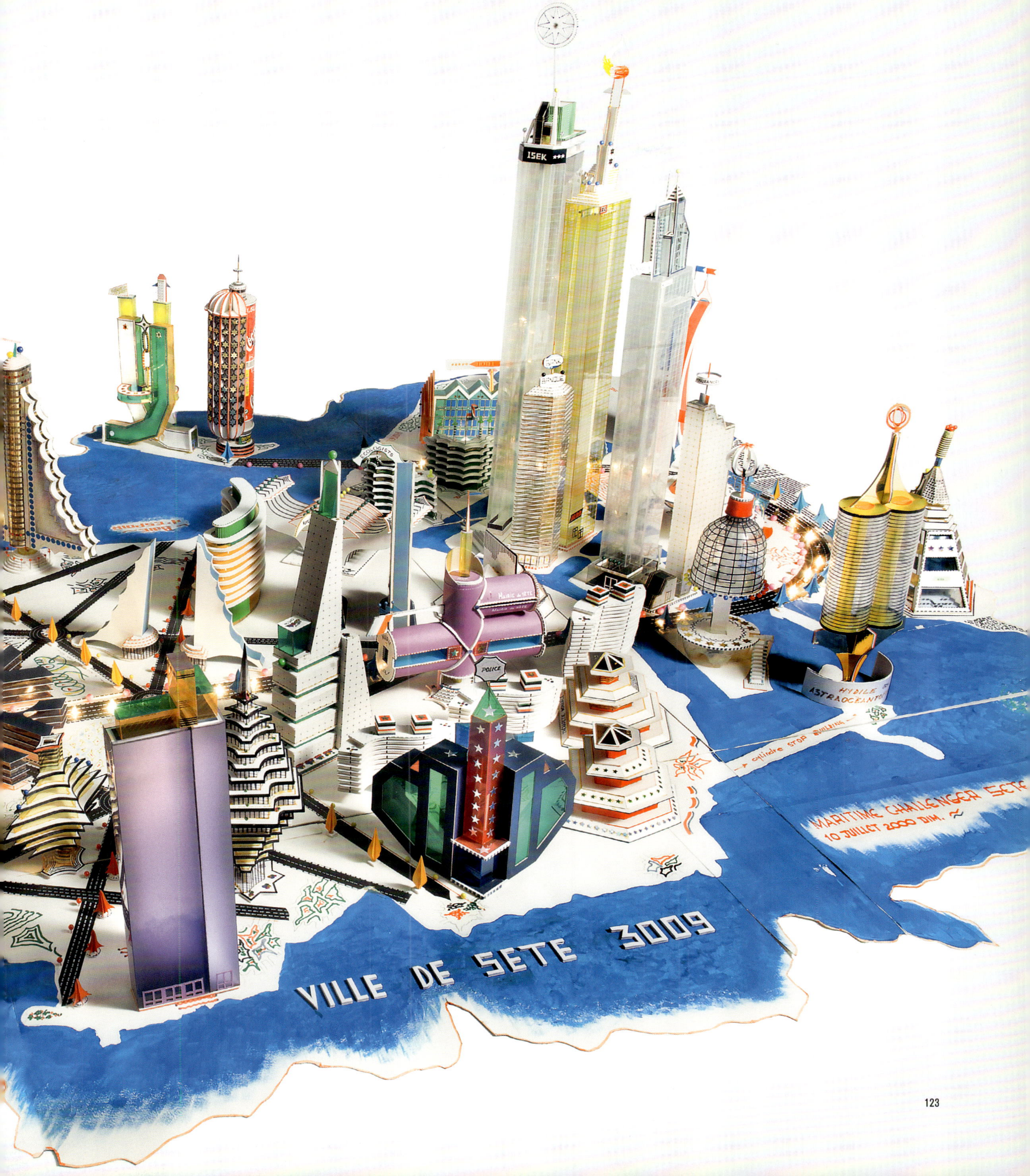
ISEK
POLICE
MARITIME CHALLENGER SETE
10 JUILLET 2000 DIM.
VILLE DE SETE 3009

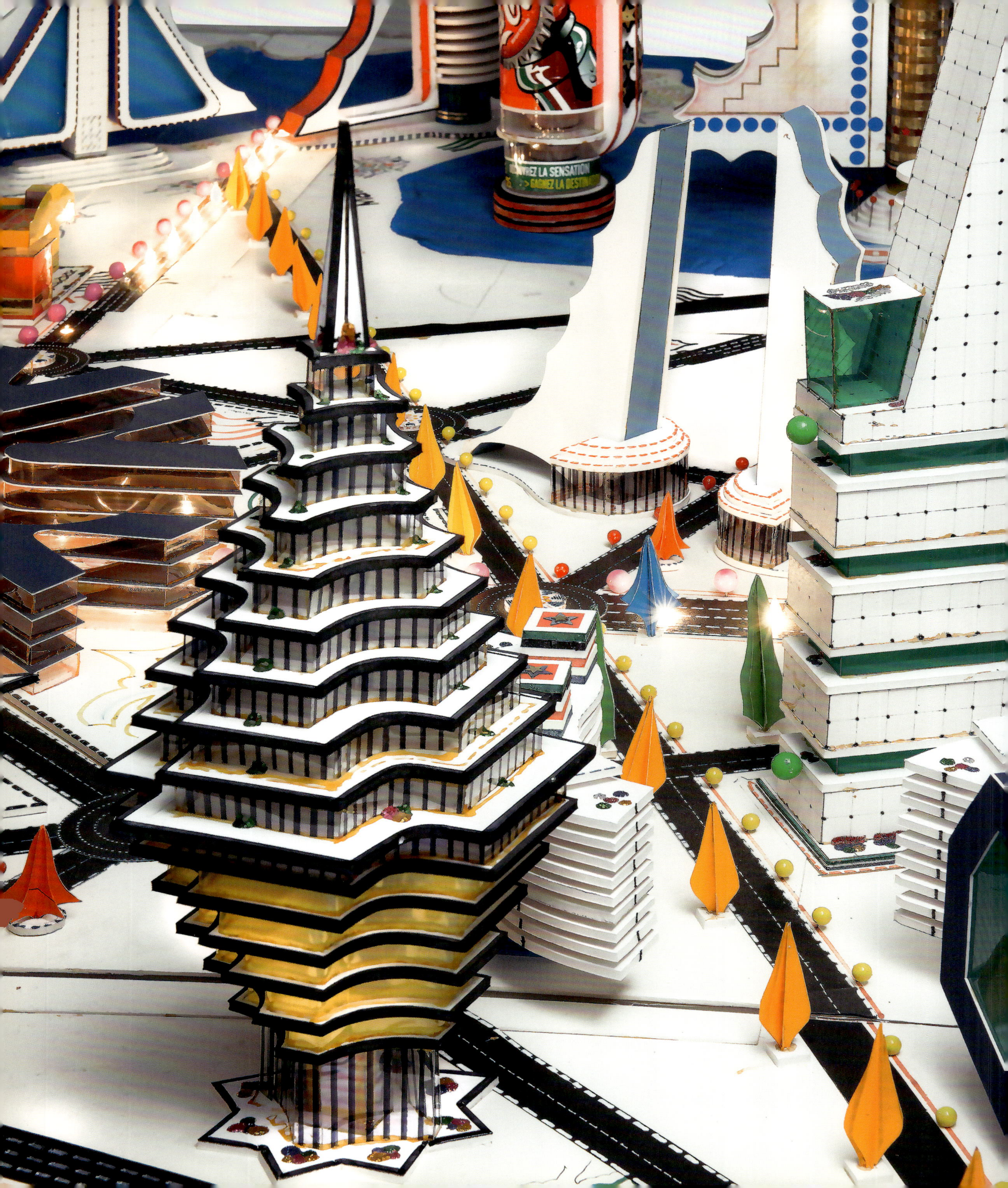
LA SENSATION

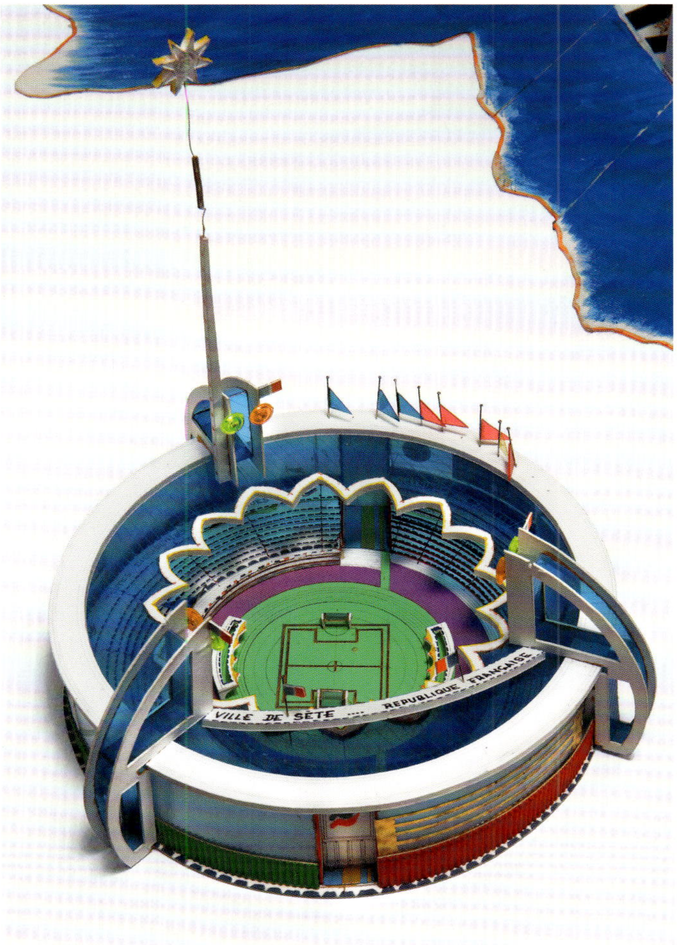
VILLE DE SÈTE ... REPUBLIQUE FRANÇAISE

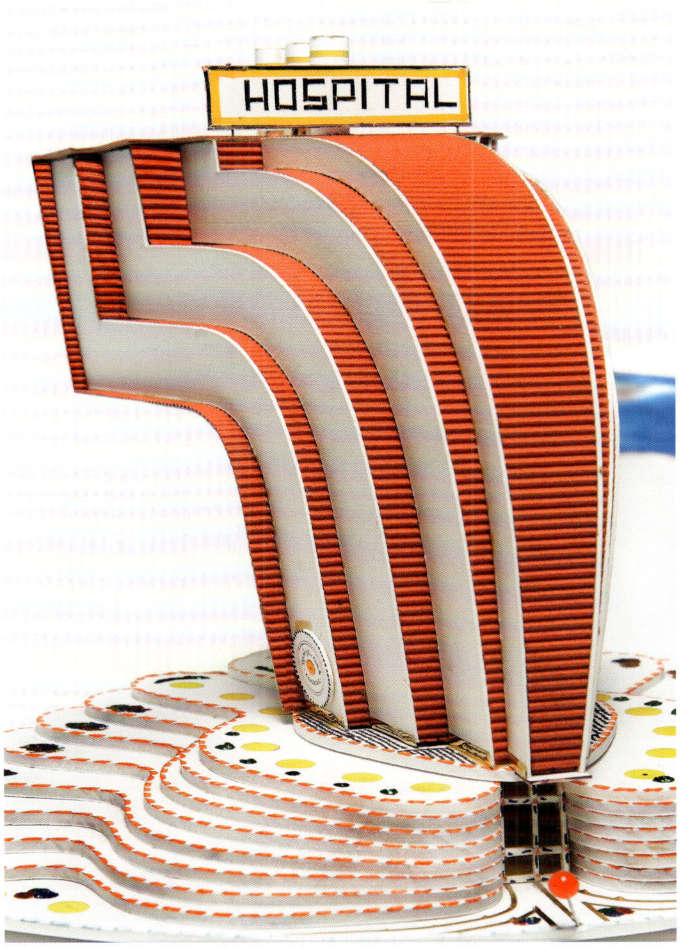
HOSPITAL

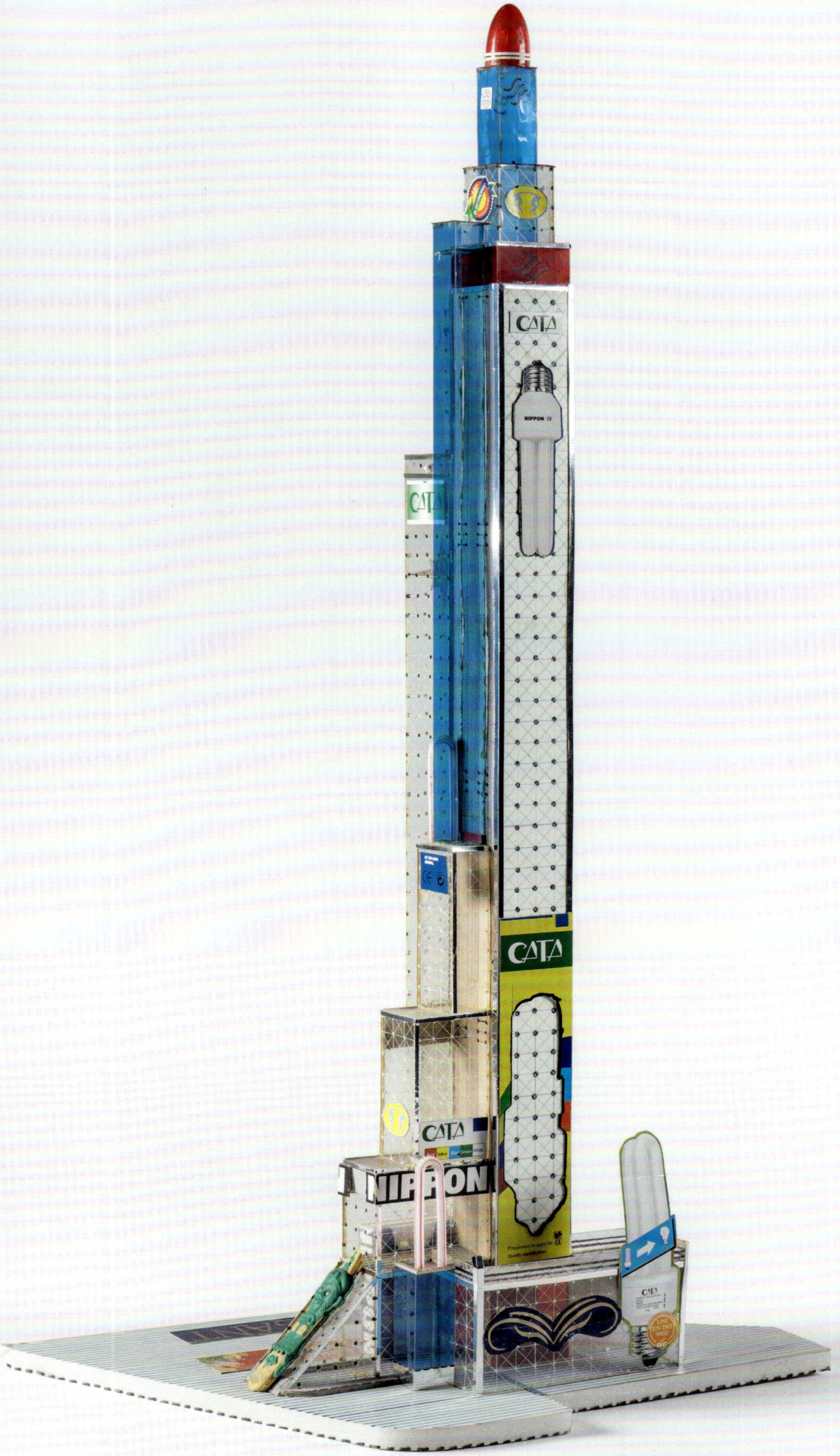

31

Nippon Tower. 2005
26 ⅜ x 13 ⅜ x 8 11/16"
(67 x 34 x 22 cm), irreg.
Courtesy Aeroplastics
Contemporary, Brussels

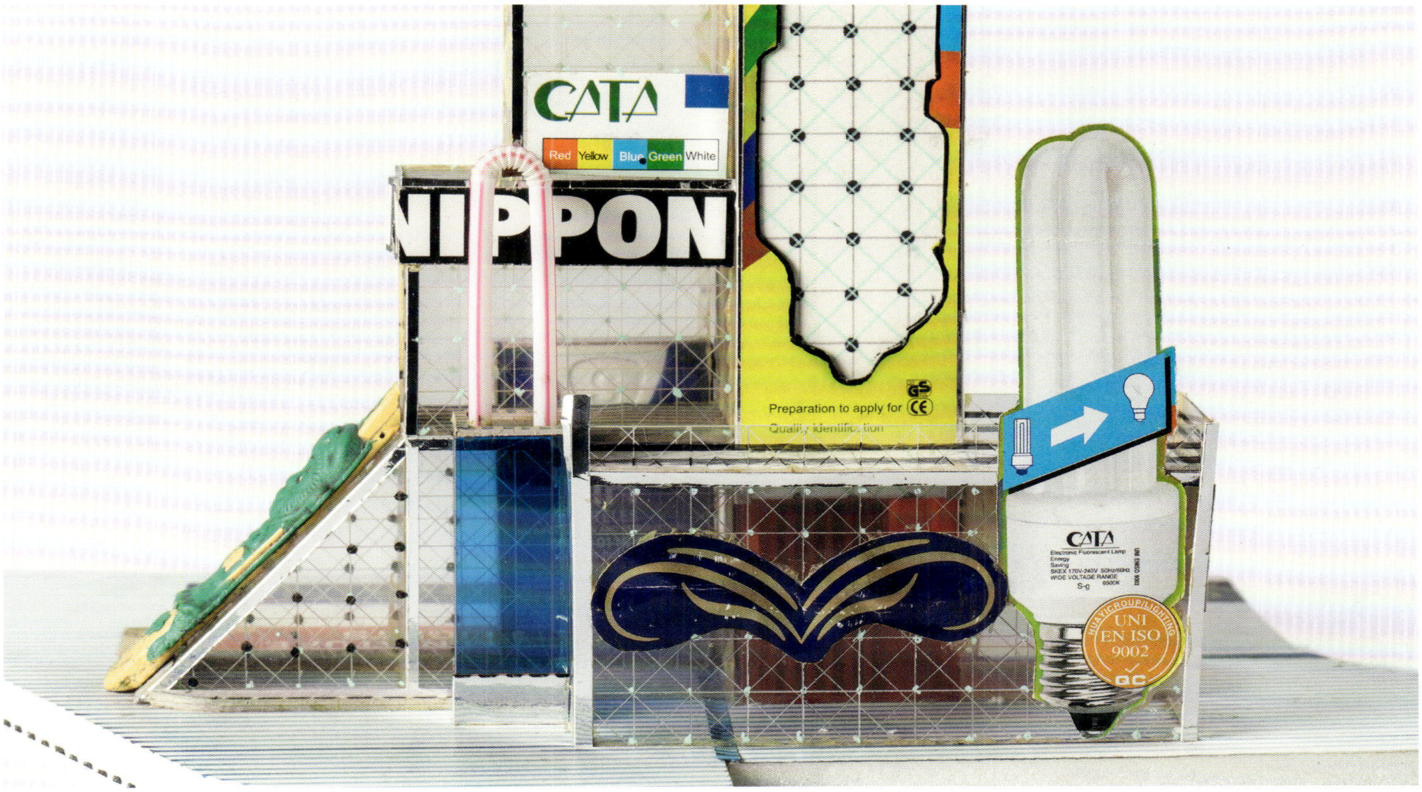
CATA
Red Yellow Blue Green White
NIPPON
Preparation to apply for
CATA
UNI
EN ISO
9002
QC

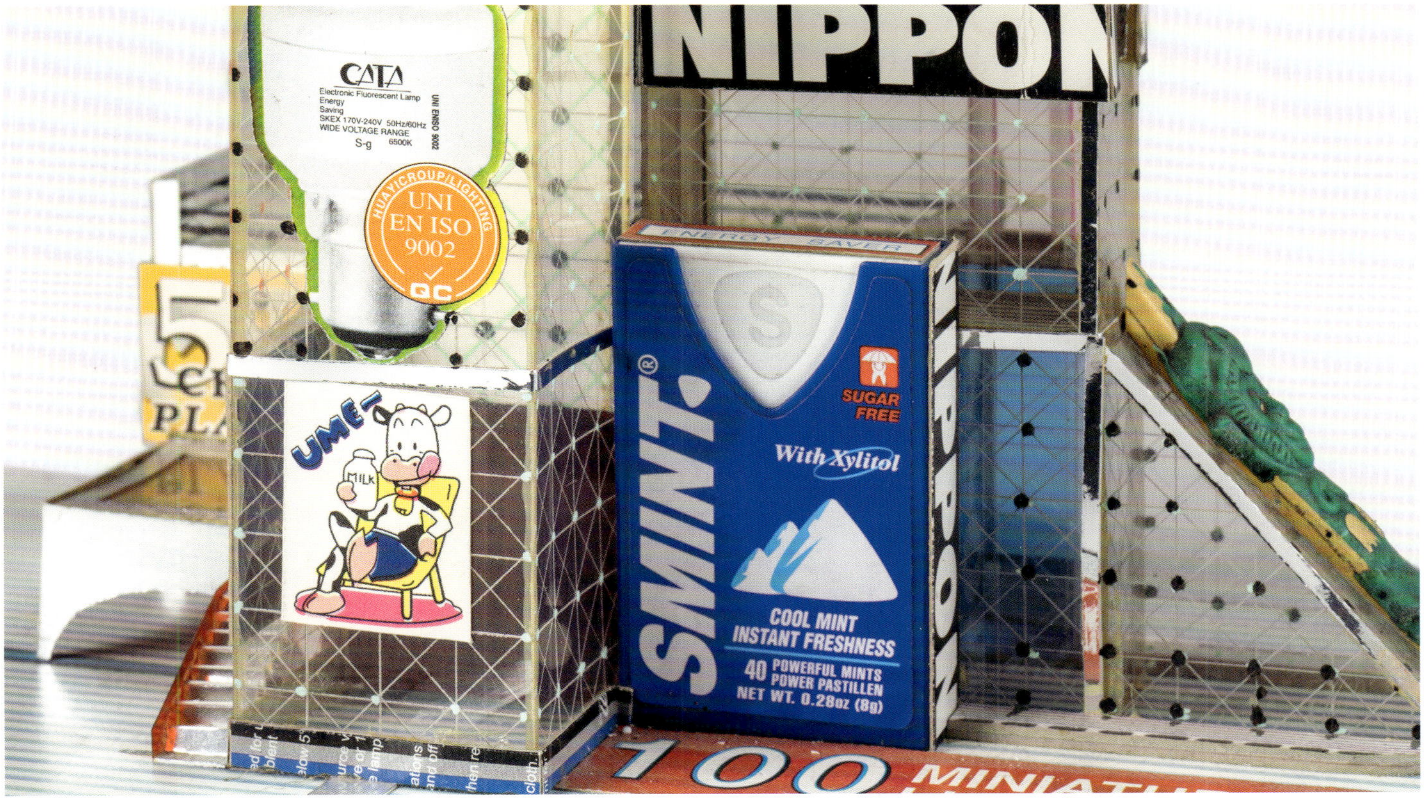
NIPPON
CATA
Electronic Fluorescent Lamp
Energy
Saving
SKEX 170V-240V 50Hz/60Hz
WIDE VOLTAGE RANGE
S-g 6500K
HUAVICROUP/LIGHTING
UNI
EN ISO
9002
QC
UME
MILK
ENERGY SAVER
SMINT
SUGAR FREE
With Xylitol
COOL MINT
INSTANT FRESHNESS
40 POWERFUL MINTS
POWER PASTILLEN
NET WT. 0.28oz (8g)
100

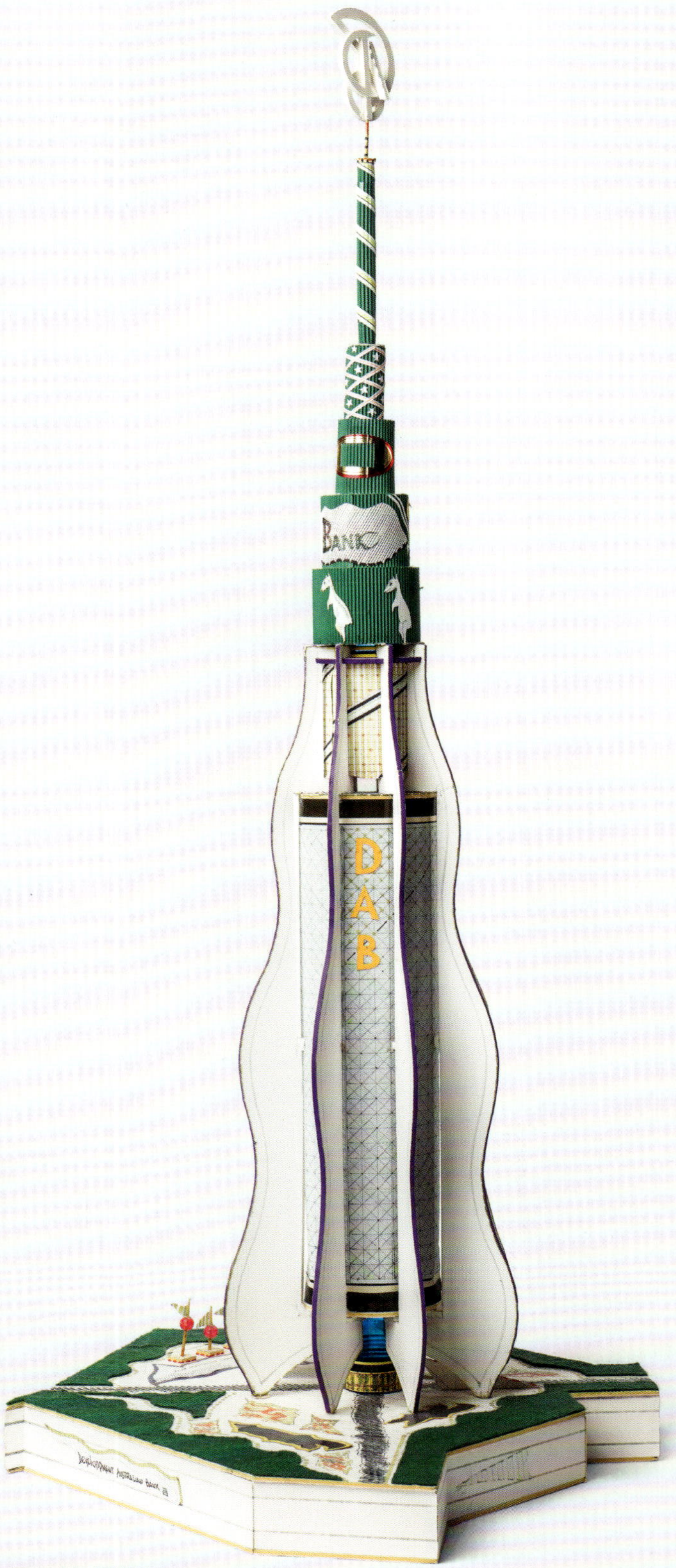

32

DAB (Development Australian Bank). 2007
39 3/8 x 18 1/8 x 16 15/16" (100 x 46 x 43 cm), irreg.
Collection LSO

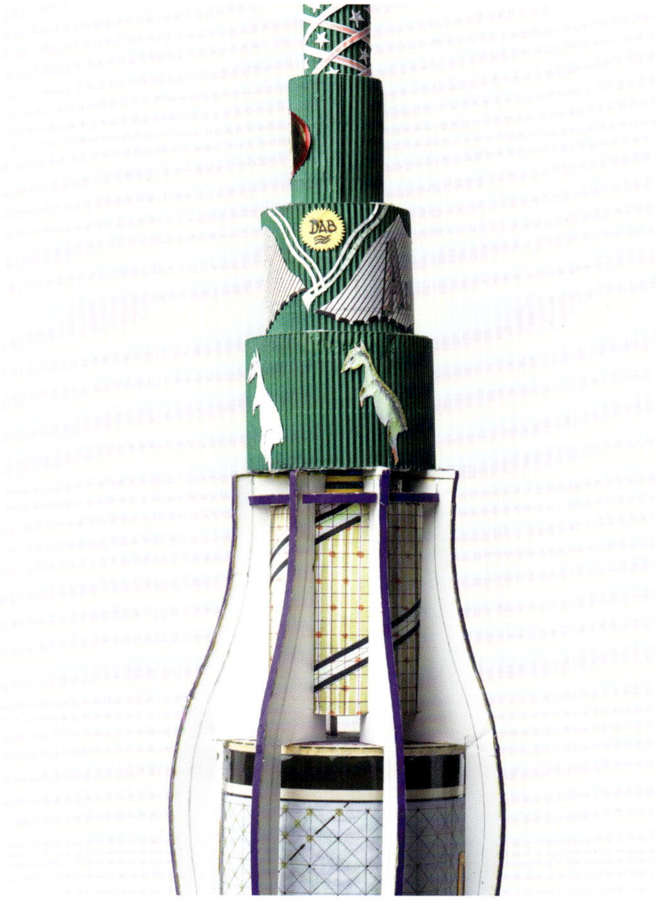

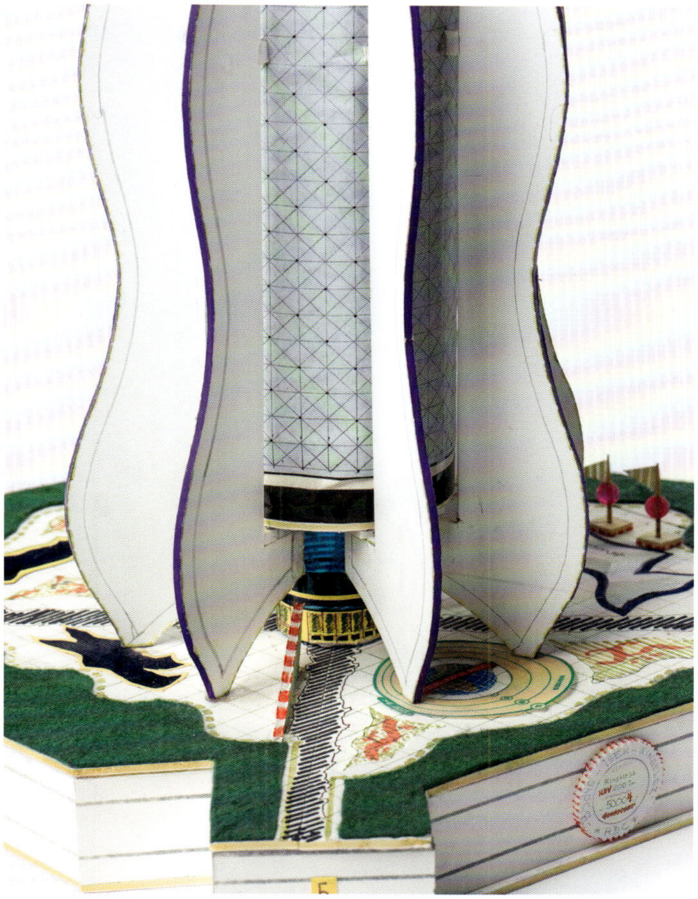

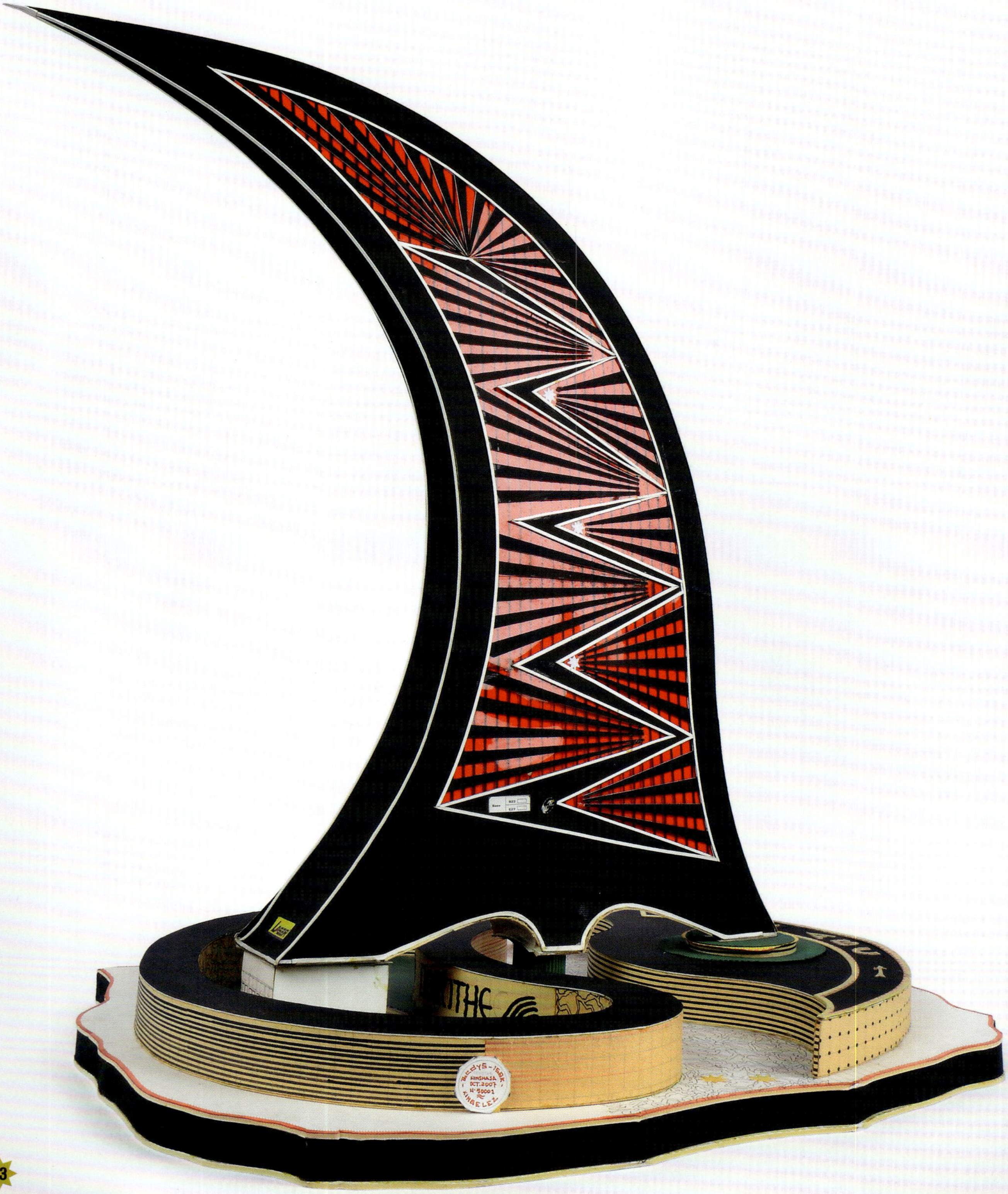

33

Dorothe. 2007
28 ⅜ x 24 13⁄16 x 19 11⁄16" (72 x 63 x 50 cm), irreg.
Courtesy The Museum of Everything

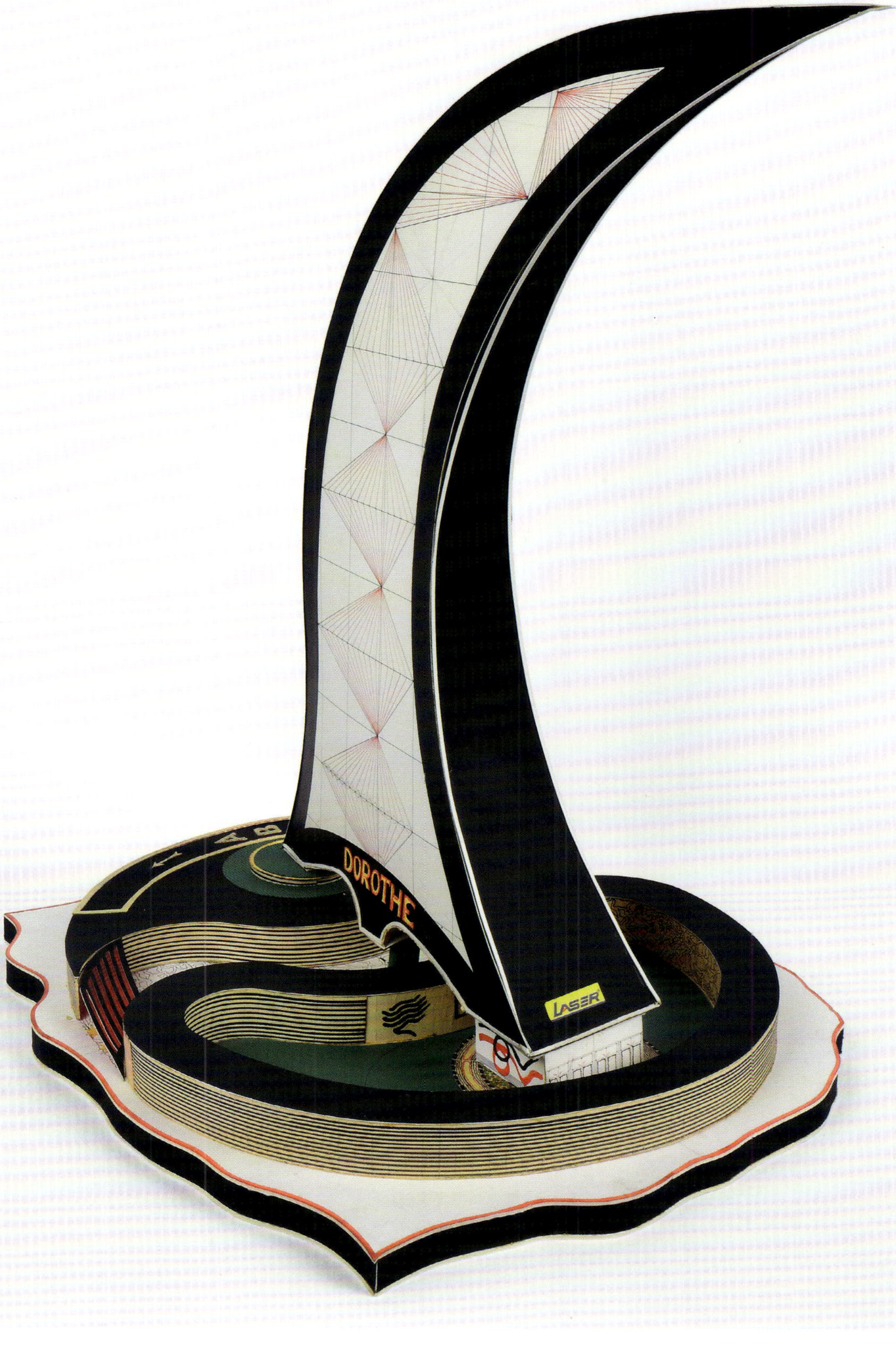
DOROTHE
LASER

SELECTED EXHIBITIONS

Compiled by Hil ary Reder

Solo Exhibitions

1992

Bodys Isek Kingelez: Architekturvisionen aus Zaire. Haus der Kulturen der Welt, Berlin. May 22–October 4, 1992.

1995

Bodys Isek Kingelez. Fondation Cartier pour l'Art Contemporain, Paris. June 23–September 10, 1995.

2001

Bodys Isek Kingelez. Kunstverein in Hamburg. March 3–May 6, 2001. Traveled to Museum Villa Stuck, Munich, with the title *Bodys Isek Kingelez—Extreme Modelle*, January 24–April 28, 2002. Organized in collaboration with CAAC—The Pigozzi Collection.

2003

Bodys Isek Kingelez. La Médiatine, Centre Culturel Wolu-Culture, Brussels. April 3–May 18, 2003.

2005

Perspectives 145: Bodys Isek Kingelez. Contemporary Arts Museum Houston. January 29–May 1, 2005.

Group Exhibitions

1989

Magiciens de la terre. Centre Georges Pompidou and Grande Halle de la Villette, Paris. May 18–August 14, 1989.

1990

WAAAAW! (A Far African Art). Kortrijk 1302 (formerly Groeningeabdij), Kortrijk, Belgium. Dates unknown.

1991

África hoy: Obras de la Contemporary African Art Collection. Centro Atlántico de Arte Moderno, Las Palmas de Gran Canaria, Spain. September 17–November 17, 1991. Traveled to Groninger Museum, Groningen, Netherlands, December 7, 1991–February 9, 1992, and Centro Cultural Arte Contemporáneo, Mexico City, February 20–June 7, 1992.

1992

Out of Africa: The Jean Pigozzi Contemporary African Art Collection at the Saatchi Collection. Saatchi Gallery, London. October 30–December 19, 1992.

1993

Ma quête d'architecture, maquettes d'architectures. Pavillon de l'Arsenal, Paris. June 1—August 1, 1993.

Home and the World: Architectural Sculpture by Aboudramane and Bodys Isek Kingelez. Museum for African Art, New York. June 6,1993–January 7, 1994.

La grande vérité, les astres africains. Musée des Beaux-Arts de Nantes, France. June 25–September 25, 1993.

1994

V Bienal de la Habana. Museo Nacional de Bellas Artes, Havana. May 6–June 30, 1994.

Crudo y cocido. Museo Nacional Centro de Arte Reina Sofía, Madrid. December 14, 1994–March 6, 1995.

1995

Dialogues de paix. Palais des Nations, Geneva. July 3–October 24, 1995.

Big City: Artists from Africa. Serpentine Gallery, London. September 21–November 5, 1995.

1996

Er bestaat geen kunst in Afrika. Stadsgalerij Heerlen, Heerlen, Netherlands. January 13–March 17, 1996.

Neue Kunst aus Afrika. Haus der Kulturen der Welt, Berlin. March 9–May 5, 1996.

Jordens huse. Øksnehallen, Copenhagen. June 5–July 14, 1996.

D'autres ajouts d'été. Musée d'Art Moderne et Contemporain, Geneva. June 7–October 27, 1996. Organized in collaboration with CAAC—The Pigozzi Collection.

Inklusion: Exklusion. Kunst im Zeitalter von Postkolonialismus und globaler Migration. Künstlerhaus, Graz, Austria. September 22–October 26, 1996.

Bomoi mobimba—Toute la vie: 7 artistes zaïrois. Collection Lucien Bilinelli. Palais des Beaux-Arts de Charleroi, Belgium. October 26–December 22, 1996.

1997

Projects 59: Architecture as Metaphor. The Museum of Modern Art, New York. April 10–June 3, 1997.

97 Kwangju Biennale: Unmapping the Earth. Various locations, Kwangju, South Korea. September 1–November 26, 1997.

Veilleurs du monde: Gbêdji kpontolè. Centre Culturel Français, Cotonou, Benin. September 8–25, 1997. Traveled to the Musée des Arts d'Afrique et d'Océanie, Paris, November 4, 1998–January 4, 1999.

Trade Routes: History and Geography. 2nd Johannesburg Biennale. Various locations, Johannesburg, South Africa. October 12–December 12, 1997.

1998

Àlbum: Una selecció dels fons de la Fondation Cartier pour l'art contemporain. Fundació Joan Miró, Barcelona. March 6–April 26, 1998.

Dak'Art 98: Biennale de l'art africain contemporain. Various locations, Dakar, Senegal. April 20–30, 1998.

Africa Africa: Vibrant New Art from a Dynamic Continent. Tobu Museum of Art, Tokyo. September 11–November 24, 1998.

Unfinished History. Walker Art Center, Minneapolis. October 18, 1998–January 10, 1999. Traveled to Museum of Contemporary Art Chicago, January 30–April 4, 1999.

1999

1 monde réel. Fondation Cartier pour l'Art Contemporain, Paris. June 29–November 13, 1999.

Kunst-Welten im Dialog: Von Gauguin zur globalen Gegenwart. Museum Ludwig, Cologne. November 5, 1999–March 3, 2000.

Carnegie International 1999/2000. Carnegie Museum of Art, Pittsburgh. November 6, 1999–March 26, 2000.

Mirror's Edge. Bildmuseet, Umeå, Sweden. November 21, 1999–February 20, 2000. Traveled to Vancouver Art Gallery, March 18–July 9, 2000; Castello di Rivoli, Turin, October 5, 2000–January 14, 2001; and Tramway, Glasgow, March 2–April 15, 2001.

Zeitwenden: Ausblick. Kunstmuseum Bonn. December 14, 1999–June 4, 2000. Traveled to Museum Moderner Kunst Stiftung Ludwig Wien, Vienna, July 5–October 1, 2000.

Collezionismi: La collezione della Fondation Cartier pour l'art contemporain. Centro Arte Contemporanea, Palazzo delle Papesse, Siena, Italy. December 19, 1999–March 5, 2000.

2000

Contra la arquitectura. La urgencia de (re)pensar la ciudad. Espai d'Art Contemporani de Castelló, Castello, Spain. April 26–June 25, 2000.

Out of Space—Schnitt Ausstellungsraum zu Gast im Kölnischer Kunstverein. Kölnischer Kunstverein, Cologne. May 13–July 2, 2000.

12th Biennale of Sydney. Museum of Contemporary Art Australia, Sydney. May 26–July 30, 2000.

Domiciles, de la maison à la ville, de la construction à la ruine. Centre d'Art de Tanlay, France. May 27–October 1, 2000.

Visions du futur: Une histoire des peurs et des espoirs de l'humanité. Grand Palais, Paris. October 5, 2000–January 1, 2001.

2000 Shanghai Biennale: Spirit of Shanghai. Shanghai Art Museum. November 6, 2000–January 6, 2001.

Afrika sana: La peinture congolaise d'hier et d'aujourd'hui. Salle d'Exposition du quai Antoine 1er, Port de Monaco. December 22, 2000–February 11, 2001.

2001

An/Sichten: Malerei aus dem Kongo 1990–2000. Museum für Völkerkunde, Vienna. February 1–July 1, 2001.

The Short Century: Independence and Liberation Movements in Africa, 1945–1994. Museum Villa Stuck, Munich. February 15–April 22, 2001. Traveled to Martin Gropius Bau, Berlin, May 18–July 29, 2001; Museum of Contemporary Art Chicago, September 8–December 30, 2001; and P.S.1 Contemporary Art Center, New York, February 10–May 5, 2002.

New Settlements. Nikolaj Kunsthal, Copenhagen. March 24–May 6, 2001.

Le monde est ma maison. Le Parvis, Centre d'Art Contemporain, Ibos, France. April 21–June 24, 2001.

Áfricas: El artista y la ciudad. Centre de Cultura Contemporània de Barcelona. May 29–September 11, 2001.

ARS 01: Unfolding Perspectives. Kiasma—Museum of Contemporary Art, Helsinki. September 30, 2001–January 20, 2002.

DC: Thomas Bayrle, Bodys Isek Kingelez. Museum Ludwig, Cologne. November 1, 2001–February 17, 2002.

2002

25a Bienal de São Paulo: Iconografias metropolitanas. Ciccillo Matarazzo Pavilion, São Paolo. March 23–June 2, 2002.

Artists Imagine Architecture. Institute of Contemporary Art, Boston. May 22–September 2, 2002.

documenta 11. Platform 5, Kassel, Germany. June 8–September 15, 2002.

Afrikanische Reklamekunst. Iwalewahaus, Universität Bayreuth, Germany. October 24, 2002–February 16, 2003. Traveled to Münchner Stadtmuseum, Munich, March 14–June 30, 2003.

2003

Fault Lines: Contemporary African Art and Shifting Landscapes. Institute of International Visual Arts, London. June 15–November 2, 2003.

Transferts. Palais des Beaux-Arts, Brussels. June 21–September 14, 2003.

The American Effect: Global Perspectives on the United States, 1990–2003. Whitney Museum of American Art, New York. July 3–October 12, 2003.

Un-built Cities. Bonner Kunstverein, Bonn, Germany. December 9, 2003–February 8, 2004.

Kongo Kingdom Art: From Ritual to Cutting Edge. Guangdong Museum of Art, China. December 30, 2003–March 31, 2004. Traveled to Shanghai Art Museum, April 21–June 4, 2004, and National Museum of China, Beijing, July 6–October 9, 2004.

2004

Black Box: Les Afriques. Le Tripostal, Lille, France. March 13–August 8, 2004.

Je m'installe aux abattoirs: La collection d'art contemporain d'agnès b. Les Abattoirs de Toulouse, France. April 9–June 13, 2004.

Africa Remix: Contemporary Art of a Continent. Museum Kunstpalast, Düsseldorf. June 24–November 7, 2004. Traveled to Hayward Gallery, London, February 10–April 17, 2005; Centre Georges Pompidou, Paris, May 24–August 15, 2005; Mori Art Museum, Tokyo, May 27–August 31, 2006; Moderna Museet, Stockholm, October 14, 2006–January 14, 2007; and Johannesburg Art Gallery, Johannesburg, South Africa, June 24–September 30, 2007.

Arti & Architettura 1900–2000. Genova Palazzo Ducale, Genoa. October 2, 2004–February 13, 2005.

2005

African Art Now: Masterpieces from the Jean Pigozzi Collection. Museum of Fine Arts, Houston. January 29–June 5, 2005.

Zeitgenössische Kunst aus Afrika und Europa im Dialog. Iwalewahaus, Universität Bayreuth, Germany. April 28–September 4, 2005.

Avenirs de villes/Futures for Cities. Site Alstom, Nancy, France. May 7–August 22, 2005.

Fantasmapolis: La ville contemporaine et ses imaginaires. Galerie Art et Essai, Rennes, France. May 11–June 18, 2005.

Africa urbis: Perspectives urbaines. Musée des Arts Derniers, Paris. May 20–September 30, 2005.

Modèles, modèles. Musée d'Art Moderne et Contemporain, Geneva. June 7–September 18, 2005.

Il teatro dell'arte: Capolavori dalla collezione del Museo Ludwig di Colonia. Villa Manin di Passariano, Codroipo, Italy. July 9–November 6, 2005.

Arts of Africa: Jean Pigozzi's Contemporary Collection. Grimaldi Forum, Monte Carlo. July 16–September 4, 2005.

2006

Kijken Zonder Grenzen. Hedendaagse kunst in het Afrika Museum, de collectie Valk en verder. Afrika Museum, Berg en Dal, Netherlands. January 31–August 31, 2006.

África: De ida y vuelta. La Casa Encendida, Madrid. March 10–June 6, 2006.

Collection of the Fondation Cartier pour l'Art Contemporain at MOT—Tokyo. Museum of Contemporary Art, Tokyo. April 22–July 2, 2006.

100% Africa. Guggenheim Museum Bilbao. October 12, 2006–February 18, 2007.

2007

TRANS CAPE: Contemporary African Art on the Move. Trans Cape Africa, Cape Town, South Africa. March 24–May 2, 2007.

Terre noire: Ousmane Sow et les tendances de la sculpture africaine d'aujourd'hui. Musée Départemental Maurice Denis, Saint-German-en-Laye, France. June 20–September 30, 2007.

Il futuro del futurismo. Galleria d'Arte Moderna e Contemporanea di Bergamo, Italy. September 21, 2007–February 24, 2008.

Anatomia dell'irrequietezza. Museo Della Citta'—Palazzo della Penna, Perugia, Italy. September 28, 2007–January 6, 2008.

Why Africa? La collezione Pigozzi. Pinacoteca Giovanni e Marella Agnelli, Turin. October 6, 2007–February 3, 2008.

2008

Less Is Less, More Is More, That's All! Présence Panchounette. CAPC Musée d'Art Contemporain de Bordeaux, France. May 30–September 14, 2008.

2009

Africa? Una nuova storia. Complesso del Vittoriano Roma, Rome. November 19, 2009–January 17, 2010.

GAGARIN: The Artists in Their Own Words. Stedelijk Museum voor Actuele Kunst, Ghent, Belgium. December 4, 2009–March 14, 2010.

2010

Dreamlands: Des parcs d'attractions aux cités du futur. Centre Georges Pompidou, Paris. May 5–August 9, 2010.

La RDC en 2060. Mercedes House, Brussels. June 10–June 30, 2010.

2011

JapanCongo: Carsten Höller's Double-Take on Jean Pigozzi's Collection. Magasin—Centre National d'Art Contemporain de Grenoble, France. February 6–April 24, 2011. Traveled to The Garage—Center for Contemporary Culture, Moscow, July 8–August 14, 2011.

La ville et les imaginaires. Fondation Blachère, Apt, France. May 31–October 8, 2011.

MärklinWorld. Kunsthal KAdE, Amersfoort, Netherlands. September 24, 2011–January 8, 2012.

Postmodernism: Style and Subversion, 1970–1990. Victoria and Albert Museum, London. September 24, 2011–January 15, 2012.

Mondes inventés, mondes habités. Musée d'Art Moderne Grand-Duc Jean, Luxembourg City. October 8, 2011–January 15, 2012.

2012

Six Yards Guaranteed Dutch Design. Museum Moderne Kunst Arnhem, Netherlands. January 29–May 6, 2012.

Ein Wunsch bleibt immer übrig: 12 Jahre Museum Ludwig: eine Auswahl. Museum Ludwig, Cologne. June 2–November 4, 2012.

Skyscraper: Art and Architecture against Gravity. Museum of Contemporary Art Chicago. June 20–September 23, 2012.

Les trésors de l'art modeste. Le Musée International des Arts Modestes, Sète, France. December 14, 2012–March 17, 2013.

2013

Alternative Guide to the Universe: Mavericks, Visionaries, Outsiders. Hayward Gallery, London. June 11–August 26, 2013.

Utopie beginnt im Kleinen—12. Triennale Kleinplastik Fellbach. Various locations, Fellbach, Germany. June 23–September 29, 2013.

Here is always somewhere else. Forum Triangulare: Euregionaal Kunstcentrum Oud-Rekem, Oud-Rekem, Belgium. July 28–September 29, 2013.

2014

Ici l'Afrique. Musée des Suisses dans le Monde, Geneva. May 8–July 6, 2014.

Mémoires vives. Fondation Cartier pour l'Art Contemporain, Paris. May 10–September 21, 2014.

Notre itinéraire. Espace Verney-Carron, Lyon, France. May 16–September 8, 2014.

Harvest. Queensland Art Gallery and Gallery of Modern Art, Brisbane, Australia. June 28–September 21, 2014.

Luminós/C/ity.Ordinary Joy: From the Pigozzi Contemporary African Art Collection. Ethelbert Cooper Gallery of African and African American Art, Harvard University, Cambridge, Massachusetts. October 21, 2014–January 8, 2015.

2015

(un)möglich! Künstler als Architekten. Marta Herford, Herford, Germany. February 21–May 31, 2015.

Making Africa: A Continent of Contemporary Design. Vitra Design Museum, Weil am Rhein, Germany. March 14–September 13, 2015. Traveled to Guggenheim Museum Bilbao, October 30, 2015–February 21, 2016; Centre de Cultura Contemporània de Barcelona, March 22–July 31, 2016; Kunsthal, Rotterdam, October 1, 2016–January 17, 2017; High Museum of Art, Atlanta, October 14, 2017–January 7, 2018; Albuquerque Museum, New Mexico, February 3, 2018–May 6, 2018; and Blanton Museum of Art, Austin, Texas, October 14, 2018–January 13, 2019.

Triennale Brugge 2015. Various locations, Bruges, Belgium. May 20–October 15, 2015.

Africa: Architecture, Culture and Identity. Louisiana Museum of Modern Art, Humlebæk, Denmark. June 25–October 25, 2015.

Villissima! Des artistes et des villes. Hôtel des Arts, Toulon, France. July 4–September 27, 2015

Beauté Congo: 1926–2015: Congo kitoko. Fondation Cartier pour l'Art Contemporain, Paris. July 11–November 15, 2015.

2050: Une brève histoire de l'avenir. Royal Museums of Fine Arts of Belgium, Brussels. September 11, 2015–January 24, 2016. Traveled to Palazzo Reale, Milan, March 23–May 29, 2016.

One More Time. L'exposition de nos expositions. Musée d'Art Moderne et Contemporain, Geneva. October 28, 2015–January 24, 2016.

2016

Wir nennen es Ludwig. Das Museum wird 40! Museum Ludwig, Cologne. August 27, 2016–January 8, 2017.

Vivre!! La collection agnès b. au Musée national de l'histoire de l'immigration. Musée National de l'Histoire de l'Immigration, Paris. October 18, 2016–January 8, 2017.

Regarding Africa: Contemporary Art and Afro-Futurism. Tel Aviv Museum of Art. December 9, 2016–May 27, 2017.

2017

Il cacciatore bianco/The White Hunter: Memories and African Representations. FM Centro per l'Arte Contemporanea, Milan. March 31–June 6, 2017.

Les initiés: Un choix d'œuvres (1989–2009) dans la collection d'art contemporain africain de Jean Pigozzi. Fondation Louis Vuitton, Paris. April 26–August 28, 2017.

Les éclaireurs: Sculpteurs d'Afrique. Fondation Blachère and various locations, Avignon, France. May 19, 2017–January 14, 2018.

The Museum of Everything. Museum of Old and New Art, Hobart, Australia. June 10, 2017–April 2, 2018.

Ray Hughes: Africa. Delmar Gallery, Trinity Grammar School, Ashfield, Australia. July 2–August 6, 2017.

On aime l'art . . . !! Un choix d'Éric Mézil parmi les œuvres de la Collection agnès b. Collection Lambert, Avignon, France. July 6–November 5, 2017.

SELECTED BIBLIOGRAPHY

Compiled by Hillary Reder

The first section of this bibliography primarily features exhibition catalogues and articles that make direct reference to Kingelez, though, in many cases, the mention is only in passing. The second section comprises literature on the history of the Democratic Republic of the Congo, Congolese art, and significant biennials and other surveys and exhibitions that included modern and contemporary African art. The last section lists the few published examples of Kingelez's writing in English translation.

25a Bienal de São Paulo: Iconografias metropolitanas. São Paulo: Fundaçao Bienal de São Paulo, 2002. Exh. cat. In Portuguese.

Ackermann, Franz, and Annelie Pohlen. *Un-built Cities.* Bonn, Germany: Bonner Kunstverein, 2003. Exh. cat. In German.

Adamson, Glenn, Jane Pavitt, and Paola Antonelli. *Postmodernism: Style and Subversion, 1970–1990.* London: V & A, 2011. Exh. cat.

Adjaye, David, Mariane Ibrahim-Lenhardt, and Henry Louis Gates, Jr. "Luminous City, Luminous Gallery." *Transition*, no. 117 (2015): 198–209.

Africas: The Artist and the City: A Journey and an Exhibition. Barcelona: Centre de Cultura Contemporània de Barcelona, 2001. Exh. cat.

Attali, Jacques. *2050: A Brief History of the Future.* Ghent, Belgium: Snoeck, 2015. Exh. cat.

Bajac, Quentin, and Didier Ottinger. *Dreamlands: Des parcs d'attractions aux cités du futur.* Paris: Centre Pompidou, 2010. Exh. cat. In French.

Bonami, Francesco. "Invisibleville: The Work of Bodys Isek Kingelez." *Nka: Journal of Contemporary African Art* 10, no. 1 (1999): 12–13.

Bodys Isek Kingelez. Paris: Fondation Cartier pour l'Art Contemporain, 1995. Exh. cat. In French.

Bodys Isek Kingelez. Brussels: La Médiatine, Centre Culturel Wolu-Culture, 2003. Exh. cat. In French.

Bonami, Francesco. *Unfinished History.* Minneapolis, Minn.: Walker Art Center, 1998. Exh. cat.

Borchert, Till-Holger, Michel Dewilde, and Philip Vandenberghe. *Triennial Bruges 2015: Contemporary Art and Architecture in the Historical City of Bruges.* Ghent, Belgium: Borgerhoff et Lamberigts, 2015. Exh. cat.

Busine, Laurent, and Stefan Liberski. *Bomoi mobimba—Toute la vie: 7 artistes zaïrois. Collection Lucien Bilinelli.* Charleroi, Belgium: Palais des Beaux-Arts de Charleroi, 1996. Exh. cat. In French.

Cameron, Dan, et al. *Cocido y crudo.* Madrid: Museo Nacional Centro de Arte Reina Sofía, 1994. Exh. cat. In Spanish and English.

Caubet, Annie, Zeev Gourrier, and Jean-Hubert Martin. *Visions du futur: Une histoire des peurs et des espoirs de l'humanité.* Paris: Réunion des Musées Nationaux, 2000. Exh. cat. In French.

Clarisse, Catherine. *Ma quête d'architecture, maquettes d'architectures.* Paris: Pavillon de l'Arsenal, 1997. Exh. cat. In French.

Cohen-Solal, Annie. *Magiciens de la terre: Retour sur une exposition légendaire.* Paris: Xavier Barral: Éditions du Centre Pompidou, 2014. In French.

Collins, Judith. *Sculpture Today.* London: Phaidon, 2007.

Daftari, Fereshteh. *Projects 59: Architecture as Metaphor.* New York: Museum of Modern Art, 1997. Exh. brochure.

Dak'art 98: Biennale de l'art africain contemporain. Cimaise 45, no. 253 (April 1998). Exh. cat.

Dany Keller Galerie. *Afrika: Skulptur heute.* Munich: Die Galerie, 1993. Exh. cat. In German.

David, Philippe, André Magnin, Paul Rabibisoa Ravoay, and Jacques Soulillou. *Africa Now: Jean Pigozzi Collection.* Groningen, Netherlands: Groninger Museum; The Hague: Novib, 1991. Exh. cat.

Dean, Tacita, and Jeremy Millar. *Place.* London: Thames & Hudson, 2005.

Deér, Katalin. *Artists Imagine Architecture.* Boston: Institute of Contemporary Art, 2002. Exh. cat.

Dialogues de paix. Paris: Association Française d'Action Artistique, 1995. Exh. cat. In French and English.

Direktor, Ruth. *Regarding Africa: Contemporary Art and Afro-Futurism.* Tel Aviv: Tel Aviv Museum of Art, 2016. Exh. cat.

Draper, Robert. "Kinshasa: Urban Pulse of the Congo." *National Geographic* 224, no. 3 (September 2013): 100–123.

Dumbadze, Alexander Blair, and Suzanne Hudson, eds. *Contemporary Art: 1989 to the Present.* West Sussex, U.K.: Wiley-Blackwell, 2013.

Dumon, Dirk. *Kingelez: Kinshasa, une ville repensée.* Brussels: Piksa, 2004. Film. In French with English subtitles.

Duplat, Guy. "Le maître des maquettes." *La libre belgique*, October 23, 2001. In French.

Dziewior, Yilmaz. *Bodys Isek Kingelez.* Ostfildern-Ruit, Germany: Hatje Cantz; Hamburg: Kunstverein in Hamburg, 2001. Exh. cat. In German, English, and French.

——, Angelika Nollert, and Christa Linsenmaier-Wolf. *Utopie beginnt im kleinen—12. Triennale Kleinplastik Fellbach.* Cologne: Walther König, 2013. Exh. cat. In German and English.

Eggers, Dave. "Eleven Encounters with Bodys Isek Kingelez." *Frieze*, no. 78 (October 2003): 94–97.

Enwezor, Okwui. *documenta 11_Platform 5: Catalogue.* Ostfildern-Ruit, Germany: Hatje Cantz, 2002. Exh. cat.

——. *documenta 11_Platform 5: Exhibition.* Ostfildern-Ruit, Germany: Hatje Cantz, 2002. Exh. cat.

——. *documenta 11_The Short Guide.* Ostfildern-Ruit, Germany: Hatje Cantz, 2002. Exh. cat.

——. *Under Siege: Four African Cities: Freetown, Johannesburg, Kinshasa, Lagos: documenta 11_ Platform 4.* Osfildern- Ruit, Germany: Hatje Cantz, 2002. Exh. cat.

——. "A Conversation with Okwui Enwezor." Interview by Carol Becker. *Art Journal* 61, no. 2 (Summer 2002): 9–27.

——. *The Short Century: Independence and Liberation Movements in Africa, 1945–1994.* Munich: Prestel, 2001.

——. *Mirror's Edge.* Umeå, Sweden: BildMuseet, 1999. Exh. cat.

——. "Between Localism and Worldliness," in "Liminalities: Discussions on the Global and the Local." *Art Journal* 57, no. 4 (Winter 1998): 32–36.

——. *Trade Routes: History and Geography. 2nd Johannesburg Biennale.* Johannesburg: Greater Johannesburg Metropolitan Council, 1997. Exh. cat.

——. "Occupied Territories": Power, Access, and African Art." *Frieze* 26 (January–February 1996): 36–41.

Fall, N'Goné, and Jean L. Pivin. *An Anthology of African Art: The Twentieth Century.* New York: Distributed Art Publishers, 2002.

Felix, Marc Leo, and C. C. Lu Henry. *Kongo Kingdom Art: From Ritual to Cutting Edge.* Taipei: National Taiwan Museum of Fine Arts, 2004. Exh. cat.

Francis, Mark, André Magnin, Jean-Hubert Martin, and Bernard Marcadé. *Magiciens de la terre.* Paris: Éditions du Centre Pompidou, 1989. Exh. cat. In French.

Frankel, David. "África hoy: Obras de la Contemporary African Art Collection," *African Arts* 24 (October 1992): 34.

García-Antón, Katya. "Dak'art 98." *Third Text* 12, no. 44 (1998): 87–92.

Gaudibert, Pierre. *L'art africain contemporain.* Paris: Éditions Cercle d'Art, 1991.

Geers, Kendell, and Ross Doran H. "Africa95: Many Stories about the Art of a Continent." *African Arts* 29, no. 3 (1996): 1–11.

Girard, Christian. "Les extrêmes architectures de Bodys Isek Kingelez." *Art Press* 136, no. 5 (1989): 47. In French.

Grant, Vera, ed. *Luminós/C/ity. Ordinary Joy: From the Pigozzi Contemporary African Art Collection.* Cambridge, Mass.: Ethelbert Cooper Gallery of African and African American Art, 2014. Exh. cat.

Grynsztejn, Madeleine. *Carnegie International 1999/2000*, vols. 1 and 2. Pittsburgh, Penn.: Carnegie Museum of Art, 1999. Exh. cat.

Home and the World: Architectural Sculpture by Two Contemporary African Artists: Aboudramane and Bodys Isek Kingelez. New York: Museum for African Art; Munich: Prestel, 1993. Exh. cat.

Hug, Alfons. *Neue Kunst aus Afrika.* Heidelberg, Germany: Edition Braus, 1996. Exh. cat. In German.

Jacob, Laurent. *Black Box: Les Afriques.* Liège, Belgium: Espace 251 Nord, Archives Actives, 2005. Exh. cat. In French.

Jacquemin, Dominique, and Clément Dirié, eds. *Collection agnès b.* Zurich: JRP Ringier, 2015.

Jaukkuri, Maarette, and Irit Rogoff. *ARS 01: Unfolding Perspectives*. Helsinki: Kiasma—Museum of Contemporary Art, 2001. Exh. cat.

Jones, Erica Perlmutter. "Imagining Heterotopia: Kinshasa and the Urban Simulations of Bodys Isek Kingelez." PhD diss., University of California, Los Angeles, 2008.

Jones, Jonathan. "Bodys Isek Kingelez: Kimbéville—City of Tomorrow." *Art & Design* 11, no. 9–10 (September–October 1996): 32–35.

Jongbloed, Marjorie, and Kasper König, eds. *DC: Thomas Bayrle, Bodys Isek Kingelez*. Cologne: Museum Ludwig, 2001. Exh. cat. In German and English.

Kasasa, Francis, and Aimé Mpana. *Afrika sana: La peinture congolaise d'hier et d'aujourd'hui*. Monaco: Comité National Monégasque de l'Association des Arts Plastiques de l'UNESCO, 2000. Exh. cat. In French.

Kasfir, Sidney L. *Contemporary African Art*. London: Thames & Hudson, 2014.

Laval-Jeantet, Marion, Benoît Mangin, and Anaïd Demir. *Veilleurs du monde: Gbêdji kpontolè*. Paris: CQFD, 1998. Exh. cat. In French and English.

Luntumbue, Toma Muteba. *Transferts*. Brussels: Palais des Beaux-Arts, 2003. Exh. cat. In Dutch, French, and English.

MacDonald, Ewen. *Biennale of Sydney 2000*. Sydney: Biennale Ltd, 2000. Exh. cat.

Magnin, André. *Arts of Africa: Jean Pigozzi's Contemporary Collection*. Milan: Skira, 2005. Exh. cat.

——. "Kingelez et ses extrêmes maquettes." *Jeune Afrique*, no. 1803 (July–August 1995): 64–65. In French.

——, Alison de Lima Greene, Alvia J. Wardlaw, and Thomas McEvilley. *African Art Now: Masterpieces from the Jean Pigozzi Collection*. London and New York: Merrell, in association with the Museum of Fine Arts, Houston, 2005. Exh. cat.

—— and Jacques Soulillou, eds. *Contemporary Art of Africa*. London: Thames and Hudson, 1996.

—— and Julia Peyton-Jones. *Big City: Artists from Africa*. London: Serpentine Gallery, 1995. Exh. cat.

Martin, Jean-Hubert, and Sally Laruelle. *Bodys Isek Kingelez: Plasticien*. Montreuil, France: Éditions de l'Œil, 2005.

Monsaingeon, Guillaume. *Villissima!: Des artistes et des villes*. Marseille: Parenthèses, 2015. Exh. cat.

Mulin, Amédé. "Bodys Isek Kingelez rêves d'architectures." *Revue noire* 18 (September–November 1995): 92. In French.

Njami, Simon. *Africa Remix: Contemporary Art of a Continent*. London: Hayward Gallery, 2005. Exh. cat.

Oguibe, Olu, and Okwui Enwezor. *Reading the Contemporary: African Art from Theory to the Marketplace*. London: Institute of International Visual Arts, 1999.

Pagé, Suzanne, André Magnin, Angeline Scherf, and Ludovic Delalande. *Les initiés: Un choix d'œuvres (1989–2009) dans la collection d'art contemporain africain de Jean Pigozzi*. Paris: Éditions Dilecta, 2017.

Pelletier, Adeline, ed. *Beauté Congo: 1926–2015: Congo kitoko*. Paris: Fondation Cartier pour l'Art Contemporain, 2015. Exh. cat. In French.

Pellizzi, Francesco. "Mésaventures de l'art: Premières impressions des *Magiciens de la terre*." *RES: Anthropology and Aesthetics*, no. 17–18 (Spring–Autumn 1989): 198–207. In French.

Perspectives 145: Bodys Isek Kingelez. Houston: Contemporary Arts Museum, 2005. Exh. cat.

Piccoli, Cloe. "La città di carta di Bodys Isek Kingelez." *Abitare*, no. 411 (September 2001): 176–78. In Italian.

Pigozzi, Jean, and André Magnin. *100% Africa: The Jean Pigozzi Contemporary African Art Collection at the Guggenheim Bilbao*. Alcobendas, Madrid: Tf Editores; Bilbao: Guggenheim Museum, 2006. Exh. cat.

Pigozzi, Jean, André Magnin, Jean-Michel Rousset, and Yaya Savane. *The Jean Pigozzi Contemporary African Art Collection at the Saatchi Collection*. London: Saatchi Collection, 1992. Exh. cat.

Reif, Rita. "Arts/Artifacts; Fanciful Dreams of Africa's Past and Future." *New York Times*, August 15, 1993.

Rinder, Lawrence. *The American Effect: Global Perspectives on the United States, 1990–2003*. New York: Whitney Museum of American Art, 2003. Exh. cat.

Rosticher, Nathalie. "L'art exporté." *Revue noire*, no. 21 (August 1996): 26–29. In French.

Rugoff, Ralph, ed. *The Alternative Guide to the Universe*. London: Hayward, 2013. Exh. cat.

Salvadé, Christine. "Le zaïrois Kingelez n'a jamais voulu être un artiste." *Le nouveau quotidien*, no. 1051, July 4, 1995, 19. In French.

Scotini, Marco, and Elisabetta Galasso, eds. *Il cacciatore bianco/The White Hunter*. Berlin: Archive, 2017. Exh. cat.

Shimizu, Toshio. *Africa Africa: Vibrant New Art from a Dynamic Continent*. Tokyo: Tobu Museum of Art, 1998. Exh. cat.

Singh, Rajvinder. "Bodys Isek Kingelez." *Kunstforum International*, no. 122 (1993): 273–75. In German.

Soulillou, Jacques, and Christian Girard. "Une internationale de l'art urbain." *autrement,* "Les capitales de la couleur," ed. Bruno Tilliette, special issue no. 9 (October 1984): 275–82. In French.

Steeds, Lucy, et al. *Making Art Global (Part 2): Magiciens de la terre, 1989*. London: Afterall, 2013.

Stein, Eva, ed. *Bodys Isek Kingelez: Architekturvisionen aus Zaire*. Stuttgart: Edition Cantz, 1992. Exh. cat.

Sultan, Olivier. *Africa urbis: Perspectives urbaines*. Saint-Maur-des-Fossés, France: Sépia, 2005.

——. *Les Afriques: 36 artistes contemporains*. Paris: Éditions Autrement, 2004. Exh. cat

Terre noire: Ousmane Sow et les tendances de la sculpture africaine aujourd'hui. Paris: Somogy Éditions d'Art, 2007. Exh. cat.

Turine, Roger Pierre. *Les arts du Congo: D'hier à nos jours*. Brussels: Renaissance du Livre, 2007.

Unmapping the Earth: 97 Kwangju Biennale. Kwangju, Korea: Kwangju Biennale Press, 1997. Exh. cat.

Valk, Felix, and Paul Luttik. *Er bestaat geen kunst in Afrika*. Heerlen, Netherlands: Stadsgalerij Heerlen, 1996. Exh. cat. In Dutch and English.

Zabunyan, Elvan, Valérie Mavridorakis, and David Perreau. *Fantasmapolis: La ville contemporaine et ses imaginaires*. Rennes, France: Presses Universitaires de Rennes, 2005. In French.

Related subjects

Araeen, Rasheed. "Dak'art 1992–2002." *Third Text* 17 no. 62 (March 2003): 93–106.

——. "Our Bauhaus, Others' Mudhouse." *Third Text* 3, no. 6 (Spring 1989): 3–14.

Blier, Suzanne Preston. "Nine Contradictions in the New Golden Age of African Art." *African Arts* 35, no. 3 (Autumn 2002): 1–6.

Brett, Guy. "Earth and Museum: Local and Global?" *Third Text* 3, no. 6 (Spring 1989): 89–96.

De Boeck, Filip, and Sammy Baloji. *Suturing the City: Living Together in Congo's Urban Worlds*. London: Autograph ABP, 2016.

De Boeck, Filip, and Marie-Françoise Plissart. *Kinshasa: Tales of the Invisible City*. Ghent, Belgium: Ludion, 2004.

Diawara, Manthia. "Moving Company: The Second Johannesburg Biennale." *Artforum* 36, no. 7 (1998): 86–89.

Downey, Anthony. "The Spectacular Difference of documenta XI." *Third Text* 17, no. 62 (March 2003): 85–92.

Cornet, Joseph-Aurélien. *60 ans de peinture au Zaïre*. Brussels: Les Éditeurs d'Art Associés, 1989. In French.

Deliss, Clémentine, and Jane Havell. *Seven Stories about Modern Art in Africa*. London: Whitechapel, 1995. Exh. cat.

Enwezor, Okwui. "Redrawing the Boundaries: Towards a New African Art Discourse." *Nka: Journal of Contemporary African Art* (1994): 3–7.

—— and Chika Okeke-Agulu. *Contemporary African Art since 1980*. Bologna: Damiani, 2009.

Fabian, Johannes. *Remembering the Present: Painting and Popular History in Zaire*. Berkeley and Los Angeles: University of California Press, 1996.

Fosu, Kojo. *20th Century Art of Africa*. Accra, Ghana: Artists Alliance, 1993.

Girard, Christian. "Profession: Africaniste," *autrement*, no. 49 (April 1983): 162–71.

Heartney, Eleanor. "The Whole Earth Show: Part II." *Art in America* 77, no. 7 (July 1989): 91–97.

Hochschild, Adam. *King Leopold's Ghost: A Story of Greed, Terror, and Heroism in Colonial Africa*. Boston: Houghton Mifflin, 1998.

Holm, Michael Juul, and Mette Marie Kallehauge. *Africa: Architecture, Culture, Identity*. Humlebæk, Denmark: Louisiana Museum of Modern Art, 2015. Exh. cat.

Ibongo Gilungula, Joseph. "La peinture populaire et publicitaire de Kinshasa (République démocratique du Congo): Éléments d'histoire culturelle de la ville et analyse iconologique des oeuvres représentatives." PhD diss., Université Catholique de Louvain, 1999. In French.

jegede, dele. *Contemporary African Art: Five Artists, Diverse Trends*. Indianapolis: Indianapolis Museum of Art, 2000. Exh. cat.

——. "Review of André Magnin, Jacques Soulillou, eds. *Contemporary Art of Africa*." H-AfrArts, H-Net Reviews, August 1997. http://www.h-net.org/reviews/showrev.php?id=1214.

Lagae, Johan, and K. De Raedt. "'Building for l'authenticité': Eugène Palumbo and the Architecture of Mobutu's Congo." *Journal of Architectural Education* 68, no. 2 (2014): 178–89.

Kawaguchi, Yukiya. *An Inside Story: African Art of Our Time*. Tokyo: Japan Association of Art Museums, 1995. In Japanese and English. Exh. cat.

Martin, Jean-Hubert. "The Whole Earth Show." Interview by Benjamin H. D. Buchloh. *Art in America* (May 1989): 151–58, 211–13.

Mboka, Mwana. *Kinshasa Then and Now* (blog). http://kosubaawate.blogspot.com/.

McEvilley, Thomas. *Art and Otherness: Crisis in Cultural Identity*. Kingston, N.Y.: Documentext, 1999.

——. "Fusion: Hot or Cold?" In *Fusion: West African Artists at the Venice Biennale*. New York: Museum for African Art; Munich: Prestel, 1993, 9–24. Exh. cat.

Oguibe, Olu. "Appropriation as Nationalism in Contemporary African Art." *Third Text* 16, no. 60 (September 2002): 243–59.

——. "In the Heart of Darkness," *Third Text* 7, no. 23 (Summer 1993): 3–8.

Okeke-Agulu, Chika. "Contemporary African Art: Beyond Colonial Paradigms: An Interview with Okwui Enwezor," *Art Papers* 26, no. 4 (July–August 2002): 6–7.

——. "Dak'art 98: An Interview with 3rd Dakar Biennale Director Remi Sagna." *Nka: Journal of Contemporary African Art*, no. 8 (Spring–Summer 1998): 24–27.

Pinther, Kerstin, Larissa Förster, and Christian Hanussek, eds. *Afropolis: City, Media, Art*. Auckland Park: Jacana, 2012.

Powell, Richard J. *Black Art and Culture in the 20th Century*. London: Thames & Hudson, 1998.

Said, Edward W. *Culture and Imperialism*. New York: Vintage, 1994.

Stanley, Janet L. *Modern African Art: A Basic Reading List*. http://www.sil si.edu/SILPublications/ModernAfricanArt/newmaa.cfm.

Tawadros, Gilane, and Sarah Campbell, eds. *Fault Lines: Contemporary African Art and Shifting Landscapes*. London: Institute of International Visual Arts in collaboration with the Forum for African Arts and the Prince Claus Fund, 2003.

Taylor, Brian B. *Reading the Contemporary African City*. Singapore: Concept Media for the Aga Khan Award for Architecture, 1983.

Thompson, Robert Farris, and Joseph Cornet. *The Four Moments of the Sun: Kongo Art in Two Worlds*. Washington, D.C.: National Gallery of Art, 1981. Exh. cat.

Van Beurden, Sarah. *Authentically African: Arts and the Transnational Politics of Congolese Culture*. Athens, Ohio: Ohio University Press, 2015.

Vogel, Susan. *Africa Explores: 20th Century African Art*. New York: Center for African Art; Munich: Prestel, 1991. Exh. cat.

Wikinshasa.org: Atlas de l'architecture et du paysage urbains. Last modified August 2, 2011. http://www.wikinshasa.org/index.php/Accueil.

Young, Crawford. *Politics in Congo: Decolonization and Independence*. Princeton, N.J.: Princeton University Press, 1965.

Young, Louis C., ed. *Contemporary African Artists: Changing Tradition*. New York: Studio Museum in Harlem, 1990. Exh. cat.

Writings by Kingelez

"Artist's Statement." In *Perspectives 145: Bodys Isek Kingelez*, 2–9. Houston: Contemporary Arts Museum, 2005. Exh. cat.

"Scale Models of Post-Modes Art." *Gagarin* 7 (2003): 68–73.

"The Essential Framework of the Structures Making Up the Town of Kimbembele-Ihunga (Kimbéville)." In André Magnin and Julia Peyton-Jones, *Big City: Artists from Africa*, n.p. London: Serpentine Gallery, 1995. Exh. cat.

CHECKLIST OF THE EXHIBITION

Kingelez's sculptures are complex amalgamations of materials, and there has not yet been an opportunity for exhaustive scientific study of the mediums of the individual objects in this exhibition. In his early years, the artist primarily used paper, paperboard, and commercial packaging; over time, as he gained access to more materials, he began to incorporate plastic, metallic foil, and a range of found objects. This list compiles the materials so far definitively identified in the works by conservators and curators, roughly organized from most to least prevalent:

Paper, colored paper, and printed paper (including wrapping paper and tissue paper); corrugated cardboard, paperboard and printed paperboard, and printed commercial packaging; wood; acrylic and plastic (including colored plastic); aluminum foil, metallic foil paper, and metallic foil cardboard; rubber foam, Styrofoam, and foamcore; ink, pencil, colored pencil, crayon, marker, and paint (including paint pen, gouache, and poster paint); adhesive, tape (including colored tape and metallic tape), and stickers; fabric (including mesh fabric), yarn, string (including colored string), thread (including metallic thread), and twine; beads (paper, wood, and plastic); balls (plastic, foam, and thread-wrapped); paper and plastic straws; copper wire, coated wire, and metal grommets; toothpicks, pins (including map pins, pushpins, thumbtacks, and other metal pins), and nails; aluminum cans, plastic bottles, and plastic and other bottle caps; and mirrors, plastic figurines, 35mm plastic slide mounts, ballpoint-pen shafts, circuit-board diodes, and electric lights.

For the dimensions of the works in the checklist below, height precedes width precedes depth. Many of the titles are French. Kingelez's poetic, idiosyncratic, and often playful phrasing and spelling make their spirit difficult to capture in translation, and, in most cases, the titles given below are those written directly on the works by the artist himself.

Untitled. c. 1980
32 15/16 x 14 7/8 x 9 5/8" (83.6 x 37.8 x 24.5 cm)
Private collection, Paris
Plate 1

Untitled. 1980
15 3/8 x 17 3/8 x 12 3/8" (39 x 44.2 x 31.5 cm)
Private collection, Paris
Plate 2

Maryland University USA. 1981
26 x 5 9/16 x 7 1/2" (66 x 14.2 x 19.1 cm)
Private collection, Paris
Plate 3

Approche de l'Échangeur de Limete Kin. 1981
32 5/16 x 13 7/8 x 16 3/4" (82 x 35.2 x 42.6 cm)
Private collection, Paris
Plate 4

Untitled. 1982
12 3/8 x 7 1/16 x 7 3/16" (31.4 x 18 x 18.2 cm)
Private collection, Paris
Plate 5

Allemagne An 2000. 1988
33 7/8 x 24 3/16 x 24 3/16" (86 x 61.5 x 61.5 cm)
Long-term loan from the Centre National des Arts Plastiques, France, to the Château d'Oiron, France
Plate 6

Paris Nouvel. 1989
33 7/16 x 24 x 27 9/16" (85 x 61 x 70 cm)
Long-term loan from the Centre National des Arts Plastiques, France, to the Château d'Oiron, France
Plate 7

Bel Atlas. 1989
33 7/16 x 26 x 17 5/16" (85 x 66 x 44 cm)
Sandro De Sanctis/African Collection
Plate 8

Stars Palme Bouygues. 1989
39 3/8 x 15 3/4 x 15 3/4" (100 x 40 x 40 cm)
van Lierde collection, Brussels
Plate 9

Mongolique Sovietique. 1989
24 7/16 x 15 3/4 x 24 7/16" (62 x 40 x 62 cm)
CAAC—The Pigozzi Collection, Geneva
Plate 10

Étoile Rouge Congolaise. 1990
33 7/16 x 36 1/4 x 19 11/16" (85 x 92 x 50 cm)
CAAC—The Pigozzi Collection, Geneva
Plate 11

Air Force. 1991
21 1/4 x 32 11/16 x 16 1/8" (54 x 83 x 41 cm)
CAAC—The Pigozzi Collection, Geneva
Plate 12

Aéromode (Aéroport Moderne). 1991
21 1/4 x 31 1/2 x 21 5/8" (54 x 80 x 55 cm)
CAAC—The Pigozzi Collection, Geneva
Plate 13

Kinshasa la Belle. 1991
24 13/16 x 21 5/8 x 31 1/2" (63 x 55 x 80 cm)
CAAC—The Pigozzi Collection, Geneva
Plate 14

Palais d'Hirochima. 1991
18 7/8 x 30 11/16 x 16 1/8" (48 x 78 x 41 cm)
CAAC—The Pigozzi Collection, Geneva
Plate 15

Belle Hollandaise. 1991
21 5/8 x 31 11/16 x 22 1/16" (55 x 80.5 x 56 cm)
Groninger Museum, Groningen, Netherlands
Plate 16

The Scientific Center of Hospitalisation the SIDA. 1991
16 15/16 x 25 9/16 x 31 1/2" (43 x 65 x 80 cm)
Groninger Museum, Groningen, Netherlands
Plate 17

Canada Dry. 1991
20 7/8 x 31 1/2 x 21 5/8" (53 x 80 x 55 cm)
CAAC—The Pigozzi Collection, Geneva
Plate 18

Miss Hotel Brussels. 1992
19 11/16 x 15 9/16 x 24" (50 x 39.5 x 61 cm)
Lucien Bilinelli Collection, Brussels/Milan
Plate 19

Reveillon Fédéral. 1992
23 5/8 x 31 1/2 x 20 7/8" (60 x 80 x 53 cm)
CAAC—The Pigozzi Collection, Geneva
Plate 20

Industria da Pharmacia. 1992
14 15/16 x 31 1/8 x 21 5/8" (38 x 79 x 55 cm)
CAAC—The Pigozzi Collection, Geneva
Plate 21

Kimbembele Ihunga (Kimbembele Ville). 1992
20 1/16 x 42 1/2 x 34 1/16" (51 x 108 x 86.5 cm)
Courtesy The Museum of Everything
Plate 22

Place de la Ville. 1993
15 3/4 x 33 7/16 x 29 1/2" (40 x 85 x 75 cm)
Courtesy The Museum of Everything
Plate 23

Centrale Palestinienne. 1993
31 7/8 x 28 3/8 x 26 3/8" (81 x 72 x 67 cm), irreg.
COLLECTION PROSPER—The Prosper Collection.
Courtesy Aeroplastics Contemporary, Brussels
Plate 24

Africanisch. 1994
19 11/16 x 22 7/16 x 24" (50 x 57 x 61 cm)
Private collection, Paris
Plate 25

Kimbembele Ihunga. 1994
51 3/16" x 72 13/16" x 10' 5" (130 x 185 x 320 cm)
CAAC—The Pigozzi Collection, Geneva
Plate 26

U.N. 1995
35 13/16 x 29 1/8 x 20 7/8" (91 x 74 x 53 cm), irreg.
CAAC—The Pigozzi Collection, Geneva
Plate 27

Ville Fantôme. 1996
47 1/4" x 18' 8 7/16" x 7' 10 1/2" (120 x 570 x 240 cm)
CAAC—The Pigozzi Collection, Geneva
Plate 28

Sports Internationaux. 1997
35 7/16 x 33 7/16 x 9 13/16" (90 x 85 x 25 cm), irreg.
Purchased 2013 with funds from Tim Fairfax, AM, through the Queensland Art Gallery | Gallery of Modern Art Foundation. Collection Queensland Art Gallery, Brisbane
Plate 29

Ville de Sète 3009. 2000
31 1/2" x 9' 10 1/8" x 6' 10 11/16" (80 x 300 x 210 cm)
Collection Musée International des Arts Modestes (MIAM), Sète, France
Plate 30

Nippon Tower. 2005
26 3/8 x 13 3/8 x 8 11/16" (67 x 34 x 22 cm), irreg.
Courtesy Aeroplastics Contemporary, Brussels
Plate 31

DAB (Development Australian Bank). 2007
39 3/8 x 18 1/8 x 16 15/16" (100 x 46 x 43 cm), irreg.
Collection LSO
Plate 32

Dorothe. 2007
28 3/8 x 24 13/16 x 19 11/16" (72 x 63 x 50 cm), irreg.
Courtesy The Museum of Everything
Plate 33

ACKNOWLEDGMENTS

This exhilarating undertaking—the first retrospective of the work of Bodys Isek Kingelez—would have been impossible without the generosity, expertise, and support of a long roster of colleagues, scholars, and friends. First I must thank our lenders, many of whom shared their experiences and memories of the artist: Lucien Bilinelli, Collection LSO, COLLECTION PROSPER—The Prosper Collection, Bruno and Gael van Lierde, Sandro De Sanctis, and other private collections. The support of CAAC—The Pigozzi Collection has been extraordinary: Jean Pigozzi constantly impressed with his generosity and enthusiasm; André Magnin, former curator, was gracious and generous in sharing information; and Elisabeth Whitelaw, Alexandra Theiler, and Corentine Guillot helped us at every turn. Our institutional partners welcomed me warmly on their campuses and assisted in making our loans possible. I send thanks to Yves Robert, Violaine Daniels, and the team at the Centre National des Arts Plastiques, Paris; Carine Guimbard and Samuel Quenault at the Château d'Oiron, France; Andreas Blühm, Marlon Steensma, and the staff at the Groninger Museum, Groningen, Netherlands; Victoire and Hervé Di Rosa, Sylvie Côte, and Pascale Grégogna at the Musée International des Arts Modestes, Sête, France; James Brett, Rosario Gallo, and Robin Mann at The Museum of Everything; and Chris Saines, Emmy Schmeider, and Ellie Buttrose at the Queensland Art Gallery | Gallery of Modern Art, Brisbane.

This catalogue represents the first in-depth study of the artist, and the contributions of David Adjaye, Sammy Baloji, André Magnin, and Chika Okeke-Agulu add immeasurably to this effort. I am grateful to those who shared their knowledge, expertise, and experience of the artist with me: Bruno Asseray, Baudouin Bikoko, Philippe Boutté, Marco di Castri and Gianfranco Barbieri, Dirk Dumon, Christian Girard, Joseph Ibongo, Jerome Jacobs, Myoto Liyolo, Jean-Hubert Martin, Jean-Marc Patras, Grazia Quaroni, and Jacques Soulillou. Augustin Bikale, in Kinshasa, kindly facilitated conversations for us there. We are grateful for the assistance of Alessandro Azzoni, Sarah van Beurden, Tiberto Brandolini d'Adda, Florence Burban, Elodie Cazes, Jean-Michel Champault, Bob Coppens and Hélène de Zagon, Diego Cortez, Ilse Dauwe, Stéphane Ibars, Hadeel Ibrahim, Hélène Joubert, Gervanne and Matthias Leridon, Albane Ménoret, Laurent Nebot, Federico Negro, John Ollman, Joan Rabascall, Liz Rudnick, and Thierry Simoens.

It has been my great fortune to work with the stellar staff at The Museum of Modern Art. Director Glenn D. Lowry has been steadfast in his support of the exhibition, as have Christophe Cherix, The Robert Lehman Foundation Chief Curator of Drawings and Prints, and Ann Temkin, The Marie-Josée and Henry Kravis Chief Curator of Painting and Sculpture, whose advice and suggestions have been critical to its success. In the Department of Drawings and Prints, Hillary Reder, Curatorial Assistant, has been an extraordinary partner, and her intellect, enthusiasm, and tenacity inflect every aspect of the catalogue and exhibition. Hanna Girma, Curatorial Fellow, has been an adept researcher and invaluable sounding board. Heidi Hirschl, former Curatorial Assistant, helped organize the project in its earliest phase. Heather Nickels, former Louise Bourgeois Twelve-Month Intern, contributed critical and exploratory research, and Charlotte Barat, Curatorial Assistant in the Department of Painting and Sculpture, kindly made herself available for all manner of research queries. Jennifer Tobias, Librarian, helped us locate many volumes that have informed our research. Roger Griffiths, Associate Sculpture Conservator, and Erika Mosier, Paper Conservator, explored Kingelez's materials with enthusiasm.

The catalogue has been realized under the guidance of Don McMahon, Editorial Director, and Christopher Hudson, Publisher, in the Department of Publications. Rebecca Roberts, Editor, has been my trusted and valued partner in shaping these texts, and Marc Sapir, Production Director, ensured the beauty of the images with his characteristic care and attention to detail. Hannah Kim, Senior Marketing and Production Coordinator, and Sara Beth Walsh, Senior Publicist, helped us publicize the catalogue and exhibition, respectively. Nancy Adelson, Deputy General Counsel, navigated rights issues with diligence and sensitivity. My thanks to Naomi Mizusaki of Supermarket for her inspired catalogue design. Ugochukwu-Smooth Nzewi commented on an earlier draft of my essay and helped it take shape. One of the great contributions of this catalogue is the beautiful new photography it contains, which allows for an enhanced understanding of the artist's oeuvre. For this, I owe a debt of gratitude to Maurice Aeschimann, Vincent Everarts, Genevieve Hanson, Florian Kleinefenn, Marten de Leeuw, Frédéric Pignoux, and Pierre Schwartz.

Ramona Bannayan, Senior Deputy Director, Exhibitions and Collections, ensured that the exhibition had the support it needed. Erik Patton, Director, and Chloe Capewell, Assistant Coordinator, Exhibition Planning and Administration, and Susan Palamara, Registrar, seamlessly supervised the logistics. Carsten Höller was an invaluable colleague in developing the exhibition design, challenging us to rethink many of our standard procedures, and the end result is better for it. Aimee Keefer, Exhibition Designer, processed these various inputs and produced a beautiful show, and Elle Kim, Senior Art Director, and Olya Domoradova, Senior Graphic Designer, gave it a compelling graphic identity. MoMA's Visitor Experience team and Aaron Louis, Director; Aaron Harrow, Design Manager; and Tal Marks, Manager, in our Audio Visual Department, were essential advisors as we navigated new technologies in virtual reality, in dialogue with Paul Jastrzebski of Oculus.

A project of this nature can be all-encompassing, and I thank my family and friends for their patience, love, support, and encouragement.

Sarah Suzuki
Curator, Department of Drawings and Prints

PHOTOGRAPH CREDITS

In reproducing the images contained in this publication, the Museum obtained the permission of the rights holders whenever possible. In those instances where the Museum could not locate the rights holders, notwithstanding good-faith efforts, it requests that any information concerning such rights holders be forwarded so that they may be contacted for future editions.

Artworks by Bodys Isek Kingelez are © 2018 Estate of Bodys Isek Kingelez, unless otherwise noted.

© David Adjaye; photograph by David Adjaye: pp. 39–40.

Courtesy CAAC—The Pigozzi Collection: p. 24 (photograph by Claude Postel); and p. 25 fig. 20 (photograph by Jean Pigozzi).

Source: Olivier-Clément Cacoub, *Architecture de soleil* (Tunis: Cérès Productions, 1974), 49: p. 17 fig. 8.

© CNAC/MNAM/Dist. RMN-Grand Palais/Art Resource, NY: p. 22 fig. 14.

© Cnap (France), droits résérves; photograph by Frédéric Pignoux, Studio Ludo: p. 48 and pls. 6 (FNAC 981001) and 7 (FNAC 981003).

Photograph by Eliot Elisofon; EEPA EECL 7748; Eliot Elisofon Photographic Archives at the National Museum of African Art, Smithsonian Institution: p. 14.

Vincent Everarts Photography Brussels: pls. 9, 19, 24, and 31.

Photograph by Marc Gemoets, 2010; source: wikinshasa.org: p. 17 fig. 7 and p. 18.

Courtesy Groninger Museum, Groningen, Netherlands: p. 23 fig. 16 (photograph by John Stoel); and p. 31 and pls. 16 and 17 (photographs by Marten de Leeuw).

Courtesy Groupe ATEPA; photograph by Pierre Goudiaby Atepa: p. 16 fig. 6.

Photograph by Genevieve Hanson, NYC: pl. 8.

© Bodys Isek Kingelez; courtesy CAAC—The Pigozzi Collection; photograph by Maurice Aeschimann: cover, pp. 8, 27, and 38 and pls. 10–15, 18, 20, 21, and 26–28.

© Bodys Isek Kingelez; courtesy Fondation Cartier pour l'Art Contemporain, Paris; exhibition view of *Vivid Memories*, Fondation Cartier pour l'Art Contemporain, Paris, May 10–September 21, 2014; photograph © Luc Boegly: p. 35 fig. 2.

Photograph by Kleinefenn: pls. 1–5, 25, and 32.

© Daniel Lainé/Gamma Rapho: p. 15.

Source: Alfred Liyolo, *Liyolo* (Switzerland: M. Hofmann Graficolor International, 1977): p. 26.

Courtesy André Magnin, Paris: pp. 21, 45, and 47 fig. 2 (photographs by André Magnin); p. 47 fig. 3 (photograph by Fredi Casco); and p. 50.

Pascal Maitre/Cosmos/Redux: p. 37.

© Musée du quai Branly–Jacques Chirac, Paris; dist. RMN-Grand Palais/Art Resource, NY; photograph by Claude Germain: pp. 23 fig. 17 and 35 fig. 3.

Courtesy Musée du quai Branly–Jacques Chirac, Paris; photograph by Sarah Suzuki: p. 22 fig. 15.

Courtesy The Museum of Everything: p. 32 and pls. 22, 23, and 33.

Courtesy Nationaal Museum van Wereldculturen, Netherlands: p. 11 fig. 1 (object number TM-5867-48) and p. 19 fig. 12 (object number TM-5829-1).

Courtesy Prisma by Dukas Presseagentur GmbH/Alamy Stock Photo; photograph by Jose Fuste Raga, 2012: p. 25 fig. 19.

© Pume-Bylex; courtesy REVUE NOIRE; photograph by Pascal Martin Saint Leon: p. 43.

© QAGOMA; photograph by Natasha Harth: pl. 29.

© Pierre Schwartz ADAGP; courtesy Musée International des Arts Modestes (MIAM), Sète, France: title pages and pl. 30.

Photograph by Hugues Sirault; source: wikinshasa.org: p. 19 fig. 11.

Sygma Collection/Getty Images; photograph by Roberto Antonetti: p. 16 fig. 5.

Courtesy Universal Images Group North America LLC/ DeAgostini/Alamy Stock Photo: p. 11 fig. 2.

TRUSTEES OF THE MUSEUM OF MODERN ART

Ronald S. Lauder
Honorary Chairman

Robert B. Menschel*
Chairman Emeritus

Agnes Gund*
President Emerita

Donald B. Marron
President Emeritus

Jerry I. Speyer
Chairman

Leon D. Black
Co-Chairman

Marie-Josée Kravis
President

Mimi Haas
Marlene Hess
Maja Oeri
Richard E. Salomon
Vice Chairmen

Glenn D. Lowry
Director

Richard E. Salomon
Treasurer

James Gara
Assistant Treasurer

Patty Lipshutz
Secretary

Wallis Annenberg*
Lin Arison**
Sarah Arison
Sid R. Bass*
Lawrence B. Benenson
Leon D. Black
David Booth
Eli Broad*
Clarissa Alcock Bronfman
Patricia Phelps de Cisneros
Steven Cohen
Edith Cooper
Mrs. Jan Cowles**
Douglas S. Cramer*
Paula Crown
Lewis B. Cullman**
David Dechman
Anne Dias Griffin
Glenn Dubin
Joel S. Ehrenkranz*
John Elkann
Laurence D. Fink
H.R.H. Duke Franz of Bavaria**
Glenn Fuhrman
Kathleen Fuld
Gianluigi Gabetti*
Howard Gardner
Maurice R. Greenberg**
Agnes Gund*
Mimi Haas
Marlene Hess
Ronnie Heyman
AC Hudgins
Barbara Jakobson*
Werner H. Kramarsky*
Jill Kraus
Marie-Josée Kravis
June Noble Larkin*
Ronald S. Lauder
Michael Lynne
Donald B. Marron*
Wynton Marsalis**
Robert B. Menschel*
Khalil Gibran Muhammad
Philip S. Niarchos
James G. Niven
Peter Norton
Daniel S. Och
Maja Oeri
Richard E. Oldenburg**
Michael S. Ovitz
Ronald O. Perelman
Peter G. Peterson*
Emily Rauh Pulitzer*
David Rockefeller, Jr.
Sharon Percy Rockefeller
Lord Rogers of Riverside**
Richard E. Salomon
Marcus Samuelsson
Ted Sann**
Anna Marie Shapiro*
Anna Deavere Smith
Jerry I. Speyer
Ricardo Steinbruch
Jon Stryker
Daniel Sundheim
Tony Tamer
Steve Tananbaum
Yoshio Taniguchi**
Jeanne C. Thayer*
Alice M. Tisch
Edgar Wachenheim III*
Gary Winnick

EX OFFICIO

Glenn D. Lowry
Director

Agnes Gund*
Chairman of the Board of MoMA PS1

Sharon Percy Rockefeller
President of The International Council

Ann Fensterstock and
Tom Osborne
Co-Chairmen of The Contemporary Arts Council

Bill de Blasio
Mayor of the City of New York

Corey Johnson
Speaker of the Council of the City of New York

Scott M. Stringer
Comptroller of the City of New York

*Life Trustee
**Honorary Trustee